Women's Career Development

WOMEN'S CAREER DEVELOPMENT

A Study of High Flyers

BARBARA WHITE, CHARLES COX AND
CARY COOPER

BLACKWELL
Business

Copyright © Barbara White, Charles Cox and Cary Cooper, 1992

The right of Barbara White, Charles Cox and Cary Cooper to be identified as authors of this work has been asserted in accordance with the Copyright, Designs and Patents Act 1988.

First published 1992

Blackwell Publishers
108 Cowley Road
Oxford OX4 1JF
UK

238 Main Street, Suite 501
Cambridge, Massachusetts 02142
USA

British Library Cataloguing in Publication Data

A CIP catalogue record for this book is available from the British Library.

Library of Congress Cataloging-in-Publication Data

White, Barbara.
    Women's Career Development: A Study of High Flyers/Barbara White, Charles Cox, and Cary Cooper.
        p.   cm.
    Includes index.
    1. Women executive—Great Britain.   2. Women in business—Great Britain.   3. Women—Employment—Great Britain.   I. Cox, Charles.
II. Cooper, Cary L.   III. Title.
HD6054.4.G7W49   1992
331.4′816584′00941—dc20   92-5696
                                                                           CIP

ISBN 0-631-186557 (pbk)

Typeset in 11 on 13 pt Plantin
by Best-set Typesetter Ltd., Hong Kong
Printed in Great Britain by T.J. Press (Padstow) Ltd.,
Padstow, Cornwall

Contents

List of Figures

List of Tables

1

The Role of Women in the Workplace and Women's Career Development

Introduction

An increasingly familiar image of the successful woman is being portrayed in the media. Headlines such as these are becoming ever more commonplace: 'Running circles round men' (*Sunday Times*, 25 February 1990); 'Business boom for enterprise women' (*Today*, June 1990). However, Blum and Smith (1988) have warned that the reality is a stark contrast to the media images. They caution us to beware of what they describe as the 'politics of optimism' which stem from the image of women's upward mobility. This optimism exaggerates the extent of women's integration and the opportunities available to them in the workplace. The danger associated with this politics of optimism is that the need for reform may be obscured, or that future policymaking may be misdirected, ultimately preventing or slowing further progress. Scase and Goffee (1989) have also remarked that the position of women at work should be the subject of detailed empirical inquiry rather than a topic for rhetorical debate. They believe that research plays a vital role in the process of policy formulation and in setting action agendas.

Women at Work

A report by the Hansard Society (1990) states that there has been a quiet revolution in women's participation in the workplace. In the 1950s women comprised less than one third of the labour force; in the 1990s, they represent almost half of the British workforce. Almost every occupation in every sector of the economy can point to an increase in the numbers of women employed. Of an estimated total workforce of 27.9 million, approximately 42 per cent are women (Institute for Employment Research, 1988). The issue of women reaching top positions, therefore, must be considered against a background in which participation in paid work is nearly as common among women as among men.

Goffee and Scase (1985) have pointed to four main factors which they claim account for this rising number of women in the labour force. First, the implementation of new technological processes within large-scale administrative and productive systems has led to the de-skilling of jobs so that highly trained male workers could be replaced to a large extent by cheaper semi-skilled workers. Second, they suggest that demographic changes have enabled women to take up paid employment; that is, they marry earlier, live longer, and have fewer children in a shorter and earlier period of their life. They also propose that a restructuring of psychological expectations has led women to look for work-related as opposed to marriage-related self-identities. The final factor influencing the upsurge in the numbers of working women is that women's incomes are needed to keep many families above the poverty line.

Despite the quiet revolution in the number of working women, many are blocked in their attempts to gain access to higher occupational positions. Although no formal distinctions are made between jobs for men and jobs for women, there is a fairly clear segmentation of the labour market in most Western countries. The Hansard Society report shows that 70 per cent of women work in lower-level clerical and service-sector jobs. Over 40 per cent of women work in jobs where they have no male colleagues. Metcalf and Leighton (1989) have provided an indication of the under-utilization of women in the labour force. Their report gives information on occupational segregation which shows that a lower proportion of women are professionals, employers, managers, and that a higher proportion are in junior non-manual and lower-level manual work. This segmentation of the labour market is often described in terms of primary and secondary sectors within a dual labour market. Barron and Norris (1976) describe those in the primary sector as earning high wages, having personal autonomy and responsibility, with good employment conditions, security and prospects of career advancement. In contrast, secondary-sector jobs offer low pay, poor working conditions, limited prospects, little autonomy and responsibility, and virtually no job security. Davidson (1990) notes that, despite the introduction of sexual discrimination and equal-pay legislation, there is still a gap between men's and women's earnings (25 per cent differential), and the law still sanctions unequal treatment in the areas of pensions and retirement. She states that, 'Over all, women at work do not enjoy the same job conditions, pay, status and career opportunities as their male counterparts.'

The Hansard Society report concludes that many women are blocked in their attempts to gain access to higher-level positions. Many women are said to encounter a 'glass ceiling' over their aspirations, allowing them to see where they might go but preventing them from getting there.

Women at the top

In any given occupation, the higher the rank the lower the proportion of women. Evidence concerning the number of women at the top is sparse, but figures produced by the Association of University Teachers (1990) suggest that the percentage is as shown in table 1.1, illustrating that women have not made a significant impact on top jobs in either the private or the public sector. Other sources suggest that the number of women in senior management positions may be even lower than those reported by the Association of University Teachers. It is difficult to obtain a realistic estimate of the number of managers in the UK, mainly because the title may incorporate a range of jobs from supervision to board-level management. The highest estimates are from reports using self-defined managers – i.e. 14 per cent of the workforce (Constable and McCormick, 1987; Handy, 1987). A report defining management more tightly suggests that managers and administrators account for 7 per cent of workers in production and 9 per cent in the service sector (Rajan and Pearson, 1986).

Table 1.1   Percentage of women in top jobs

Head teachers	40%
Publishing directors	22%
Circuit judges	17%
Heads of BBC regions	10%
Senior managers in industry	7%
Under-secretaries in Civil Service	5%
University vice-chancellors and principals	2%

Source: Association of University Teachers (1990)

At present the estimated proportion of women in management varies according to occupation, but is approximately one in nine (Marshall, 1984). Reflecting the gender segmentation of the labour market, women are most likely to be in management positions in occupations which have traditionally been women's realms, such as retail and catering (Novarra, 1980). More recently, Nicholson and West (1988) have conducted an extensive longitudinal survey of women in management. They found that the women in their sample were concentrated in the public sector and under-represented in the industrial sector. Even in sectors where women are well represented as employees, they are under-represented in management (e.g. building societies; Ashburner, 1989). In nursing, where 90 per cent of nurses are women, 46 per cent of chief officers (the most senior post in each district) are men (Hutt, 1985). A perhaps rather surprising statistic reported by Hakim (1981) is that the proportion of women in positions of power actually declined between 1911 and 1971, and the number of women in senior management roles is currently estimated at 1–2 per cent (Fraker, 1984).

Prospects for women in the 1990s

The Hansard Society report stated that, 'As a nation, we are committed by our public philosophy and by law to eliminate discrimination against women in the political and public life of the country, and to ensure genuine equality of opportunity for women in all aspects of life.' In addition to this public philosophy, Davidson (1990) points out that the opening of a free European market in 1992 will inevitably pressurize British employers to comply with the European Community directives on equal opportunities. Although there is some concern over equal opportunities, apprehension is growing over predicted skill shortages in the 1990s. The number of young people entering the workforce between 1988 and 1995 is projected to drop by 25 per cent (Metcalf, 1988). Also, the Institute for Employment Research (1988) has predicted that employment will increase by 1.75 million between 1987 and 1995, and that 90 per cent of this increase will be among women workers. Therefore, British organizations will have to acknowledge that they can no longer afford not to utilize the skills of women throughout their working lives.

Coinciding with the increasing numbers of women in the labour market has been a change in the structure of employment in Britain. Employment in manufacturing has declined, while service-sector employment, in which the majority of women workers are located, has increased. Of the 1.75 million new jobs anticipated by 1995, one million will be in professional and related occupations, bringing the proportion of the labour force employed in these sectors to just under 25 per cent by the middle of the decade (Institute for Employment Research, 1988). The evolving structure of the labour market therefore means that more high-status jobs will be available.

To summarize, there has been a growth in traditionally female-dominated sectors of the labour market, an increase in the number of high-level jobs, and a decline in the number of young people entering the labour force. Given these changes, it seems reasonable to expect that women may find it easier to reach top jobs in the 1990s. As the Hansard Society report suggests, economic necessity may compel employers to recognize that the best man for the job in the 1990s is a woman.

In the light of this potential opportunity for women to reach positions of power and influence, it seems appropriate to investigate the issues facing women as they strive for top jobs. The focus of the research reported here is on the process of career development among women who have achieved recognized success in corporate, public and professional life. The aim is to understand the characteristics of those who make it to the top and to see how they achieved their success. In looking at the experiences of successful women, one of our intentions is to identify the barriers to the appointment of women to top jobs. Some barriers will be unique to a particular occupation and so will require special attention if they are to be eradicated; however, women also face more general barriers to success which transcend differences of occupational sector. It is these more general barriers, and the way in which they have been overcome by successful women, which we set out to investigate. It is hoped that such an investigation will lead to a greater understanding of what needs to be done to allow all women to achieve their full potential.

The Successful Women

The sample studied for this research consisted of forty-eight women who had achieved extraordinary levels of career success. These women were executives and entrepreneurs in commerce and industry, and senior members of high-status professions (e.g. lawyers, management consultants, high-level politicians, accountants). The sample reflected, therefore, different business and industrial settings. The sample is illustrative rather than representative of the ways in which women participate in business, the occupations ranging from traditional to non-traditional (Table 1.2). As the aim was to gain insight into the career and personal experiences of successful women, a wide distribution was desirable.

Occupational success

Focusing on the upward mobility of women and the entrance of women into management and other high-status fields has been criticized because it is said to overlook the bases of stratification among employed women. Blum and Smith (1988) claim that such a focus produces an optimism which reflects the position of women in the upper strata to the detriment of women who have not achieved such occupational success. As researchers, we are warned to be aware that we may contribute to this false sense of optimism.

Demonstrably successful individuals have been selected for investigation in accordance with Osipow's (1983) claim that much of the research on the career development of women may have been inconclusive because it mixed respondents of varying levels of success. The objective of the research was to gain a more complete understanding of the dynamics of women's careers. The aim was to focus on mid-career status, taking a long-term view of work and

Table 1.2 Occupational distribution of women in the sample

Newspapers (company owner)	1 ⎫
Editors (news, magazine, television)	3 ⎪
Printing (company owner)	1 ⎬ 7
Television broadcaster	1 ⎪
General management (television)	1 ⎭
Banking	3
Accountancy	5
Solicitors	3
Marketing/PR/Advertising (company owner, general management)	8
Catering (company owner, general manager)	4
Computing (company owner, general manager)	2
Manufacturing (company owner)	4
Miscellaneous	9

personal life. This approach is based on the recommendations of Valliant (1977) and Levinson et al. (1978), who have emphasized that the examination of careers that are well under way is essential. The intention of the research was also to identify the characteristics of the women who have made it to the top and the way in which they did it. By focusing on the experiences of successful women, it may be possible to identify the barriers en route to the top, and the ways in which they may be overcome. It is hoped that the findings may reveal practical recommendations which may help other women to overcome subordination within the labour market. In this sense, our research does not neglect women in the lower occupational strata.

Defining success

Derr (1986) defines 'career success' as 'both being able to live out the subjective and personal values one really believes in and to make a contribution to the world of work.' This definition incorporates both psychological success, which Hall (1976) describes as 'an individual's feeling of success', and external measures of success. When identifying subjects for research on success, one is limited to selection on the basis of observable external measures. Such external measures might be levels of income or occupational status. Due to the diversity of careers to be explored in the current research project, success was peer driven – that is, a career was seen as being successful if it was considered to be so by prominent women's groups established for high-flying women.

Identifying the successful women

The sample was contacted via well-established women's business networks in different regions of the country. Networks are best defined in terms of their stated aims (Women in Enterprise Directory, 1989):

1 To reduce women's sense of isolation in a business world that is still essentially masculine.
2 Not merely to act as a social support group, but also to offer all advantages of traditional male networks.
3 To bring together like-minded women to give them the opportunity to enjoy the social and sisterly benefits that ensue.

An attempt was made to achieve a nationwide sample; however, the main networks involved in the study were located in London and the south-east, Bristol and the north-west. The chairperson of each of the networks was invited to assist in identifying successful women as potential subjects for the project. It was made very clear that to qualify for inclusion in the sample the women must have achieved positions of eminence within their occupational fields. All the networks contacted agreed to co-operate in the research. The names, addresses and telephone numbers of the successful women were usually forwarded by mail.

Contacting the sample

Having collected the names of potential subjects, a letter was sent directly to each woman requesting her participation in the research. The letter outlined briefly the purpose of the research, and described what would be involved should she decide to take part in the project. The women were told that there would be an interview lasting approximately one hour, exploring their background and career history. They were also informed that they would be asked to complete a set of questionnaires at a time convenient to themselves. It was emphasized that all the information given would remain anonymous. This letter was followed by a telephone call to obtain their reactions to the request. All except two agreed to take part in the study. The two women who declined claimed to be overloaded with other commitments and, therefore, did not have time to be interviewed. This excellent response rate minimized any self-selection bias.

Collecting the Data

We decided that an investigation of the careers of successful women would best be conducted by collecting detailed information about the personal experiences of a relatively small number of women. This approach was considered to give a greater understanding of the dynamics of women's careers than could be obtained by a more quantitative, questionnaire-based study. The aim was, however, to move beyond the anecdotal state of much of the work on successful women. A balance must be struck between anecdotes and survey questionnaires, which impose an already structured perception of the world of work based on male-centered notions, without attempting to discover the female perspective.

The interview schedule used for this research was designed within the framework of the Sonnenfelt and Kotter (1982) model of career development (see figure 1.1, p. 14). The organization of the interview did not correspond exactly to the nine components of the model, owing to the need to achieve a more natural, conversational sequence. The data collected are reorganized and discussed under the following headings.

Childhood

The objective here was partly to obtain some biographical data on the sibling position, parental occupation and hence the social class of the women. In addition, this section focused on the qualitative nature of the parent–child relationship. The role of early socialization experiences and their part in determining career orientation was explored in some detail. This covered factors such as identification with mother or father, parental expectations and encouragement of achievement striving. The interview also sought evidence of critical events during childhood which were perceived as character building or particularly influential in developmental terms.

Education

Education is said to be strongly linked to the type and extent of vocational participation. Therefore the level and the subject of education were investigated. Data were also collected on gender segregation, education and the level and type of professional qualifications. The issue of whether the acquisition of qualifications was part of a long-term career plan was explored.

Personality and motivation

The personality traits which were of interest were assessed mainly by means of psychometric tests. There was, however, a limit to the number of objective tests that the respondents could realistically be expected to complete.

Locus of control Locus of control was assessed using the Spector (1988) work locus of control scale and Makin's (1987) career-locus questionnaire. In addition, the women were also asked directly whether they felt that luck had played an important role in their working lives.

Need for achievement   This was assessed using Smith's (1973) quick measure of achievement motivation. The issue of motivation was examined more generally within the framework of the expectancy/valence theory. The aim was to explore women's understanding of the contingency between performance and outcomes – i.e. what people have to do to be promoted. Information was sought on the 'pushes and pulls' acting on women embarking upon careers, and the value (or valence) they placed on different career outcomes.

Gender identity   The possibility that women may mute their awareness of the potential disadvantages of being female was explored. Women were asked to express their views on feminism, and the advice they would offer to other aspiring career women. Affiliation to networks and views on their utility were explored in an attempt to assess concern for women as a group or their need to maintain an individual status.

Other aspects of personality and motivation which were assessed by psychometric tests alone included managerial self-efficacy and creative style.

Work history

This section was concerned with obtaining information about career concepts. In accordance with Driver's (1979) recommendations, the women were asked to describe their career decision-making story. This story included the timing of career moves and the decision-making processes underlying each move. The extent of parental involvement in career choices and of conscious decision-making and career planning were discussed in order to determine the career concept. The possibility of changes in the career concept over time was also examined. In addition, the women were asked for their current definitions of a 'job' and a 'career'.

Power and politics

This aspect of the research explored the process of organizational socialization and the role of organizational politics. Although it is acknowledged that organizational politics have negative connotations for many individuals, it was thought that the best way to confront this issue would be to ask direct questions. The women were asked whether they were aware of organizational politics and whether they used such politics. To clarify the definition of organizational politics, the respondents were also asked to describe what they perceived to be political strategies. The possibility that participation in team sports could be related to a willingness to engage in organization politics was assessed. Participants were also asked to complete a political styles questionnaire (Kakabadse, 1986).

Non-work – family history

Family responsibilities were explored in this section. Patterns of occupational behaviour were investigated, with particular attention given to the timing of marriage and childbirth. The priority placed on family and work roles was explored, together with the changes in these priorities over time. Issues of role conflict and overload were investigated along with coping mechanisms adopted. Questions on the contribution that partners made to childcare, the running of the household and the extent to which the women employed paid home help were also included.

The Successful Career

There is a general lack of uniformity in the definition of career, which Driver (1988) suggests is due to lack of agreement among theorists over two basic issues. First, do career choices change over time or stay constant, and, second, are career choices externally generated or are they internal processes?

Sonnenfelt and Kotter (1982) have presented a conceptual framework for organizing career-development theory, based on two very similar dimensions. The first relates to whether concepts of the *environment* are static or dynamic; the second relates to whether concepts of the *individual* are static or dynamic. On the basis of these two dimensions, Sonnenfelt and Kotter have outlined four stages in the maturation of career theory.

1 *The social-structure approach.* This began in the 1930s and attempted to identify external determinants of occupational attainment, such as social class.
2 *The personality-trait approach.* This began in the 1920s and looked at the relationship between internal factors, such as personality and vocational choice. This view was largely one of a static individual in a static world.
3 *The career-stages approach.* In the 1950s a more dynamic approach was adopted which acknowledged that an individual's career changes and that

different stages are marked by different needs, concerns, commitments, aspirations and interests. However, the notion of developing one's career over an entire lifetime is relatively recent (Hall, 1976). Adulthood is no longer viewed as a static period, but a period of change and development.

4 *Life-cycle theory*. Work in the 1970s provided a more extended and dynamic view of the career stages, recognizing that career stages reflect and interact with the individual's life, past, present and future. Hall (1976) defined career as an 'individually perceived sequence of attitudes and behaviours associated with work related experiences and activities over the span of a person's life.'

Sonnenfelt and Kotter note that in the process of becoming increasingly dynamic, career theory has gained more variability and complexity along two dimensions. One dimension runs across time, the other across life space. Career outcomes are said to be the result of interactions among occupational, personal and family factors throughout one's lifetime. Driver (1988) concurs with this belief and comments that there is a growing consensus that career includes both work and non-work activities. The definition of career proffered by Derr (1986) reflects this consensus. She describes career as 'a long-term work history characterised by an intended and intentional sense of direction that allows for and honours aspects of one's personal life'.

What is career development?

Vondracek et al. (1986) have emphasized the need to be aware that change and development are not equivalent. Whenever development occurs there is change, but not all changes can be classified as developmental. It is proposed that changes must be successive and have systematic character for them to be termed developmental changes. The successive aspect of development derives from the observation that changes as seen in the present are in part influenced and constrained by changes that occurred in the past. Gutek and Larwood (1987) propose that the notion of development, when applied to careers, implies that a series of jobs represents some progress: for example, climbing a hierarchy, increased salary, increased recognition and respect, and greater freedom to pursue interests.

Having established the meaning of the terms 'career' and 'development', it is possible to arrive at a comprehensive definition of career development. The operational definition used in the research reported here is:

A successive and systematic sequence of attitudes and behaviours associated with work-related experiences, which acknowledges the individual's personal life, over the entire span of the life cycle.

A Career-development Model

A model to guide the research was required which emphasized the reciprocities between the individual, her environment and the active contribution the individual makes to her own development over time. In accordance with the definition of career outlined earlier, the model must acknowledge work and non-work factors. The model of career development outlined by Sonnenfelt and Kotter (1982), shown in figure 1.1, appeared to meet these conditions and provides a useful framework within which to organize previous research on women's career development.

This model, however, has received some criticism on the grounds that it centres on individual and environmental factors, which are believed to influence career outcomes leading to a preoccupation with isolated effects. These critics (Mihal et al., 1984) call for a descriptive process model that goes beyond a listing of influencing factors to describe the process by which careers develop.

These criticisms have been overcome in this research by considering the processes operating within each of the nine component factors outlined in the models. Certain components of the model will be treated in greater depth when it is perceived that previous literature and research has neglected to explore the contribution of the component to career success.

Do we need a separate theory of women's career development?

Perun and Beilby (1981) complain that little has been done to explain changes in women's lives in developmental terms, or to incorporate them into theories of the development of occupational behaviour. This complaint resounds throughout the literature on women's career development. Tinsley and Heesacker (1984) comment that, although not completely bereft of theory, the topic of women at work as studied by psychologists is hardly theory driven. Fitzgerald and Betz (1983) are concerned about the implications of this lack of theory: 'There is a lack of comprehensive conceptualisations or theories which are capable of producing meaningful, testable hypotheses regarding the development of women's careers'.

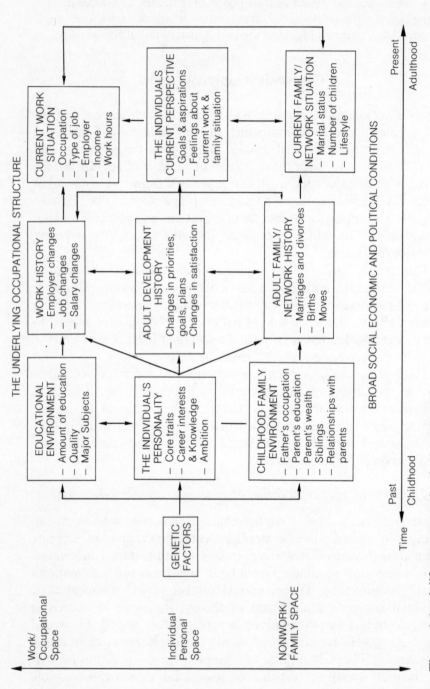

Figure 1.1 A lifespan career-development model
Source: Sonnenfelt and Kotter (1982)

In 1981 Perun and Beilby stated that research on adulthood in women had focused on the family cycle at the expense of the work cycle. The outcome was that no formal theory of women's occupational behaviour existed. Theoretical advances have been made since 1982, although most have received some criticism. Three main theoretical trends, outlined below, have guided research on women's career development.

The classic model

Traditionally, career-development theorists (e.g. Super, 1957; Ginzberg, 1951) have based their models on studies of men. The result is what has been termed the 'classic model', in which career patterns are typified by the careers expected of successful males. In 1967 Tyler claimed that 'Much of what we know about the stages through which an individual passes as he prepares to find his place in the world of work might appropriately be labelled the vocational development of white middle class males.'

Many models propose that there are two early career stages (e.g. Hall, 1976; Schein, 1979). During the 'education and exploration' phase (ages 15–25) the individual learns job-related skills and maps career possibilities, then chooses a career. In the following 'identification and establishment' phase (ages 25–40) young men identify with that career and begin to move in it. The third stage (ages 40–60) is 'maintenance and stagnation', which leads to disengagement and retirement. A small number of men may avoid stagnation by continuing to grow successfully in their careers or by changing direction (Driver, 1979).

Wortley and Amatea (1982) note that attempts to generalize about normative patterns of adult development are based on the premise that, while the nature, duration and timing of an individual's career pattern may vary, certain pathways and tasks are predictable. They do comment, however, that, although adults as a group face multiple role changes that necessitate adaptation, it would be an error to say that the stages are fixed and uninfluenced by individual differences. They also point out that gender prescribes behaviour more prominently than age at any given time. Perun and Beilby (1981) also comment on the inappropriate age structure of the classic model when applied to women. They suggest that the determinants of the occupational behaviour of women are different from those of men, and that the trajectory of the work cycle of women is less predictable than that of men.

Gilligan (1979) argues that proponents of the classic model fail to take account of the experience of women, 'implicitly adopting the male life as the norm they have tried to fashion women out of masculine cloth'. The classic model ignores the unique social and family situation of women, and places no significance on demands on women external to the work environment. As such, it cannot accommodate female experience.

Neoclassic model

The neoclassic model does acknowledge that competing family demands and individual preferences may interact with organizational needs, and thereby affect careers. Early attempts to address the work cycle of women include Psanthas (1968) and Zytowski (1969). These theories emphasized the role of marriage, motherhood and home-making. These models are based on the assumption that women's career roles would be relegated to a subordinate position, in the belief that home-making and work roles are mutually exclusive. Forrest and Mikolaitis (1986) believe that such a perspective per-petuates the belief that women are bound to men and children in their lives.

Super (1984) claims that the career patterns of men are essentially applicable to women if they are modified to take marriage and childbearing into account. He describes patterns for women as stable home-making, conventional (working followed by marriage), stable working, double-tracking and interrupted, unstable and multiple trial (the patterns for men were fewer and included stable, con-ventional, unstable and multiple trial). Within this model, questions are addressed of how absences, their timing and spacing affects women's development. Super also hypothesized that there is no difference in the part self-concept plays in male and female career development. It is proposed that both make decisions on the basis of their self-concept and their concept of the circumstances in which they live. Several authors (e.g. Putnam and Hansen, 1972; Richardson, 1974) have criticized this proposal, suggesting that self-concept may be implemented differently by men and women. Perun and Beilby (1981) state that 'we cannot assume that the process of self concept development . . . is identical for both sexes.'

Astin (1984) has presented a sociopsychological model of occupa-tional behaviour. The basic work motivation is said to be the same for men and women, but they make different choices because of their early socialization experiences and because structural opportunities are different.

In an invited response to Astin's theory, a number of limitations were identified. Gilbert (1984) questioned whether the model sufficiently addressed the realities of the career development of women. Gilbert points to a 'schism' between our current institutional structure and the demands of family roles. Even when women make the required changes in sex-role beliefs and behaviour, and expect to include active participation in both occupational and family roles, the problem of societal structure still arises. For example, a woman may be hampered in her efforts to combine family and work by the belief that to be successful one must work extraordinary hours in the office. Gilbert asks, 'Can a concept of career that includes involvement in family and occupational roles realistically co-exist with social institutions that embody the values of a patriarchal society?'

Kahn (1984) also criticized Astin's model on the grounds that it relegated family issues to a subordinate position: 'If we adopt Astin's theoretical stance and view work as the principal activity of life (subsuming both career and family cycles), then do we risk relegating social and familial relationships to background factors which are responsive and subordinate to work?'

Astin's model does represent, however, an advance on earlier theoretical formulations in that it looks at the way in which social forces reshape occupational decisions, and at the impact of this on contemporary women and their occupational behaviour. The model will be outlined in greater detail later in this book.

Researchers have begun to question whether the neoclassic model is enlightened enough. Following a review of the literature, Osipow (1983) comments that, although there exist similarities between the sexes in the career-development process, there are enough differences to warrant attempts to develop distinct theories, 'at least until such a time as the sexual equality of career opportunity exists and the results have permeated society at all levels'.

Dual-development model

The dual-development model suggests that the understanding of women's careers requires an acknowledgement that women have fundamentally different situations in developing careers than men have. Issues such as sex discrimination, the structure of opportunities and recent emphasis on equal opportunities may have altered the patterns of women's career development from that of men. Therefore, not only do we need to consider family and competing demands which are external to the work environment, but we also need to account for phenomena within the workplace which may distinguish men from women (Brooks, 1984). Larwood and Gatticker (1986) propose that women's career development does not merely lag behind that of men, but that it may proceed in a different manner.

Gutek and Larwood (1987) outline four major reasons why women's careers differ from those of men. First, different expectations of the appropriateness of jobs for each sex affect the types of jobs men and women prepare for and select. Second, husbands and wives differentially prepare to accommodate each other's careers (that is, wives are usually more adaptive). Also, parental roles differ for men and women, in that the mother's role requires more time and effort. Finally, compared with men, women face more constraints in the workplace which are detrimental to their career advancement.

Prospects for research

Following a discussion of the literature, Gutek and Larwood (1987) comment that a clear picture of the career-developmental process for women has not yet emerged. They suggest that it may be premature to develop a theory of women's occupational behaviour, as it is barely a decade since changes in women's role at work began. They conclude that more research is needed. Tinsley and Heesacker (1984) express similar reservations. They state that in some cases it is clear that research investigates timeless phenomena. In other instances, however, the findings need to be replicated using data from a more contemporary sample of women.

Vondracek et al. (1986) suggest that the paucity in current research may be attributed to two main causes. First, it is developmental, but insufficiently contextual. (In some cases it is also insufficiently developmental because little research has been carried out on life-course changes in women's lives.) Such research has led to person-centred explanations of women's occupational behaviour. It is often suggested that socialization practices encourage the development of personality traits or behaviour which are contrary to the demands of senior occupational positions (e.g. fear of success; Horner, 1972), and unwillingness to take risks (Hennig and Jardim, 1978). Putnam and Heinen (1985) point out that there are numerous inherent difficulties in applying the trait approach to the study of women. They believe the trait approach to be antiquated. Approaches to leadership which emphasize personality traits without also considering situational factors have been abandoned after twenty-five years of inconclusive research on male leaders. Reviving the approach for women is likely to be no more productive. They also warn that, without female role models, women become more dependent on expert prescriptions for effective managerial behaviour than do their male counterparts. The development of a universal set of traits will force aspiring career women into a predetermined mould, which may be contrary to their particular strengths and inappropriate in the given situation.

Second, the research is situational, but not sufficiently developmental. Historical and sociological research has not paid heed to intra-individual differences as they influence and are influenced by the context in which they are embedded. Almquist (1977) noted that

> The most current research is macrosocial rather than microsocial, based on large scale, impersonal, aggregated and static data rather than small scale, personal disaggregated and dynamic findings. From this we get a very firm appraisal of the position of women in the labour force but we do not know the processes by which they attained it.

Perun and Beilby (1981) claim that to understand the changes in women's lives we need a theoretical perspective which synthesizes the outcomes of macro-level processes with individual-level behaviour.

After sampling research studies in applied industrial psychology, Acker (1987) concluded that men are over-represented as subjects of study. Much of the work on career development has used college-educated, white, middle-class men as a standard against which others are compared. Women are often studied to see how they depart from the male standard (see Davidson and Cooper, 1987). Gutek and Larwood (1987) complain that, although it is likely that women's careers will be different from those of men, it does not mean that every study of women's career development should involve a comparison with men. They emphasize that there are internal dynamics to women's careers which also warrant examination. Therefore, while drawing comparisons with the findings from studies of high-flying men, the following discussion will also attempt to address issues of particular relevance to women.

The aim in the current study, therefore, is to begin to compensate for the lack of theory-driven research. Having reviewed the literature, we have introduced theory from general organizational psychology, which it is hoped will further our understanding of women's work behaviour. In addition, models which relate specifically to the issue of women's career development are tested for their explanatory validity when applied to the careers of successful women.

2

Childhood

Introduction

The interest and research which has focused on events during childhood is based on the enduring belief, embedded in many theories of development, that they have a bearing on events in later life. This inference is derived from the notion that prior development of the individual may constrain the potential of later influences to change the individual. Therefore, it seems reasonable to propose that women's childhood experiences may provide some of the antecedents of success at work.

Childhood events form a central component of Astin's (1985) model of career choice and work behaviour which was formulated to enhance understanding of women's behaviour at work. The model includes Roe's (1956) concept of need and the importance of early childhood experiences in shaping occupational interests. It is claimed that the model can be used to explain the occupational behaviour of both genders, based on the premise that the basic work motivation is the same for men and for women. They make different occupational choices, however, due to early socialization and because opportunities are different for men and women. Astin defends her proposition that a single theory should be able to account for the work behaviour of men and women by pointing out that they share a common human condition and live together in the same world of personal obligations and social conditions.

Astin goes on to argue that if men and women are working for essentially the same reasons, then we need to identify the variables that translate motivation into different work expectations and hence different work outcomes. Astin's model incorporates four major constructs: motivation, expectations, sex-role socialization and the structure of opportunity.

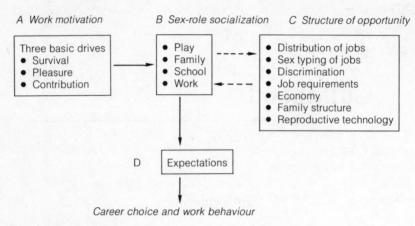

Figure 2.1   Model of career choice and work behaviour
Source: Astin (1984)

The model represented in figure 2.1 entails four major principles. First, work behaviour is described as a motivated activity to satisfy three basic needs: survival, pleasure and contribution. Second, career choices are based on expectations of accessibility of alternative forms of work and their capacity to satisfy needs. Third, expectations are shaped by early socialization and in part by the perceived structure of opportunity. Finally, expectations can be modified by changes in the structure of opportunity and this change in expectations can lead to changes in career choice and in work behaviour.

Astin's contention that childhood socialization is an important influencing factor in occupational behaviour has been the topic of much research. More specifically, research on high flyers has tended to focus on the quality of the relationship between children and their parents (e.g. Cox and Cooper, 1988).

Parental Relationships and Self-concept

Most theories of vocational development incorporate constructs of 'identity' or 'self-concept'. For example, Super (1957) suggests that the adequacy of a career decision will partially depend upon the similarity between the individual's self-concept and the vocational concept of the career that he/she chooses. Holland (1985) also proposes that individuals prefer to work in an environment where their identity is expressed and valued.

Gender differences in identity formation

It is often proposed in the literature that clear sex differences exist in self-concept. The origins of these differences are said to be located in early childhood relationships with parents. Chodorow (1978) suggests that because women are generally the primary care-givers during the early years of a child's life, both sexes begin life being dependent on a woman and as a result their primary identification is with the mother. Parsons (1965) and Lynn (1969) confirm that both males and females form their first attachment to their mother. It is proposed that a boy must separate and differentiate his identity from that of his mother. A boy is said to acquire a 'positional identity' which requires separation from the mother and the learning of specific behaviours modelled by a more remote father. In contrast, a girl's identity development is based on sameness with the mother. A girl's identity is described as a 'personal' one which is continuous with her earliest attachments and is based on relationships with other people.

Gilligan (1982) used Chodorow's concepts of attachment and separation to delineate the different modes of self-definition. She conducted extensive interviews which revealed sex differences in experience and understanding of the relationship between self and other. These differences were reflected in self-descriptions. Women reflect their sense of identity primarily in terms of their connection to others, for example helping, supporting and not hurting others. Gilligan comments that, although many of the women she interviewed were 'highly successful and achieving women', they tended not to mention their achievements in describing themselves; rather they focused on the conflict that they felt between achievement and care. Relationship problems are construed in terms of how to respond with care for others. Women develop empathy which enables them to understand the viewpoint of others.

The sense of identity reflected in the self-descriptions of the men in Gilligan's study were distinctly different. Men emphasize their sense of separateness as opposed to their sense of 'being' in relation to others. Men derive their sense of identity by differentiating themselves from others in terms of abilities and attributes. Relationship problems are construed as issues of competing rights of individuals which are resolved according to standards of fairness. A man assesses how he would like to be treated if in the other's position, rather than attempting to identify with the other.

Identity and role orientation

The development of personal identity may be part of the evolution process involved in the creation of what Bernard (1978) conceptualizes as two worlds. Bernard states that the majority of people inhabit a one-sex world – women have their world and men have theirs. The female world is said to be based on status and love and/or duty, while the male world is based on what Bernard calls the 'cash-nexus' contract (the exchange of work for financial reward).

It would seem plausible to interpret the 'love/duty' ethos of the female world as the outcome of the female personal identity. The most pervasive function associated with the love/duty ethos is a stroking function. Bernard (1971) outlines this function as showing solidarity, raising the status of others, giving help, rewarding, agreeing, complying, understanding and passively accepting. Emotionally supportive behaviour is viewed as the keystone of women's relationships with others. More recently, Bernard (1981) has documented a decline in the dominance of the love/duty ethos among women and it is proposed that women are becoming increasingly involved in the cash-nexus world.

Identity mode of self-definition and motivational needs

It can be argued that the socialization experiences of women during childhood may influence their mode of self-definition and hence their orientation towards involvement in the male-dominated cash-nexus world. This argument is further reinforced by the proposal that there is a link between the modes of self-definition and motivational needs. The 'separate' sense of identity is created by differentiating self from others in terms of abilities and attributes. The standard of self-assessment is one of individual achievement and success. This form of identity is likely to engender a need for achievement. In contrast, the 'connected' self is assessed in terms of the quality of care given and the ability to maintain the inter-connectedness of people. This form of identity can logically be associated with a need for affiliation. Hoffman (1972) has pointed out that there is a lot of evidence that women have greater affiliative needs than men, which is consistent with Gilligan's (1982) finding that men have separate identities while women have connected identities.

The dysfunctional nature of need for affiliation

In 1972 Horner introduced the concept of 'fear of success' which was said to be applicable largely to women. Horner found that women demonstrated poorer performance in competitive tasks than when working alone. This finding lead Horner to conclude that women were afraid of success because they feared social rejection or loss of femininity. Success in a competitive situation may also be seen to be at odds with the stroking function associated with the love/duty ethos. The affiliative motive was said to be dysfunctional to success, as Horner suggests: 'out-performing a competitor may be antagonistic to making him a friend.'

Hoffman (1972) points out that need for affiliation is not necessarily dysfunctional. Fear of success will operate only if achievement goals are incompatible with affiliative goals. For instance, excellence in school is rewarded by approval of parents, teachers and peers. Hoffman goes on to argue that the qualities required for sustained top performance as an adult are not 'part of a girl's make up'. The rationale behind this statement is that girls strive for approval and so perform well at school; they do not, however, become involved in the task itself because they are less motivated by striving for mastery. Performance may also decline because success in occupational endeavours is not highly valued by parents. The research of Standley and Soule (1974) into the personal and vocational histories of women in male-dominated professions supports this argument. They found that parents were less committed to their daughter's career than to her academic pursuits. The explanation offered by Standley and Soule is that parents may have been interested in academic credentials to announce their daughter's worth and, once stated, priorities turn to traditional values of housewifery.

Hoffman attempts to describe the origins of sex differences in achievement motivation. He suggests that there are four factors associated with early parent–child interactions which cause boys to learn 'effectance' (that is, how to have an impact upon the environment) through mastery while girls learn effectance through eliciting help and protection from others:

1 Girls receive less encouragement in early independence striving.
2 Girls receive more parental protection.

3 Girls are under less social and cognitive pressure to establish an identity separate from their mother.

4 Girls encounter less mother–child conflict.

Insufficient independence training   All infants are said to be dependent, but, as the child matures, independence striving will increase. White (1960) has called this independence striving the 'effectance motive' – that is, the child's need to have an effect upon the environment. Early independence exploration requires a secure affective base. The independence and competence orientation will be learnt most effectively with the parent present so that, as the child explores and moves towards independence, safety is still in sight. Baumrind (1971) goes on to point out that a secure base is necessary but not sufficient for the development of independence behaviour. The child also requires opportunities for independence behaviour and parental encouragement. Hoffman (1972) contends that the female child is often given inadequate parental encouragement in independence strivings. Collard's (1964) findings support this contention. Mothers of four-year-olds were asked at what age they would permit certain behaviours which were linked to independence granting and achievement induction. The mothers of girls responded with significantly later ages than the mothers of boys.

Protectiveness   As the child explores and moves towards independence, Hoffman (1972) claims that parents feel a combination of anxiety and pleasure. The parents of boys demonstrate their pride in the child's achievement *per se*, while the parents of girls show greater anxiety. Parental indication of anxiety may be detrimental to the child's exploratory attempts because the child will doubt his/her own competence. Hoffman suggests that indirect evidence may be drawn from the finding that, despite the greater maturity and sturdiness of female children, parents think of them as being more fragile.

As a result of anxiety felt towards the female child's independence striving, the mother may exhibit over-help. The mother responds too quickly with help, with the result that the child does not develop the ability to tolerate frustration. As a result, the child withdraws from the task rather than tackle the problem and tolerate the temporary frustration. Crandall and Rabson (1960) state that this withdrawal behaviour is more characteristic of female children. They found that in conditions of free play girls were more likely to withdraw from threatening situations and were more likely to seek help from adults.

Kagan and Moss (1962) report that this pattern of dependency is reinforced in later socialization and that childhood dependency predicts adulthood dependency in females, but not in males.

Separation of identity As discussed earlier, a boy's separation from his mother begins earlier and is more complete than a girl's. A girl is encouraged to maintain identification with her mother and, as a result, is not as likely to establish an early independent self. A boy develops a separate sense of identity while a girl develops a connected sense of identity. The connected identity mitigates against the early experience of coping with the environment independently, which Hoffman (1972) claims is crucial in the development of competence and self-confidence.

Mother–child conflict Heinstein (1965) has shown that boys experience more conflict with their mothers than girls. These encounters are said to facilitate a separation of self from the mother. Hoffman (1972) suggests that one implication of this is that girls need a little maternal rejection if they are to become independent and self-confident. Stein and Bailey (1973) reach similar conclusions:

> Perhaps the major theme that emerges from the socialisation data is that the childrearing practices that are conducive to feminine sex-typing are often antagonistic to those that lead to achievement oriented behaviour. A female child is most likely to develop achievement behaviour and independence when her parents are moderately warm and moderately to highly permissive, and when they reinforce and encourage achievement related efforts. Some concomitant features of the practices in the families of highly achievement oriented females are moderate punitiveness, high demands on the child and acceleration attempts by the mother.

Hoffman emphasizes that maternal hostility need not be equated to rejection but to an absence of 'smother love'. Girls may experience too much maternal rapport and protection during their early years. The outcome is that, as adults, they are unwilling to face stress and they have inadequate motivation for autonomous achievement. The developing female will continue to depend upon adults to solve her problems and hence she needs to maintain affective ties with others.

Fitzgerald and O'Crites (1980) have criticized the work of Hoffman on the grounds that it is patronizing to suggest that women strive for approval rather than mastery. They also claim that Hoffman's theory does not allow for the behaviour of those women who do display the modal masculine pattern of achievement behaviour. However, on the basis of the earlier discussion of Hoffman's work it would seem that this criticism is largely unjustified. Hoffman does not treat women as a homogeneous group and he does allow for the possibility of variation among women in achievement motivation.

The Quality of the Parent–Child Relationship among Successful Women

Analysis of our interviews with successful women in industry and professions revealed a variety of parent–child relationships; however, a consistent theme emerged from their descriptions. In most cases the parent–child relationship facilitated the development of an early sense of independence and self-sufficiency.

Approximately 30 per cent of our sample of successful women described their relationship with their parents as being stable and close knit. The women also emphasized that their parents had supported and encouraged achievement, and that they had promoted autonomy of decision-making. Five of these women did mention, however, that their parents had been strict in their child-rearing practices. One said, for example:

> My mother was very strict and rather Victorian. There was a lot of love there but my parents were hard. We never knew that we had money, we were not given luxuries and we were expected to work hard.

This description of parent–child relations matches the outline of parental behaviours which are said to promote achievement striving and independence in female children reported by Stein and Bailey (1973). It would seem that a large proportion of the parents of successful women are warm, moderately permissive, they encourage and reinforce achievement-related efforts and in some cases they are also moderately punitive. This parental strictness was invariably perceived positively in retrospect as being a source of character building.

The general recollection of childhood reported by this group of women as being a happy period is consistent with the reports of male high flyers in the study by Cox and Cooper (1988). In contrast, a large proportion of the successful women (44 per cent) experienced a problematic relationship with their mothers or they had a remote relationship with both their parents. One woman said:

From the age of eight it became difficult because I was separated by
virtue of my education and intellectual interests. The isolation grew as
I got older. I became conscious of the gap between family life in the
middle class and my own background. I resented the lack in my own
family. There was a lack of common ground and an inability to
communicate.

This lack of bonding in the parent–child relationship could have
encouraged the development of a separate sense of identity among
these women. Hoffman (1972) claims that this increases the probability of early experiences of coping with the environment independently, which is said to be essential in the development of
competence and self-confidence.

Over one fifth of the successful women interviewed mentioned
that they had experienced a particularly poor relationship with their
mothers. For example:

I had an extremely difficult relationship with my parents. I was born
by Caesarean section and the bonding between my mother and myself
was flawed. I think that my mother secretly believed that I was not
her child because I was so tall and she was small. Then, because of the
war, I spent some time with my grandparents. I often felt that I might
have been adopted. My mother died this year and it has never been
resolved. I had to prove that I could achieve in order to gain her
approval.

In Hoffman's terms this mother–daughter conflict should act to
facilitate the early separation of self from the mother. Similar
patterns of hostile mother–daughter relations have been observed in
other studies of successful women. In a review of the literature,
Bardwick (1971) found that high-achieving females had hostile
mothers while high-achieving males had warm mothers. Tangri
(1972) provided further support for this argument in her finding
that mothers of achievement-oriented females fostered emotional
independence rather than dependency. In adulthood these achievement-oriented females were less close to their family origins than
more traditional females.

Without maternal rapport and protection during their early years
these women may have learnt to be more independent and self-
confident. It can be speculated that the mothers of these women
would be unlikely to exhibit over-help, enabling the child to develop
tolerance of temporary frustration in tackling problems. Evidence to

support this speculation may be drawn from a study by Kagan and Moss (1962), who report that the daughters of hostile mothers were less likely to withdraw from stressful situations. This ability to tolerate stress might constitute an important attribute in the 'high pressure working lives' of women at the top, as discussed by Cooper and Davidson (1982).

Kets de Vries (1980) offers an alternative explanation of the processes linking parent–child relations and future career success. He observed that a central problem for many male entrepreneurs is their relationship with their father. In a similar way, successful women report difficulties in their relationship with the same-sex parent. Kets de Vries states that the entrepreneur's father is portrayed as remote, rejecting and unpredictable. This relationship is said to increase the likelihood of insecurity, self-esteem problems and lack of self-confidence. Kohut (1971) claims that this lack of integration and the fragmentation of parental images results in the absence of a cohesive self. Kets de Vries goes on to suggest that the inability to identify with parental figures encourages that adoption of a strategy described as 'conformist rebelliousness'. This strategy is defined as an urge to rebel which is restrained by forces which necessitate compromise. Such individuals often possess controlled hostility and suspicion towards people in authority as a result of their earlier experience of perceived control, rejection and inconsistencies in parental actions. These problems may lead to identity confusions and difficulties with career choice. The individual often drifts between jobs testing his/her abilities. The individual is said to adopt a reactive mode characterized by attempts to exert control over the environment which in childhood had proved to be unreliable. On reaching the top, or upon becoming an entrepreneur, the individual gains control over a tangible entity – i.e. the enterprise. Although Kets de Vries focuses on the entrepreneur, it is possible that individuals who strive to reach the top of their organization may be motivated by a similar drive to control their environment.

Identification with the father

One of the outcomes of separation of self from the mother is that the girl may then develop a closer identification with her father. Block (1977) states that it is more common for fathers to train their daughters in traditional femininity. They show greater concern with the affective and interpersonal development of their daughters than with achievement-related behaviour. Data on career-oriented women suggest, however, that paternal encouragement can be an important antecedent of achievement orientation (Tangri, 1972). An influential study of senior women managers by Hennig and Hackman (1964) found a regular pattern in the family history of these successful women. All the women recalled childhood as being happy. They also spoke of a closeness and warmth in relations with parents. A very special relationship was said to exist between fathers and daughters. Fathers and daughters shared activities which are traditionally regarded as appropriate for fathers and sons. When growing up the women enjoyed participating in outdoor activities and play with their fathers.

In an extensive review of the literature on sex-typing, Huston (1983) concludes that 'Sex-typed activities . . . provide an environmental context for learning personal and social behaviour such as dependence and independence'. Huston also emphasizes the role of play in the context of masculine and feminine personal social behaviour. Lever (1978) makes several observations about children's play which can be associated with the formation of expectations about need gratification. Boys are said to play outdoors, which gives them greater freedom and independence. Girls play inside the home, which is private and less subject to scrutiny while playing outdoors is open to surveillance and recognition. Boys also engage in competitive games more often than girls. Competitiveness and the drive to achieve are said to be reinforced by such games.

Hennig and Hackman state that the relationship with their father added another dimension to childhood from which the girls derived attention, approval, reward and confirmation. It was an added source of learning through which the girls gained a role model with whom they could begin to identify. To their fathers they were girls, but they could do much more than ordinary girls did. These girls developed what are traditionally thought of as male characteristics: drive to achieve, an orientation to a task, enjoyment of competition and capacity to take risks. The role traditionally associated with girls was found to be too constraining. They fought for greater freedom and their fathers actively supported them.

Influential parent among successful women

The consequence of the poor mother–daughter relations was that many of the women formed closer relationships with their fathers.

Another eight women claimed that they had been closer to their fathers, although they did not have a problematic relationship with their mothers. These women said that their fathers had treated them as sons that they did not have. They were encouraged to use their initiative and to be financially independent. They were also led to believe that they could be successful if they chose to be, as is illustrated by the following quotation:

> I was always very fond of my father. I enjoyed doing things with my father. I suppose I was a bit of a tomboy really and we both liked sport, whereas none of the rest of the family did, so we had quite a lot in common. I would go with him when he was doing jobs at the weekend and he would let me get on and do things and use my initiative.

In addition, 35 per cent of the successful women identified their fathers as being the most influential parent in terms of their development. These women felt that they were similar to their fathers in temperament. As one senior woman said, 'I had a good relationship with both of my parents but I'm very like my father temperamentally. I was brought up to be very independent and strong willed and my father is the same.'

These reports bear striking resemblance to the findings of Hennig and Hackman (1964). The women executives in their study reported a very special father–daughter relationship in which they shared activities traditionally regarded as appropriate for fathers and sons. Research (e.g. Lever, 1978) suggests that the games that boys and fathers play reinforce competitiveness and the drive to achieve. Like those in the current sample, the women interviewed by Hennig and Hackman also suggested that their fathers made them believe that they could do more than girls were traditionally able to do. The role associated with girls was found to be too constraining. These women fought for greater freedom and their fathers actively supported them. The lack of emphasis on appropriate sex-role behaviour in childhood is thought to have led these women to develop what are often regarded as innate masculine traits. Hennig and Jardim (1978) point out that the development of these traits may be better understood if seen as based on knowledge, skills and competence, which boys develop by virtue of the activities and relationships in which they engage and the rewards they receive for mastery of these things. These processes may also have been operating among the successful women in the current sample. As a result of their childhood activities, these women have developed knowledge, skills and competencies which help them to tackle the male-dominated world of work.

Maternal influence – a positive model of femininity

The women in Hennig and Hackman's (1964) study did not recall their relationship with their mother in great detail. The women emphasized that both parents shared the same aspirations for their daughters. The typical mother provided a warm, caring and socially sanctioned feminine model, while the father confirmed his daughter in believing that these were not binding models of behaviour but a matter of choice. The result was that these women were able to adopt traditionally male traits without abandoning their femininity

Marshall (1984) makes a distinction between public and private worlds which may be invoked to clarify the maternal influence on the women managers in Hennig and Hackman's study. Marshall suggests that women's sphere of influence is often restricted to the private world (home). Their position in this world can serve to moderate male domination experienced within the public world of work. Marshall states that in the private arena women have the opportunity to establish their identity, skills and influence which are recognized and valued by other family members. As Bardwick (1979) suggests, 'When we feel pride in the qualities, values and accomplishments that have historically been ours, we will have finally given up our minority status'.

Twenty-six per cent of the successful women felt that their mothers had been most influential in their development. Their mothers were often described as having very strong characters and driving energy which their daughters had found to be a positive influence. As one woman said, 'My mother has a very strong character. She has a lot of drive and energy and she pushed me to do everything that I could do. Without her drive I think that I would have been a different person.' Such reports are consistent with the conclusion of Stein and Bailey (1973) that females are most likely to exhibit achievement behaviour given acceleration attempts by the mother. In addition, the strong maternal figure may have provided a positive feminine role model. Marshall (1984) suggests that by positively valuing their mother's role these women may have gained the initiative to develop an appreciation of their own feminine strengths and abilities, leading to a sense of self-acceptance which is not contingent upon male approval. By maintaining their femininity these women may have created a more androgynous role for themselves, taking the best of both male and female worlds. Although men have been slow to incorporate the caring, love/duty ethos of the private sphere into their cash-nexus, public world, women are rapidly moving to incorporate work into their world.

It would seem that successful women do not have to buy into the male world entirely. The outcome is the availability of a more diverse set of life-role options for these women. Their family background creates an atmosphere in which women can choose the roles they are attracted to rather than adopting culturally prescribed roles.

Childhood Experience

Interviews with 'change makers' (Cooper and Hingley, 1983) and with 'high flyers' (Cox and Cooper, 1988) have emphasized the importance of childhood experiences. Frequently there is a tale of childhood deprivation which is recalled vividly and is often thought to be significant in later development. The main issues which are discussed have centered on overcoming hardships – for instance, escape from poverty, death of a parent or living away from parents.

Cooper and Hingley suggest that these early adverse experiences are wounding to the developing personality. This wound is said to lead to the creation of 'a healthy scar tissue which is stronger than normal and protects the damaged area'. In psychological terms, the personality defends itself by reinforcing valuable aspects of the psyche, compensating via defence mechanisms. Several of those interviewed in the change-makers study reported feelings of strength through adversity. The early personal trauma leads to the successful testing out of survival skills which creates a fundamental feeling of strength, self-sufficiency and independence which they claim is useful in later life.

Cox and Cooper (1988) found evidence of childhood deprivation in their study of forty-five male managing directors. Their research indicates a prevalence of separation and loss of parents during formative years. The effect of the early death of the father leads to the development of an early sense of responsibility. Separation from parents on being sent to boarding school was recalled as significant in that it helped the boys to develop independence and an ability to cope with life on their own. The male high flyers developed a sense of strength through adversity. They coped successfully with early traumatic events, which, it is proposed, set a pattern for successfully coping with future life events.

The majority of the successful women were also able to identify childhood events which they considered to have had an impact on their later development. Eight women said that they were motivated to overcome limited family origins. The element of escape from poverty was mentioned by high flyers (Cox and Cooper, 1988) as an important motivator in early life. This financially impoverished background applied to only a minority of the high flyers, as was the case for the successful women in the present study. Rather, several women remarked that their family origins were limited in terms of academic stimulation.

Thirteen of the successful women claimed that they had fought to overcome a weakness in their character such as a lack of self-confidence. They were aware of their weakness and subsequently attempted to overcome it. It is possible that this early experience of acknowledging weakness and learning how to improve coping could set a pattern of future self-development and a willingness to accept personal challenges. As Cox and Cooper (1988) have suggested, it is not the events which an individual encounters which are important to his or her development, but how he or she responds to them.

The remaining women identified positive experiences in their childhood which they felt had made an impact upon their development. Seven women said that their family had an ethos of equity, independence, high standards and a belief that one could do anything that one chose to do. Forrest and Mikoliatis (1986) believe that such patterns of non-sexist socialization are likely to lead both sexes towards a balanced capacity for dealing with issues of separation and connection of identity. Hence a balance between male and female worlds may be achieved. Their hope for the future is that gender will lose its importance as a factor predicting the nature of an individual's vocational development.

Ten women said that they had encountered people who had inspired them to be successful. It is possible that these people provided an important role model and sources of efficacy information.

Social Economic Status

Social economic status (SES) is one of the most consistent predictors of occupational level among men. Goodale and Hall (1976) claim that sons are likely to inherit their father's occupational level.

However, Cox and Cooper (1988) reported no class bias among their sample of forty-five British managing directors.

The data on the influence of parental SES on women's career development have been more inconsistent. Astin (1968) and Burlin (1976) found that higher SES is related to a stronger career orientation and innovation. Cartwright (1972) and Russo and O'Connel (1980) found that women in male-dominated professions were significantly more likely to have fathers who had worked in professions. Studies which have reported the social background of women managers suggest that they have predominantly middle-class origins (Hennig and Jardim, 1978; White, 1989). Conflicting results have been found in studies of female entrepreneurs. Research on American female entrepreneurs (Hisrich and Brush, 1987) has shown that the majority have a middle-class background. The limited data on British female entrepreneurs indicate that they have somewhat different social origins. In a small-scale study, White (1989) found that the majority had a working-class background (as measured by father's occupation).

Fitzgerald and Betz (1983) suggest that the failure of SES to be as predictive of women's careers as it is of men's may be in part explained by differential expectations of the sexes in society. Although high SES families are likely to encourage and facilitate achievement-related behaviour in their sons, the extent to which they do so in their daughters will depend upon their attitudes towards working women and the possible absence of sons in the family. As suggested by Goodale and Hall (1976), parental interest and support may moderate the relationship between SES and career achievement in women.

Father's occupations and SES

Based on the interviewer's guide to social grading (Monk, 1973), social class was determined in our study according to the father's occupation. Grade A households account for about 3 per cent of the total. The head of the household is a successful business or professional man, senior civil servant or has considerable private means. Grade B households account for about 12 per cent of the total. In general, the head of the household will be quite senior but not at the very top of his business or profession. Grade C1 constitutes about 23 per cent of the total. It is made up of families of small tradespeople and non-manual workers who carry out less important administrative, supervisory and clerical jobs. Grade C2 makes up 32 per cent of the total. It consists mainly of skilled manual workers, all of whom have served an apprenticeship. Grade D consists entirely of manual workers, generally semi-skilled or unskilled. The grade accounts for 21 per cent of families. Grade E represents those at the lowest level of subsistence and accounts for about 9 per cent of the total.

The distribution of the families of the successful women in comparison with the general population is shown in table 2.1.

A large proportion of our successful women (75 per cent) have middle-class origins compared to only 38 per cent of the general population. This finding is consistent with other studies of female managers which have shown that they have predominantly middle-class origins (Hennig and Jardim, 1976; White, 1989). It also supports the argument put forward above that higher SES is related to stronger career orientation and innovation (Astin, 1968; Burlin, 1976). In the case of successful women, SES does seem to be predictive of career orientation. It is possible, as Fitzgerald and Betz (1983) suggest, that the effects of SES are mediated by parental attitudes towards female achievement. The majority of successful women in the present study did have parents who condoned women's participation in the world of work.

Parental Ambitions and Expectations

The majority of the successful women (75 per cent) felt that their parents had been ambitious for them to succeed. Thirteen of these

Table 2.1 Socioeconomic status of successful women

Social class	Frequency	%	General Population
Grade A: upper middle class	9	18.75%	3%
Grade B: middle class	19	39.58%	12%
Grade C1: lower middle class	8	16.66%	23%
Grade C2: skilled working class	9	18.75%	32%
Grade D: semi-skilled and unskilled working class	3	6.25%	21%
Grade E: lowest level of subsistence	0	0.00%	9%

women remarked that this ambition was limited to their education. As one successful woman said:

> I think that they realized that I was quite bright. Until I was five we lived with my grandparents and they spent a lot of time with me educationally so that I could read and write by the age of five, which was quite advanced. They felt that I was bright so I was pushed academically.

These women were expected to get a good education and, if possible, to go to university. The research of Standley and Soule (1974) into the personal and vocation histories of women in male-dominated professions also found that parents were less committed to their daughters' careers than to their academic pursuits. It is suggested that the parents were interested in academic credentials to announce their daughters' worth, then, once stated, their priorities turned to traditional values of housewifery. In fact, eight of the women in the sample said that they were ultimately expected to marry and to have children. As one woman recounts, '[My parents] were not ambitious for me in any defined way. My father's ambition was for me to go to university to study something safe. My mother's ambition for me was not formalized. It was expected that I would marry.'

Seven women said that, although their parents were ambitious for them to be successful, that ambition was limited to the parents' realm of experience. These women felt that they had been disadvantaged by their parents' inability to give them occupational guidance. Nine women said that their parents expected them to enter a specific profession. In contrast, a larger proportion of successful women claimed that their parents had no rigid expectations for them, except that they should do what made them happy. A similar response was obtained from the postal survey sample. Sixty-eight per cent said that their parents were supportive of what they had chosen to do. It is possible that these patterns of parental expectations will result in either 'conferred' or 'constructed' identities.

Marcia (1966) suggests that if an individual's family and social environment permits and encourages decision-making about occupations, then the individual's identity will be a synthesis of childhood experiences. If family and social environment prescribe an occupation, then identity will be the sum of childhood experiences. A conferred identity can be said to happen as one becomes increasingly aware of one's characteristics and one's position in the world.

In comparison, the identity is constructed when the individual begins to make decisions about who to be, with what groups to associate, and what occupational direction to pursue. Self-constructed identity involves the superimposition of a decision-making process on a conferred identity. Waterman (1982) claims that a constructed identity will be promoted by democratic parenting which is said to lead to the consideration of a number of vocational alternatives followed by a commitment to one. It is necessary to examine parental involvement in choice of career to determine whether these parent expectations lead to conferred or constructed identities among successful women. This is discussed in more detail in chapter 5.

Ten women claimed that their parents had been indifferent to their success. A small number of women stated that their parents had actually hindered their careers by forcing them to leave school prematurely to make a financial contribution to the household. For some of these women this perceived lack of parental concern stimulated them to prove to themselves that they could be successful.

Maternal Employment

One of the most extensively studied and consistent correlates of career orientation is maternal employment. The focus on the role of the mother in women's career development is based on the assumed importance of the same-sex parent in influencing development.

Working mothers are said to provide a positive role model for their daughters. Daughters of employed women are found to have less stereotyped views of feminine and masculine roles than daughters of home-makers (Broverman et al., 1970; Hoffman, 1972), which is believed to result in aspirations to non-traditional occupations (Almquist, 1974; Tangri, 1972). Working mothers also provide a model of the integration of work and family roles (Almquist and Angrist, 1971). Banducci (1967) found that daughters of working mothers more often planned to combine the roles of mother and careerist than daughters of non-working mothers.

Stein (1973) found that adolescent and college-aged children of employed mothers tend to be more achievement oriented than children of home-making mothers. Hoffman (1972) also showed that daughters of working mothers had greater self-esteem and a more positive evaluation of female competencies than daughters of housewives.

Vondracek et al. (1986) have criticized much of the research on the effects of maternal employment on the grounds that it is over simplistic. Little attention has been given to the reason for employment, to satisfaction with life roles and work situation, or to the social support received. The mother's involvement or commitment to a career may be more important than the fact of employment outside the home. It is also pointed out that the findings are largely restricted to middle-class women employed in relatively high-status jobs. The results of these studies may not generalize to working-class women who work because of necessity rather than the attractiveness of the rewards.

Maternal employment of successful women

Sixty-five per cent of the women in our sample had mothers who were employed outside the home. Over half of these mothers worked continuously throughout their daughter's childhood, without taking a significant career break. The remaining 35 per cent of the mothers were full-time housewives. These proportions of working mothers are high when compared to the numbers of women who were working outside the home at that time. Davidson and Cooper (1987) document a steady increase in the participation of women in the labour force, from 42 per cent in 1971 to 49 per cent in 1985. In 1987 over 60 per cent of women were working full or part time. It is probable that the mothers of these successful women were somewhat unconventional at that time. As other authors have suggested, it is probable that employed mothers presented a less stereotyped view of feminine and masculine roles than housewives. This is said to encourage a career orientation rather than a home-making orientation.

The relationship between maternal employment and combination of roles is shown in table 2.2. This reveals quite clearly that maternal employment is not predictive of the decision to combine motherhood and a successful career.

Table 2.2 Maternal employment and children

	Children	No Children
Working mother	15	16
Non-working mother	9	8

As mentioned above, Vondracek et al. (1986) have called for a closer examination of the nature of maternal employment, particularly the mother's satisfaction with life roles, and social support. They suggest that mothers who combine roles effectively present a more viable role model to their daughters. The current study failed to examine the mother's job satisfaction. This is an issue to be explored in more depth in future research. In terms of social support, the women were asked whether their mothers employed home help. Twenty-eight per cent of the working mothers of women in the group employed home help. This did not, however, appear to contribute to the decision of women in the main sample to combine the roles of mother and careerist.

The Influence of Siblings

The number of siblings that a child has, his/her place among the children (that is, birth order), and relationships with brothers and sisters constitute important aspects of the child's learning situation in the home. The child may learn patterns of loyalty, helpfulness, protection, or of conflict, domination and competition, which may later be generalized to other social relationships.

A large proportion (54.2 per cent) of the women in the study were first-born or only children. This finding is consistent with numerous other studies which have noted the predominance of first-born children (including only children) among high achievers (Eysenck and Cookson, 1970; Helmreich et al., 1980). Handy (1976) has stressed the importance of birth order, with youngest and eldest being more assertive than those in between. Studies of women who have succeeded in male-dominated occupations have produced similar findings (Auster and Auster, 1981). In a study of women managers enrolled in the MBA programme at Harvard Business School, Hennig and Hackman (1964) found that twenty out of twenty-five were first-born or only children. Later studies of both American and British female entrepreneurs have shown a large percentage to be first-born (Hisrich and Brush, 1987; Watkins and Watkins, 1983).

An explanation for the association between birth order and achievement orientation may be derived from findings in developmental psychology. Mussen et al. (1979) suggest that first-born children are likely to be treated differently from those born later.

Oldest children do not initially have to share their parents and so they tend to receive a lot of parental attention and affection, to have their needs gratified quickly and to receive help promptly when in distress. This secure environment enables the child to explore and move towards independence while security is still in sight. It is possible that first-born children may be over-indulged or over-protected, which can lead to a pattern of dependency (Kagan and Moss, 1962). Alternatively, parents may treat their first-born more like an adult than they do their later-born children; they may expect more of the child, who may be pushed harder to accomplish. First-born children may be given the responsibility of looking after younger siblings before they are ready for such responsibility, and they alone must face the problem of losing only-child status. The arrival of a new sibling may threaten the first-born's security and relationship with parents. These early experiences of responsibility and of pressure to achieve may encourage first-born children to test their abilities and to gain mastery experiences which should enhance their feelings of competence and self-confidence. To determine whether the parents of the women in the present sample responded to their first-born with over-indulgence or by encouraging competence it is necessary to refer to the results on the quality of the parent–child relationship.

A significant proportion (46 per cent) of the successful women were middle or youngest children. Later-born children are likely to encounter a different home environment. They interact differently not only with their parents but also with their older siblings. Mussen et al. (1979) state that those who are born later tend to regard themselves as less competent than their older siblings and they may suffer feelings of inadequacy. It is possible that these feelings of inadequacy suffered could inhibit later children from striving for career success. However, the sex of the older siblings represents an important variable which mediates the effects of birth order on achievement striving. Koch (1972) studied 384 subjects, aged five–six, from two-children families. The four types of sibling combinations were represented (older boy–younger girl, older girl–younger boy, two sisters and two brothers). She found that, in general, the children with brothers had more masculine traits. The girls with brothers, as compared to the girls with sisters, were more ambitious, more aggressive and did better on tests of intellectual abilities. Girls with older brothers displayed more 'tomboyish' traits than girls with older sisters. These results are explained in terms of identification and imitation processes. In many cases the older sibling is viewed by the younger as stronger, more competent and in control of important goals that the younger one wants to achieve, but is not yet able to. The younger sibling is said to strive to become similar to the older by attempting to adopt the latter's behaviour. The majority (68.2 per cent) of the later-born women in the current sample had an older brother, which might suggest that they would also have imitated and identified with their brother's behaviour, resulting in the acquisition of what are traditionally considered to be masculine traits, such as an achievement orientation. This is supported by the observation that the women in the sample who had brothers were more likely to report sibling rivalry. Only thirteen of the successful women felt that they had competed with their siblings, and eleven of these women specified that they had competed with a brother. As one woman recalled, 'There was always competition for attention, particularly from my father who was always more interested in my two older brothers than in me.'

The absence of sibling competition among the remainder of the sample was explained in terms of outright superiority, which removed the need to compete, or having a totally different outlook, which avoided any conflict of interests. Several women said that they felt supportive towards their siblings rather than competitive. For example, one woman said,

> Both of my sisters are teachers. One of them teaches art and the other is a headmistress and they are both very happy. I, of course, have been much more financially rewarded through what I have chosen to do and I try to share that with my sisters. There is no sort of competition between us.

A Note of Caution

Although this discussion has centred on the role of childhood and its influence on later development, it must be remembered that socialization alone does not determine individual vocational development. Astin (1984) points out that if socialization alone determined work expectations then there would be little change; once set, expectations would remain stable. In addition, little social change would occur. The same values would be handed down from generation to generation with little variation. Social and individual change does occur, however, propelled by what Astin calls the structure of opportunity. Socialization and the structure of opportunity are interactive. Socialization is claimed to limit change in the structure of opportunity, while the structure of opportunity influences values transmitted via socialization. It is Astin's view that early socialization practices have not changed as rapidly as women's occupational behaviour. She draws attention, therefore, to the structure of opportunity and other factors which play a role in women's career development.

It can be seen, however, that early childhood does have an influence on later attitudes and behaviour, particularly in motivating and stimulating our successful women. Indeed, as John Milton suggested, 'The childhood shows the man [in this case the woman], as morning shows the day'.

3
Education

Introduction

Walsh and Osipow (1983) have stated that educational level is one of
the most powerful predictors of career achievement in both men and
women. Women's educational level certainly seems to be strongly
related to the type and extent of their vocational participation.
Higher education is related to greater participation in the labour
force among women, whether they are married or not (Blaska, 1978).
It is also related to a stronger career orientation and career salience
(Astin and Myint, 1971), and to the choice of pioneer as opposed to
traditional careers (Almquist, 1974). The data on high flyers do not,
however, support the contention that a high level of education is a
prerequisite for outstanding career success. In a study of forty-five
British chief executives, Cox and Cooper (1988) found that only
50 per cent had reached degree level, four had postgraduate qualifications, three had started university but had not completed the
course, and the remainder had left school between the ages of fourteen
and sixteen. Those who left school took up apprenticeships or
entered professional offices and continued their education via
evening classes. Six of the managing directors had no formal qualifications. The educational level reported in this study is lower than
that reported elsewhere. For instance, Margerison (1980) found that
65 per cent of British managers had at least a first degree. The
Wall Street Journal (1987) reports even higher levels of education
among American managers: 6 per cent high school, 40 per cent
university graduates, 35 per cent masters and 13 per cent doctorate.
These disparate response rates may be explained in terms of the
methodology employed to obtain the information. Both Margerison
and the *Wall Street Journal* used a postal survey method from which

one might expect a differential response rate (that is, the more highly qualified managers are more likely to respond). This type of response bias would not be possible given the interview method employed by Cox and Cooper.

Cox and Cooper suggest that the low level of qualifications among British chief executives may have been exaggerated by the age of their sample, most of whom were middle aged (fifty–sixty years old). It is proposed that the next generation of managing directors will show a higher proportion of graduates as the trend to continue in education increases. What the high-flyers study does show is that higher education has not in the past been necessary for success in industry. The converse may also be true, in that qualifications alone do not provide an automatic ticket to a successful career. Elias and Main (1982) present evidence which shows that some women may be employed in jobs for which they are massively over-qualified.

Women's qualifications

Women's participation in higher education has been increasing at a much faster rate than men's. The numbers of students in full-time higher education courses in the UK rose by 17 per cent between 1980/81 and 1987/8, to stand at 627,000. Over two thirds of the increase in the numbers can be attributed to the increase in the number of female students. In 1987/8, 55 per cent of full-time higher-education students were male, compared to 60 per cent in 1980/81 (Social Trends, 1990). In 1984 women comprised 43 per cent of candidates accepted through the Universities Central Council on Admissions (UCCA), as compared to only 31 per cent in 1970.

Between 1970/71 and 1987/8 the number of students in part-time higher education more than doubled. This increase has taken place almost entirely among those aged over twenty-five years. Women accounted for 39 per cent of part-time students in 1987/8, compared to 14 per cent in 1970/71.

During the period between 1981 and 1987 the number of post-graduate degrees awarded rose by 24 per cent, and first degrees by 15 per cent. In 1987, 45 per cent of first degrees and 37 per cent of postgraduate degrees were awarded to women, compared with 39 per cent and 35 per cent respectively in 1981 (Social Trends, 1990).

Gender segregation of education

Crompton and Sanderson (1986) suggest that many of the quali-fications acquired by women are gender-related, in that women anticipate the gender segregation of subsequent employment. There is growing concern over the under-representation of women in many vocational, technical and scientific education programmes at all levels. Figures from the UK Joint Metriculation Board show that over twice as many boys as girls follow science A-levels, and boys outnumber girls four to one for entries to A-level physics. Women are not represented evenly in higher education. Less than 4 per cent of women students are on engineering courses, compared with 25 per cent of men. Women are slightly less well represented in the sciences; the difference is greater for physics than for the biological sciences. Meanwhile 40 per cent of women study arts, languages or education, compared with only 18 per cent of men (Hirsh and Jackson, 1990).

The Education of Successful Women

Type of school

Over half the successful women in our sample attended a grammar school, and only 21 per cent went to a comprehensive or a secondary-modern school. Seven of the successful women had a private education, and a small proportion experienced a mixture of schools. When compared with the statistics for the general population, shown in table 3.1, it can be seen that a much higher percentage of successful women had a grammar-school education. This is still the case after accounting for changes in the education system.

In 1971, before the large-scale movement towards comprehensive education, a lower proportion of people none the less attended

Table 3.1 Percentage of pupils in public-sector secondary education: by type of school in England

Type of school	1971	1981	1989
Middle-deemed secondary	1.9	7.0	6.3
Modern	38.0	6.0	3.9
Grammar	18.4	3.4	3.4
Technical	1.3	0.3	0.1
Comprehensive	34.4	82.5	85.9
Other	6.0	0.9	0.4

Source: Social Trends (1991)

grammar school than comprehensive. This is a reflection of the fact that grammar schools were designed to take only the top 20 per cent of the ability range. Therefore, the observation that a large proportion of successful women had attended grammar schools could indicate that they are of above-average ability. Functionalists argue, however, that educational attainment in advanced societies is linked to occupational status. Halsey (1977) reported that occupational status is increasingly dependent upon education; but he also noted that the effect of the father's occupational status upon the child's educational attainment is also rising: 'The direct effect of the class hierarchy of families on educational opportunity and certification has risen since the war'.

Therefore, social background has an increasing effect on educational attainment at a time when the bonds between education and occupational status are tightening. Halsey concludes that 'education is increasingly the mediator of the transmission of status between generations'. Privilege is passed on from father to child via the education system. This conclusion is consistent with the finding that a large number of the women who attended grammar schools also came from middle-class backgrounds.

Today in the UK, the majority of children (85.6 per cent) experience their secondary education in a comprehensive school. Bellaby (1977) defines comprehensive schooling as 'the educating of all children of secondary school age in an area in one school.' The transformation of the tripartite institutionalized structure of education was first proposed in the 1944 Butler Education Act, and by 1965 the ideology of comprehensive education had become politically powerful. It was argued that comprehensive schools were more egalitarian. Selective schools were said to reinforce existing disparities between social classes, while comprehensive schools were said to improve the opportunities of socially disadvantaged children. The comprehensive school was seen as a place for children of all abilities, who would help one another. They would represent a cross-section of society, an integrated society within a school, assisting the integration of society in general. This ideal has not been achieved in the majority of instances, as the basis for deciding the intake is the catchment area, which can often lead to 'one class' schools (Rutter et al., 1979).

On a rather more positive note, Neave (1975) has suggested that comprehensive schools increase the opportunity for working-class children to go to university. He also notes that a high proportion of the '11-plus' failures who were later to go on to university following a comprehensive education were working class (44 per cent). Neave claims that these children would probably not have gone to university if they had attended a secondary-modern school. It seems, therefore, that the evidence is somewhat inconclusive as to whether education can be seen as a mechanism for the maintenance of privilege rather than a means for role allocation based on meritocratic principles. Owing to the shift towards comprehensive education, it is probable that the next generation of successful women will have a very different educational background to the women in the current sample. This is supported by the observation that the group of women who had a comprehensive education had a lower mean age than the women who attended the other types of schools.

Co-education

The majority of successful women (79 per cent) attended single-sex schools. This finding could be a product of the fact that a large number of the women also had a grammar-school education. The change to comprehensive schools has coincided with a move to co-educational schools. In 1978 over 70 per cent of schools were co-educational, and since then the numbers have increased. In a recent article in the *Sunday Times*, Colin Hughes (1990) questions whether the tide is about to turn in favour of all-female education. He reports that numerous studies in Britain and on the Continent have shown that women are more likely to achieve academic and career success, particularly in male preserves such as mathematics, science and engineering, if they attend all-female education institutions. Quite why this is the case Hughes says, is a matter of debate. He states that the female students feel that they benefit from having fewer social distractions. They also point out that women studying in co-educational establishments feel that their male classmates receive more sustained attention from tutors, even when the women are brighter and more interested in learning. Consciously or otherwise, teachers in co-educational environments are reported to treat men as more serious and more important students. When that competition is removed, the women immediately benefit. Other researchers provide evidence which suggests that Hughes may be rather overstating his case. Morrison and McIntyre (1978) state that boys tend to perform better in co-educational schools. Girls tend to perform better in maths in co-educational schools than in single-sex schools. In other subjects, however, there is no discernable pattern. They conclude that the 'within-group' differences swamp the 'between-group' differences that appear between single-sex and co-educational schools.

Level of education

As a group, our successful women have attained a high level of education. Approximately 50 per cent have a degree, compared to only 6 per cent of women in general (see table 3.2). In addition, several women have further professional and business training. Only two of the women have no formal qualifications. These findings show successful career women to have slightly better qualifications than male high flyers (Cox and Cooper, 1988). Fifty per cent of the male chief executives in Cox and Cooper's sample had a degree. The remainder had left school at fourteen or sixteen, and had obtained professional training while working.

Subject of education

The subject distribution of the qualifications obtained by the women in our sample is given in table 3.3. It should be noted that some of the women had studied subjects in more than one area.

Crompton and Sanderson (1986) have suggested that the qualifications obtained by women are gendered. This is also the case among successful women. Table 3.4 shows the proportion of men and women in a range of educational domains. These figures were compiled from statistics gathered by the Education Department in 1987 and 1988, and have been used to classify occupations as pre-

Table 3.2 Percentage of qualifications among the British population, 1987

Type of qualification	Male	Female
Degree or equivalent	13	6
Higher education below degree	17	14
GCE A-level or equivalent, or apprenticeship	51	25
GCE O-level or equivalent	60	42

Source: Social Trends (1989)

dominantly male, female or neutral. An educational domain was seen to be male or female if approximately 65 per cent or more of the students taking this subject were typically male or female. The majority of the successful women studied what could be described as neutral or predominantly female subjects. Most of the successful women in our sample had professional/vocational qualifications, or they had studied business/administration/social science. It is therefore possible that Crompton and Sanderson were correct in their

Table 3.3 Subject of education

Subject	Number of women
Education (teacher training)	3
Medicine/dentistry/health	1
Engineering/technology	0
Agriculture	0
Science	5
Administration/business/social science	16
Professional/vocational	23
Languages	3
Arts	1
Music/drama/design	1

Table 3.4 Sex segregation in subject of education

Subject	% Male	% Female	Classification
Education	29.67	70.32	female
Medicine/dentistry/health	61.10	68.90	female
Engineering/technology	88.80	11.16	male
Agriculture	67.46	32.53	male
Science	68.84	34.16	male
Administration/business/social science	42.10	57.88	neutral
Protessional/vocational	35.90	64.00	female
Language/literature	31.89	68.10	female
Arts	43.45	56.54	neutral
Music/drama/design	52.80	47.70	neutral

supposition that women anticipate the gender segregation of sub-sequent employment.

Crompton and Sanderson make a link between particular types of education and characteristic career paths. They draw on Dex's (1984) categories of women's employment behaviour to illustrate that most women experience discontinuous careers. Using life-history data, Dex described five typical career paths, encompassing market and non-market work:

1 The phased career – women who return to work after all births, usually part-time.
2 The domestic career – no return to work after childbirth.
3 Restricted family careers – early return to work after a family break, usually for financial reasons.
4 Unexpected or unplanned careers – a discontinuous pattern resulting from unexpected factors, e.g. divorce.
5 Continuous career – childless or returning to work after all births.

Crompton and Sanderson suggest that the increase in the extent of women's participation in the labour force may have enhanced the salience of career planning, and the increase in the numbers of women obtaining qualifications may be a manifestation of this planning. The results of the current study are somewhat inconclusive as regards successful women. Fifty-four per cent of the women in our sample said that they chose their education with a career in mind. The remainder said that they had no specific career in mind when they selected their subject of study. A typical comment was:

> I didn't have a career in mind when I chose my education. I picked subjects which I enjoyed. I got a love of numbers from my father; if he had had an education he would have been a superb mathematician. We used to play a lot of number games and I was fascinated. Maths was a well-respected subject and I felt that if I did it well it would be regarded as a good thing to have done. I had a simplistic view of life.

Crompton and Sanderson propose, however, that women in general tend to opt for qualifications which facilitate the 'discontinuous careers' outlined by Dex. This possibility is reflected in the statement of one of the successful women: 'I did teacher training because I didn't know what I wanted to do and it would always be something to fall back on.'

Brown (1982) suggested three strategies underlying individual choices and actions in relation to employment:

1 The entrepreneurial strategy – resources are developed such that self-employment is possible.
2 The organizational strategy – advancement is sought within an employing organization.
3 The occupational strategy – skills are acquired to enable movement between employers.

Crompton and Sanderson claim that qualifications can be thought of as lying along a continuum relating to these employment strategies. Pure occupational qualifications give a licence to practise and they have universal validity (e.g. professional exams). At the opposite end of the continuum are pure organizational qualifications which are seen as a necessary element of a linear career. They may include 'in-house training', which is used to identify individuals as promotion material. These qualifications are not transferable to other settings. The point is made that it is often difficult to make a clear distinction between organizational and occupational qualifications, and there is considerable overlap in the middle of the continuum.

Crompton and Sanderson (1986) state that occupational qualifications may be used to pursue both entrepreneurial and occupational career strategies. These qualifications are a universal guarantee of competence, which facilitate upward movement or movement between employers. In contrast to entrepreneurial and occupational careerists, only those anticipating a continuous linear career will have undertaken organizational qualifications, based on the assumption that a bureaucratic career will follow from loyal and continuous organizational service. Crompton and Sanderson claim that, although there are large numbers of women employed by bureaucratic organizations, they have not, in general, acquired the relevant qualifications which would signal upward mobility. Although increasing numbers of women are gaining qualifications, this may not lead to increasing numbers of women with continuous organizational careers. Rather, it appears that women are obtaining occupational qualifications which are more congruent with discontinuous occupational careers or entrepreneurial careers.

These claims are borne out by the findings of the present study. Thirty-five per cent of our successful women had acquired occupational qualifications (e.g. solicitors, accountants). A much smaller proportion (10 per cent) had organizational qualifications (e.g. local-government exams, museum exams). It is possible that women's occupational qualifications may be more in tune with the economic climate in Britain in the 1990s. Scase and Goffee (1989) make a case for the development of 'transferable skills', based on the changes which have taken place in the nature of management roles.

Scase and Goffee document the changing context of work, careers and lifestyles over the last forty years. In the post-war decades, growth facilitated the expansion of business, corporations and state-owned institutions, and managers were optimistic about their career opportunities and an improved standard of living. They expected to be geographically mobile and were prepared to accept the associated costs to their personal lives. These were seen as the price which had to be paid for the rewards of a successful career. Personal identity and self-worth were assumed to be derived from occupational and career accomplishments.

It was not until the late 1960s that these prevailing attitudes were challenged. Young people began to offer alternative views to their parents' materialistic achievements. They saw the rational pursuit of profit as leading to the irrational use of natural resources which was damaging to the environment (Dickson, 1974). They also began to question the 'affluent society', which was seen to foster ideals negating the development of human potential and creativity (Marcuse, 1968). Career success was seen to be meaningless, because it produced rewards which were solely materialistic. Scase and Goffee point out, however, that while some young people may have opted out, the majority proceeded to pursue relatively conventional career strategies. Managers in both public and private sectors continued to derive satisfaction from their jobs, in so far as these were located within clearly defined career structures, where individual progress could be measured according to age, experience and achievement.

Scase and Goffee claim that the real change in managerial attitudes began during the 1970s, and that this change was precipitated by three main factors. First, they state that the 'excessive' influence of the trade unions led to much debate about whether managers were capable of exercising control in the workplace. Second, they suggest that the oil crisis in 1973 weakened the British economy as a whole, as it was organized on the availability of cheap energy resources. Finally, Scase and Goffee claim that the rapid increase in the rate of inflation during the late 1970s eroded personal savings and living standards. These developments undermined the optimism of many managers concerning career success and high standards of living.

The successive election of Conservative governments in the 1980s led to radical economic and industrial reforms. As organizations were pressured to become more cost effective, managers were also urged to achieve higher levels of measurable performance (Regional Rewards Survey, 1985). Demands for greater efficiency meant that managers could no longer be assured of relatively secure jobs with reasonably predictable career prospects (Handy, 1984). The adoption of 'flatter', relatively decentralized structures, often made possible through technological advances, has resulted in a reduction in the size and extent of management hierarchies (Buchanan and Boddy, 1983). In response to highly competitive markets and the need for innovation, looser forms of organizational structures have developed, reducing dependency on rules and fixed procedures. Scase and Goffee (1989) comment that changes of this kind have had important repercussions for the nature of managerial work roles. Managers must now cope with operational uncertainties, and because of flatter structures their career opportunities are restricted. Goffee and Scase argue that managerial careers are becoming less confined to a single or a limited number of organizations. Managers will be forced to make more frequent moves between jobs, often becoming self-employed or redundant (that is, they will have discontinuous careers). Individuals will be compelled to develop personal talents and skills which are transferable to a number of different settings (Nicholson and West, 1988). It is therefore likely that in the future more people will have to follow occupational as opposed to organizational careers. The successful women in the current study appear to be in tune with the changing context of career. Many of them have acquired occupational qualifications which are transferable credentials, giving objective proof of their competence.

Several women in the sample did plan to acquire more qualifications. They felt that further education, particularly an MBA, would help them to run their businesses more effectively or that it would speed up their career progression. As one woman manager said:

> I have thought about doing an MBA but I feel I haven't got the time and I don't want to spend my spare time studying. I would do an MBA because I'm in upper-middle management and I think that a management qualification would help my career progression.

Or as one of the female entrepreneurs commented:

> I feel that I need an MBA. I want to take the company to the stock market and I think that as the company director I need credibility. I

need to get the business understanding to take us to the really 'big time'; I want to understand all the processes.

In this sense the MBA might be seen as a qualification which falls in the middle of the organizational–occupational continuum. In one sense it is perceived as useful for an entrepreneurial career. Alternatively, it may be perceived as an organizational qualification, giving an indication of promotion intentions with the goal of pursuing a bureaucratic career.

Conclusion

Educationally successful women appear mainly to be the product of single-sex schools. They show levels of qualification which are well above average, in gender and/or career-related subjects. They also show a trend towards acquiring management qualifications.

4
Personality and Motivation

Introduction

There is very little evidence of any clear-cut relationship between a particular type of personality and success. Cox and Cooper (1988), for example, found that their group of successful chief executives showed a very wide range of different personalities as measured by a standard and widely used personality test. They did score slightly higher than average on intelligence, assertiveness, emotional stability and self-sufficiency, but this is not a particularly surprising finding. In view of the likelihood that successful women also show a wide variation in personality, we decided to concentrate our investigation on three major areas of personality and motivation, which previous research and our own hypotheses suggested might be important. These were:

1 *Locus of control*. This is concerned with the individual's perception of who controls the rewards he/she receives; essentially whether they are internally or externally controlled.
2 *Need for achievement*. Since the women in the study were all high achievers, it seemed appropriate to look at achievement motivation and its possible origins.
3 *Self-efficacy*. The amount of effort an individual expends on an activity will affect his/her probability of success. The effort one is likely to put in depends on one's perception of one's ability to do the task or job in question. We therefore wanted to investigate these successful women's perceptions of their managerial self-efficacy.

In this chapter we discuss the above factors and our findings in relation to each. We then suggest how they possibly combine to determine the motivation of successful women.

Locus of Control

Rotter (1966) defined locus of control as the disposition to perceive the rewards that one receives in life either as a consequence of one's own behaviour or as the result of extrinsic factors. Those who believe that they exercise some control over their destiny are described as having an internal locus of control. In contrast, individuals with an external locus of control believe that their rewards are controlled by luck, chance, fate or powerful others. The degree of an individual's internal/external locus of control can be represented as a continuum. The individual's position on this continuum will determine the degree to which he/she perceives success or failure as being contingent upon personal initiative.

The link with success

Andrisani and Nestel (1976) have commented that the construct of locus of control is particularly well suited to research on employment success. Following a survey of the literature, they conclude that there is strong evidence to suggest that an internal locus of control reflects a propensity to influence one's environment, which they believe is a mark of initiative and competence. Shapero (1975) has also argued that individuals with an internal locus of control, who feel that they have some influence over the events in their lives and that their personal destiny comes from within, tend to be more self-reliant and independent. These authors imply that characteristics such as competence, initiative, self-reliance and independence are related to success at work. Andrisani and Nestel argue that the individual's internal belief that success results from hard work and that failure is the individual's responsibility is firmly rooted in the Protestant work ethic.

Lefcourt (1982) points out, however, that there is not a simple one-to-one relationship between locus of control and achievement. Rather, it is suggested that locus of control plays a mediating role in determining whether a person becomes involved in the pursuit of achievement. The logic behind the arguments presented by Andrisani and Nestel (1976) and Shapero (1975) is that disbelief in the contingency between one's own efforts and outcomes should preclude achievement striving. Lefcourt, however, suggests that locus of control may be seen as relevant to the willingness to defer gratification. The process of planning and working for deferred goals would seem tolerable only if the individual believed that he/she was able to determine the results of his/her efforts. In contrast, externals find the path from the initiation to the completion of their plans fraught with unpredictability and uncertainty. They are, therefore, more likely to opt for the certainty of immediate gratification. This logic is consistent with the tenets of expectancy-valence theory advanced by Porter and Lawler (1968), which states that the expectancy that effort will lead to success is crucial in generating motivation to work.

Internal locus of control can be perceived as a necessary condition for intrinsic motivation. Using a framework based on the motivator-hygiene theory of Herzberg et al. (1959), Haywood (1968) suggests that individuals differ in their ability to respond to intrinsic and extrinsic incentives. Intrinsically motivated individuals seek to maximize their satisfaction through the responsibility, excitement, challenge and learning derived from the task itself. Extrinsically motivated individuals seek to limit their dissatisfaction by focusing on ease, comfort, safety and things derived from non-task conditions. The internally controlled individual who believes he/she can affect his/her environment will act to enhance feelings of competence and self-determination. In comparison, externally controlled individuals would rarely be intrinsically motivated because of their belief that they cannot affect their environment. As a result, they do not engage in activities which lead to feelings of competence and self-determination.

While few studies have systematically explored the role of locus of control as a contributor to success at work, the research which does exist supports the thesis that an internal locus of control is a precursor of success. In a large-scale longitudinal survey, Andrisani and Nestel (1976) looked at the relationship between locus of control and various dimensions of occupational success. They found that over a two-year period internals experienced more favourable employment circumstances – i.e. they achieved a more pronounced advancement in their annual earnings and job satisfaction. Andrisani and Nestel also reported cross-sectional data which suggested that internals are in higher-status occupations, they earn more money and tend to be more highly satisfied with their work than externals. Waddel (1983) showed that women who achieved higher-status positions tended to have an internal locus of control. Forty-seven female entrepreneurs were compared with a group of female managers and secretaries, the findings revealed that female entrepreneurs and managers are more likely to have an internal locus of control than secretaries or the population in general. Brockhaus (1980) also found that internality among entrepreneurs was related to success in business.

Neubauer and Werner (1979) has added the dimensions of stability and controllability which interact with locus of control in predicting achievement-related behaviour. Internal causes are divided into those that are constant – e.g. ability – and those which may vary – e.g. effort. External factors may remain stable – e.g. task difficulty – or they may vary – e.g. luck. People who perceive outcomes in achievement activity as determined by variations in effort rather than by their constant ability level are more likely to persist in the face of failure. This is because the causes of failure are seen as variable and within their personal control.

Research on the process of attribution has shown that the dimensions of stability and controllability influence the attributions made by others for women's achievement. Garland and Price (1977) found that men with positive attitudes towards women as managers assumed that their success was a result of effort and ability. Those with a negative attitude towards women as managers attributed their success to good luck or the ease of the job. Colwill (1984) claims that there is a danger that women will apply this sex-typed model to themselves and so attribute their own successes to luck. The implications of such attributions could, she suggests, be 'devastating', for the following reasons:

1 To attribute success to luck leaves one's self-esteem unaltered.
2 Predictions of future success also remain unaltered, so women may not increase their expectations of themselves as a result of their achievements. As Bandura (1977) has pointed out, people who do not expect to perform an activity will be less likely to engage in that activity. If they do try, they will show less persistence in the face of adversity and will be more likely to fail.
3 To attribute success to luck is to learn nothing.
4 Even if women only verbally attribute success to luck and mentally to ability, others may believe what they say.

Having drawn our attention to the devastating implications of sex-typed attributions, Colwill points to some good news. In a comprehensive study of male and female managers, Harlan and Weiss (1980) found no sex differences in attributions of achievement. The majority of their sample attributed success to hard work and good performance.

The locus of control of successful women

Locus of control was examined using measures specifically designed for application in the work domain. The scale designed by Spector (1988) produces a single score indicating work-related locus of control (WLCS). The successful women were found to be more internal than the normative populations quoted by Spector (shown in table 4.1). This finding is consistent with earlier work which has shown that individuals in high-status, high-earning positions have a more internal locus of control than those in low-status, low-earning positions (Andrisani and Nestel, 1976).

Procuik and Breen (1975) suggest that the relationship between locus of control and success can be further elucidated by exploring the dimensional structure underlying the trait. Three dimensions have emerged from factor-analytic studies:

1 *Internality*. The belief that one has control over one's career
2 *Powerful others*. The belief that career is under the control of powerful others
3 *Chance*. The belief that career is controlled by luck or fate.

The three-factor scale employed in the present study was the Career Locus Questionnaire designed by Makin (1987), which is a variant on the original Levenson (1973) scale. The results shown in table 4.2 suggest that successful women have a strong belief in their own ability to control their own career, when compared with the sample of male managers tested by Makin. Procuik and Breen suggest that individuals are 'true internals'; individuals who perceive their

Table 4.1 Normative data for work-related locus of control

Sample	N^a	Mean	SD^b
MBA and industrial psychology students	151	41.7	9.6
Sales staff (department store)	41	36.8	9.9
Mental-health agency employees	101	39.2	11.9
Department store managers	292	38	9
Mental-health facility employees	160	39.4	9.1
Municipal managers	496	36.9	9.6

[a] N = sample size
[b] SD = standard deviation
Source: Spector (1988)

Table 4.2 Internality, powerful others and chance: successful women compared with a sample of 84 upwardly mobile male managers

Scale	Male managers		Successful women	
	Mean	SD	Mean	SD
Internality	19.11	4.22	12.56	3.45
Powerful others	16.00	5.53	12.14	5.71
Chance	13.75	4.43	11.86	4.97

Source: Makin (1987)

careers as being under the control of powerful others are 'defensive externals'; and those who believe that their career is dictated by chance are 'true externals'. Procuik and Breen observed that true internals had more success than defensive externals, while defensive externals had more success that true externals. Working within this framework, it is possible to classify the successful women as true internals. This result supports the findings of Procuik and Breen, as the women in the main sample had achieved outstanding success within their fields, whereas the male managers in Makin's sample were less successful. The consistency in the reserch findings might suggest that the key factor in locus of control in determining the degree of career success is the level of internality.

Due to the lack of existing comparative female data relating to the three-dimensional measure of locus of control, forty secretaries completed the questionnaire. This data showed that the successful women in the main sample were significantly more internal than the secretaries on all three scales (results shown in table 4.3). Waddel (1983) also found that female managers and entrepreneurs had a more internal locus of control than secretaries.

The differences between the successful women, the moderately successful women and the secretaries may be interpreted in terms of their relative positions within the labour force. Having reached the top of their organization or their profession, it is not surprising to find that these women have a strong belief in their ability to control their own careers. Very often the successful women have legitimate power to control their own destiny which would reinforce a personal

Table 4.3 Secretaries compared with successful women

Scale	Mean	SD	T-test value	p^a
Internality	14.55	5.25	2.187	0.05
Powerful others	15.85	5.88	2.832	0.005
Chance	14.8	5.39	2.6	0.01

[a] p = probability

sense of internality. The secretaries display a stronger belief in chance factors, such as luck or fate, than either the main sample or the postal survey sample. This may be a reflection of the segmentation of the labour force. Secretaries may be considered to constitute a group within the secondary labour force (Barron and Norris, 1976). A position with limited autonomy and prospects and little job security is not likely to engender feelings of control over one's career. In general, the two groups of women were more internal on all the scales than the male samples quoted in the normative data. The only exception was that of the secretaries, who had a stronger belief in chance factors. The lends support to the labour-segmentation hypothesis.

As mentioned earlier, Colwill (1984) has observed that male managers will often attribute the success of women to luck, while the success of men is attributed to hard work. She warns that there is a danger that women will apply these attributions to themselves with quite serious consequences. If they attribute their success to luck, women will not raise their expectancy of future success which in expectancy/valence terms would leave motivation unchanged. In addition, women would learn nothing about how they achieved success, leaving self-esteem and self-efficacy beliefs unaltered. The failure to raise self-esteem would inhibit career growth.

When asked during the interviews, 60 per cent of the successful women felt that luck had played an important role in their careers. This would seem to indicate that rather a large proportion of women attribute their success to luck, which in Colwill's terms could be detrimental to their careers. Further clarification of this issue revealed that many of the women qualified their assertion that luck was important by also commenting that hard work was more important. These women felt that one needed luck to be in the right place at the right time, and to be given opportunities. On being given a lucky break, it was important to have the ability and application to capitalize on it. Thirty-five per cent of the successful women considered that people make their own luck. One said:

> Success hasn't got a lot to do with luck. I've never relied on luck. Occasionally you get a lucky break, but it's because you've been hammering on doors. Things may happen unexpectedly and they're a surprise, but they're not luck because you put the footings in.

These beliefs that hard work is vital for achieving success are consistent with the internality scores derived from the measures of locus of control. They are also in line with Colwill's (1984) finding that the majority of successful female managers attributed their success to hard work and good performance. When asked how they had achieved their success, a large proportion of the women in the current study said it was due to tenacity and perseverance combined with hard work. Only 14 per cent of the women attributed most of their success to luck and simply being in the right place at the right time. The general feeling is well summarized by the following quote:

> Success is ninety per cent slog and ten per cent inspiration. I'm not one of those people for whom things just fall into place. If I have done things, the time has not always been right, which has left me fighting even harder, but I think success is about rising to the challenge. Someone asked me which of my characteristics I would bequeath to my children and I said my bloody-mindedness. I just will not be pushed.

Familial origins of locus of control

Several studies have investigated the relationship between parental child-rearing practices and the development of locus of control. Katkovsky et al. (1967) conducted a study with families participating in the Fels Research Institute longitudinal study of human development. Their results suggested that, in general, 'A child's beliefs in internal control of reinforcements are related to the degree to which parents are protective, nurturant and non-rejecting.

A supportive, positive relationship between a child and its parents is said to foster an internal locus of control, while a relationship characterized by punishment, rejection and control encourages an external orientation. Davis and Phares (1969) interviewed university students about their parents' attitudes and childrearing practices. They found that extreme internals recalled parents as having positive involvement with them, with less rejection, hostile control, inconsistent discipline and less withdrawal than did extreme externals. Lefcourt (1982) suggests that the findings of research show impressive consistency, given the different age groups in the samples and the diversity of procedures and measures employed for ascertaining locus of control and familial relationships. It is proposed that warmth, supportiveness and parental encouragement are essential for the development of an internal locus of control.

Nurturance should not, however, be equated with pampering. If a child receives social reinforcement on a random, if over-abundant schedule, he/she will fail to perceive the connection between behaviour and reinforcement. Indiscriminate reinforcement can lead to feelings of helplessness or a very external locus of control. In addition, MacDonald (1971) claimed that nurturance and protectiveness in parental behaviour are conceptually and empirically distinct. Devereaux et al. (1969) suggests that nurturance is subsumed under supporting, but protectiveness is subsumed under a controlling dimension. The child requires a certain degree of security and insulation in which to explore his/her environment and so develop a sense of him/herself as a causative agent. This safety and security may become arresting if parents do not later accept the movement towards independence that the security engenders. Overprotective childrearing practices, preventing children from being exposed to challenges and activities which might require coping behaviour, may have the effect of suffocating the child's natural curiosity and intrinsic motivation. Maslow (1954) has discussed these issues in the outline of his hierarchy of needs. He states that curiosity and exploration through the desire for self-actualization rest upon a more basic foundation of safety and security.

Crandall (1973) found that coolness and criticality on the mother's part was positively associated with an internal locus of control. This did not imply rejection or neglect. Crandall suggests that the internal individual has experienced a greater 'push from the nest' than the external individual. This push is said to put the individual into more active intercourse with his/her physical and social environment, giving more opportunity to observe the effects of this behaviour uninfluenced by maternal intervention:

It may be that warm, protective, supportive maternal behaviours are necessary for the assumption of personal responsibility during childhood, but in the long run, militate against internality at maturity. Perhaps internality at later developmental stages is best facilitated by some degree of maternal 'coolness', criticality and stress so that offspring were not allowed to form overly indulgent affective relations with their mother, but were forced to learn objective cause and effect contingencies, adjust to them and recognize their own instrumentality in causing those outcomes.

Familial origins and locus of control among successful women

Rather surprisingly, only 30 per cent of the successful women described their relationship with their parents as close and trouble free. Several women did mention that they had not been spoilt and that their parents had been strict. This reflects an important distinction between nurturance and pampering. The women were made aware of the contingencies between their actions and their rewards, which would enhance their belief in their ability to influence their environment.

A larger proportion of the successful women reported a problematic relationship with their parents, which seems to be inconsistent with their scores on the scales measuring locus of control. However, these results may be reconciled. Twenty-three per cent of the women felt that their parents were aloof. This forced the women to become independent at an early age, which may have provided the opportunity to explore and develop their sense of self as a causative agent. Another 21 per cent of the successful women reported mother–daughter conflict. This may have provided a push from the nest, allowing exploration of cause–effect relations without the influence of maternal intervention.

It must be pointed out that not all individuals would necessarily respond to parental aloofness by becoming self-sufficient. As mentioned earlier, Maslow (1954) has pointed out that safety and security are precursors of exploratory behaviour motivated by the desire for self-actualization. It is possible, however, that there are individual differences in the need for safety and security. We may speculate that the successful women appear to have relatively low needs for security, although this issue was not explored in the current study.

Need for Achievement

Psychological writings on the concept of achievement striving can be traced back over a century. James (1890) describes man's self-regard as being determined by self-imposed goals, the achievement of which leads to feelings of well-being and elevation, while failure brings about frustration and humiliation. The formalization of the achievement-motive construct derives primarily from the work and theory of Murray (1938). Murray conducted an in-depth study of fifty men from which he developed a taxonomy of personality needs, defined as hypothetical constructs reflecting psychological 'forces' which direct behaviour. One of these forces was the need for achievement (nAch). Murray defined this motive as

> the desire or tendency to do things as rapidly and/or as well as possible. [It also includes the desire] to accomplish something difficult. To master, manipulate and organise physical objects, human beings or ideas. To do this as rapidly and independently as possible. To overcome obstacles and attain a high standard. To excel one's self. To rival and surpass others. To increase self-regard by the successful exercise of talent.

McClelland (1951, 1955) was heavily influenced by Murray's need systems in his own attempts to explain individual differences in tendencies towards striving for success in life. McClelland focuses on the effect associated with the achievement motive, defining nAch as the positive or negative effect aroused in situations that involve competition with a standard of excellence, where performance in such situations can be evaluated as successful or unsuccessful (McClelland et al., 1953). The tendency to strive for success is postulated to be a relatively stable personality trait rooted in experiences in middle childhood.

The essence of the Murray–McClelland definitions of the achievement motive are central to the work of many other researchers in the field. Atkinson (1964) talks of nAch in terms of the capacity to take pride in accomplishments. Achievement behaviour is not just the motivation to achieve, but also the motivation to avoid failure. Together these two motivational tendencies determine whether a person will ultimately approach or avoid an achievement task. The two motives are said to be a function of two situational variables: perceived probability of success and the incentive value of success.

Those who have high nAch tend to approach those tasks for which there is either reasonable probability of success and to avoid those which are too easy (because they are not challenging and hence do not offer opportunities to demonstrate competence) or those which are too difficult (because of fear of failure).

The relationship between personality trait and task difficulty has been developed into a theoretical formulation by Atkinson and Feather (1966). It is stated that achievement-oriented activity is undertaken by the individual with some expectation that his/her performance will be evaluated in terms of some standard of excellence. Further, it is suggested that achievement-oriented activity is influenced by the resultant of a conflict between two opposing tendencies: the tendency to achieve success and the tendency to avoid failure. Achievement-oriented activities are usually also influenced by other extrinsic motivational factors. Atkinson and Feather propose that the tendency to approach or to continue a task is a simple product of the initial level of achievement motivation, the probability of success of the task and the incentive value of the task.

McClelland (1961) has claimed that individuals with high achievement motivation have a tendency to:

1 attempt tasks which seem moderately difficult;
2 persist in the face of difficulties;
3 show evidence of good performance and achievement over time.

Women and the need for achievement

O'Leavry (1977) has noted that, although situational variables are important in the conceptualization of nAch, most research has focused on the personality component. When females do not respond to instructions which are designed to arouse the achievement motive, they are said to have lower need for achievement than men (Veroff et al., 1953). Some have argued that this type of research is based on a male model of achievement and that women may have fundamentally different motivations to men. Hoffman (1972) suggests that women are often motivated by need for affiliation rather than need for achievement (an issue which was discussed at some length in relation to childhood). Other researchers have suggested that women strive for excellence in the social arena (Stein and Bailey, 1973), or that they vicariously achieve through their husbands (Tangri, 1972).

The origins of achievement motivation

Astin (1985) does not believe that women's motivations are fundamentally different from those of men; rather they are said to be influenced by childhood socialization and the structure of opportunity. Farmer (1985) presents a similar view of the factors influencing achievement motivation. Drawing on Bandura's (1977) social-learning theory, Farmer has developed a model of the factors contributing to achievement motivation. Achievement motivation is conceptualized as having three components:

1 *Aspiration*. Level of occupation or education to which an individual aspires. Aspiration is thought to be largely predetermined by given and unchangeable influences, such as social status and ability (Gottfredson, 1981). Farmer also found that for working women support has a significant influence on aspiration. McClelland and Winter (1969) also made the point that achievement motivation can be learnt and is not entirely predetermined by childhood experiences. Such learning has been brought about through training programmes and in some instances as a result of being placed in a position in which achievement-motivated behaviour is expected and rewarded.

2 *Mastery motivation*. The tendency of an individual to choose difficult, challenging tasks and to keep struggling to master the task once started. Atkinson (1958, 1978) viewed mastery motivation as fairly well established in childhood. Maehr (1974) believed mastery motivation to be influenced by background factors, such as culture and social economic status. Spence and Helmreich (1978) found that men score higher on this type of motivation. In accordance with Maehr's predictions, Farmer's research showed that social economic status had a significant effect on mastery, although race did not. Age did not have a significant effect on mastery motivation, which is consistent with Atkinson's view that it is established early in a child's life.

3 *Career centrality*. The extent to which the individual sees involvement in a career as central to his/her adult life. Super (1980) suggests that career-committed persons are those who are motivated to pursue their own development in one occupation or a series of occupations as their interests and opportunities change, over a long period over time. Career commitment involves a future orientation and a concern with long-range planning. Raynor (1978) suggests that this future orientation is essential for effective career striving on the part of achievement-oriented people. Successful individuals should show a tendency to be highly aware of both future career paths and the instrumentality of particular courses of action for attaining career advances.

Farmer found that age was not a significant influence on long-term career commitment, which suggests that career centrality is set early in life. Personal variables exerted the strongest influence on career commitment. The biggest effect was related to home-making commitment. Low home-making commitment was related to high career commitment in young women. This relationship was not observed among young men, a result consistent with earlier research findings (Atkinson and Raynor, 1978). The sex differences found for career centrality were greater than those found for mastery and aspiration. Farmer suggests that long-range career motivation is more vulnerable to competing role priorities than mastery and aspiration.

The men and women in Farmer's study had equal aspiration scores, but the women scored lower on mastery. She suggests that this may account for some of the differences in achievement which later favour men. However, Farmer is optimistic for the future because aspiration and mastery were influenced by environmental conditions, including perceived support for women working. Driver (1988) has commented that Farmer's work has rather 'stand alone quality'. He proposes that it would be interesting to integrate the dimensions of motivation with career concepts, a possibility which was explored more thoroughly in our study.

Need for Achievement in Successful Women

Need for achievement is a psychological variable which has often been invoked to explain individual differences in tendencies towards striving for success in life. Murray (1938) claimed that people with a high need for achievement show a desire to do things as rapidly and/or as well as possible, to overcome obstacles, to attain high standards, to excel themselves and surpass others. Upon successfully demonstrating their talent, these individuals are said to experience increased self-regard.

Given the above definition, it is not surprising that this construct has often been linked with career success. Boardman, et al. (1987) used an in-depth interview technique to determine the level of need for achievement among black and white successful women. These interviews were analysed for pervasive themes in the subject's life, characterizing many of her thoughts. The results showed that 94 per cent of the women in the sample were rated as having a 'strong' need for achievement.

The current study employed a more objective measure developed by Smith (1973) to determine the level of the need for achievement among successful women. This scale has been shown to discriminate between a sample of successful men selected from *Who's Who* and a group of less successful men. Unfortunately, the data on these two samples were not available for comparison. In the absence of normative data, the scale was administered to a group of female middle managers and women running their own small businesses, a group of male and female candidates for an MSc in organizational psychology and a group of secretaries.

In general, t-tests (shown in table 4.4) revealed no significant differences between the successful women and any of the comparative groups. The only significant difference observed was between the successful women and the sample of secretaries. The successful women were found to have significantly higher need for achievement than the secretaries, at the 0.05 level of probability.

These results suggest that the scale employed may not discriminate sufficiently between women who are moderately successful and women who are extremely successful. Alternatively, it could be that the women in careers rather than jobs have a similar need for achievement. The data available from the objective measure do not, therefore, provide enough information to determine whether need for achievement is a vital characteristic in outstanding career success in women.

It may be possible, as Fitzgerald and O'Crites (1980) suggest, that achievement motivation is not an adequate construct for explaining

Table 4.4 Normative data for the nAch scale compared with the successful women

Sample	N	Mean	SD	T-test value	p
Successful women	44	7.20	1.44		
Secretaries	40	6.41	1.71	2.27	0.05
MSc candidates	19	7.42	1.04	0.60	n.s.[a]
Female managers	12	6.92	1.44	0.59	n.s.
Female entrepreneurs	12	6.50	1.76	1.42	n.s.

[a] n.s. = not significant

women's career behaviour. They claim that, although classical theories of achievement motivation have been successful in predicting and explaining achievement-related behaviour in males, they are less satisfactory when aplied to females. If this is the case, then a measure designed on the basis of classical theories may not present a clear picture of women's need for achievement. Further validity testing is required on female samples to determine the usefulness of the scale in testing need for achievement among women. In addition, more normative data must be collected from both men and women, across a range of occupational positions.

There is evidence of high need for achievement among the reports the successful women gave concerning their sources of motivation. Sixty-nine per cent of the women claimed to be self-motivated, expressing a strong need to do a good job and to be the best in their field. Thirty-one per cent of the women claimed to be motivated by the desire for recognition for doing a good job. These motivations reflect Murray's (1938) definition of need for achievement: the women strive to excel themselves and to attain a high standard; in doing so they will increase their self-regard. It is feasible that in striving to enhance their self-regard in the work arena, women with a high need for achievement may be more prone to expansion of the career sub-identity at the expense of other sub-identities.

As mentioned earlier, Farmer (1985) has broken down the construct of need for achievement into three components: mastery, aspiration and career centrality. The reports of the successful women showed them to be high on all three components. This finding lends further support to the contention that successful women do have a high need for achievement (the results pertaining to the three components will be discussed in detail in relation to career decision-making).

Farmer suggests that the three motivational dimensions are interdependent in the process of career development, but how they interact is not well understood. She employed quantitative measures of the three motivational components, enabling her to test the relationship between them statistically. The current research has adopted an entirely different approach. Qualitative interview data have been interpreted by drawing on theory relating to mastery, aspiration and career centrality. The findings have then been used to speculate on the relationship between the components of need for achievement (shown schematically in figure 4.1).

A characteristic of individuals with high mastery motivation is

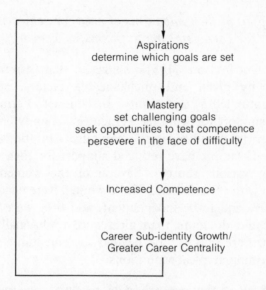

Figure 4.1 A tentative model of the relationship between the three components of career and achievement motivation

that they are more active in seeking opportunities to test their competence. They will also tend to set challenging goals, the achievement of which is important for their self-concept. Individuals with high mastery motivation also demonstrate perseverance in the face of difficulties. In the case of successful women, this perseverance eventually results in success. A large proportion of the successful women believed that their career success was due to tenacity and perseverance.

In his model of sub-identities, Hall (1976) suggests that as the individual acquires competence relevant to his/her career role, through the setting and achievement of challenging goals he/she will experience career sub-identity growth – in Farmer's terms, the individual develops greater career centrality. Therefore, it would seem that the level of career centrality is partially determined by the level of mastery motivation directed towards career. Whether the individual directs his/her mastery motivation towards his/her career will to a certain extent be dictated by personal aspirations. This is consistent with Farmer's finding that aspiration predicts achievement and career commitment.

The origins of the components of need for achievement and career striving in successful women

Aspiration   Gottfredson (1981) suggests that aspiration is pre-determined by given and unchangeable factors, such as social economic status (SES) and ability. In contrast, Farmer (1985) has found that support for working women (e.g. family encouragement, women's networks and mentors) may raise aspirations. The women in the current sample have received support for their career-related efforts from various sources. Several of the women had a close relationship with their fathers. These women were encouraged to use their initiative and to be independent, and they were led to believe that they could do more than girls were traditionally able to do. These women are said to look beyond the constraints of the female sex role, forming atypical aspirations.

Mastery   Most of the research data to date suggest that mastery motivation is established in childhood (e.g. Atkinson 1958, 1978; Farmer 1985). The development of mastery motivation among successful women was discussed at some length in relation to child-hood. Approximately 30 per cent of the women described their relationship with their parents as being warm. Their parents en-couraged and reinforced achievement-related efforts and in some cases they were moderately punitive. Stein and Bailey (1973) suggest that such parenting styles lead to the development of achievement and independence striving.

In comparison, 44 per cent of the women felt that their relation-ship with their parents had been remote, several women mentioning a mother–daughter conflict. The lack of bonding between the child and its parents is said to initiate the development of a separate sense of identity. The individual needs to differentiate him/herself from others in terms of abilities and attributes. This need may be equated with mastery motivation. Hoffman (1972) states that this need increases the probability of early experience of coping with the environment independently, which is essential for the development of competence and self-confidence.

Evidence concerning the development of mastery motivation is apparent in much of the writing on successful people. In their study of change makers, Cooper and Hingley (1983) found that many reported early traumas which had lead to the successful testing out of survival skills. This gave a basic feeling of strength and self-sufficiency. Cox and Cooper (1988) found that a large number of the high flyers that they interviewed had experienced the loss of a parent or had been separated from their parents for a significant amount of time during their childhood. The high flyers felt that these childhood events had given them the ability to cope with life alone, generating an early feeling of independence and self-reliance.

The consistent theme which runs through the reports of all these groups of successful people is the sense of independence and self-sufficiency. This early separation of self from the parents facilitates the development of a positional identity (Chodorow, 1978), which in turn engenders a high need to achieve and to have an independent impact upon the environment.

Career centrality Farmer (1985) found that career centrality was set early in life. She reports that home-making commitment has the biggest effect on career centrality. Low home-making commitment is related to high career centrality. Farmer suggests that long-range career planning is more vulnerable to competing role priorities than mastery or aspirations. This appeared to be the case among the successful women. As they resolved their role conflicts, their careers became more central to their lives. The decision to resolve the conflict in favour of career is described in more detail in the discussion of strategy formulation in career decision-making.

Self-efficacy

Self-efficacy (SE) is defined by Bandura (1977) as the conviction that one can successfully execute the required behaviour to produce the [desired] outcomes. Bandura believes that self-efficacy is central to one's beliefs about one's abilities to exercise control over events that affect one's life. SE is said to effect how people feel, think and act. Efficacy judgements vary on three dimensions: level, generality and strength. The level of SE expectations refers to the range of tasks within a particular category of which the individual feels capable. SE might be limited to simple tasks, moderately difficult tasks or demanding tasks, within a behavioural field. Generality of SE expectations refers to the range of behaviours to which a given level of expectation of efficacy will apply. Finally, the strength of efficacy expectations relates to how resolute the expectations are. Weak SE expectations are easily disaffirmed by failure experiences, whereas strong SE expectations cause people to persevere in the face of difficulties (Bandura and Cervone, 1986).

The link with success

Several studies have examined the validity of Bandura's theory that self-efficacy operates as a causal factor in human functioning. Since its inception, SE theory has been applied to a very diverse range of human behaviour, including the treatment of phobias (Bandura et al., 1982; Lee, 1984; Williams and Watson, 1985), alcoholism (Rollnick and Heather, 1982), contraceptive use (Levinson, 1982), and gymnastics (Lee, 1982). Studies on causality of SE expectations with respect to behaviours that are not problematic or related to physical endurance have also been conducted.

Moe and Zeiss (1982) asked subjects to complete a measure of SE expectations relating to social skills. The subjects were given the choice of demonstrating a social skill for which they had high SE or a skill for which they had low SE expectations. Significantly more of the subjects chose to demonstrate the social skill for which they had high SE expectations. Taylor and Betz (1983) investigated the role of SE expectations in the treatment of career indecision. They found that levels of SE were predictive of levels of career indecision. Barling and Beatie (1983) found SE expectations to be predictive of sales performance. Finally, Herriot and Winter (1988) found SE ratings to be predictive of the success and failure of army recruits in basic training.

It is clear from the evidence stated above that efficacy expectations are a major determinant of behaviour and behaviour change. The influence of SE on behaviour is proposed to operate in one of three different ways: through the choice of behaviours, through one's persistence at a task, and through one's thoughts and emotional reactions.

Choice of behaviour

Judgement of personal efficacy can shape developmental trajectories by influencing the selection of activities. People tend to avoid activities which they believe exceed their coping capabilities. The power of SE beliefs to affect the course of an individual's life is most clearly revealed in studies relating to career decision-making and career development. The stronger a person's self-efficacy, the more career options he/she considers possible, the greater the interest he/she shows in them and the better he/she prepares educationally for different occupational pursuits (Betz and Hackett, 1986).

Hackett and Betz (1981) suggest that self-efficacy theory might be a useful conceptual framework in which to view women's career development. They note that external barriers to women's career progression, such as discrimination and lack of support systems, present obstacles which require strong SE expectations to overcome. They also hypothesize that women generally lack strong efficacy expectations in relation to traditionally male occupations, and that this may contribute to women's continuing under-representation in occupations traditionally dominated by men, although they may not differ in actual ability. Hackett and Betz conducted a study which was reported to support their hypothesis. A sample of 134 female and 101 male undergraduates were asked to indicate their SE with regard to ten traditionally male occupations and ten traditionally female occupations. They were then asked to indicate their interest in the occupation and whether they had considered pursuing it. The subjects were also given ability tests to control for differences in ability. The results were claimed to show significant gender differences in SE with regard to traditional occupations. Males reported equal levels of SE for both traditionally male and female occupations. Women reported significantly higher levels of SE for traditional occupations and significantly lower levels with respect to nontraditional occupations. Only a small minority of traditionally male occupations – e.g. physician, lawyer – showed no gender differences. This was explained by the existence of at least a minority of women in such occupations. SE expectations were also shown to be related to the perceived career options for males and females.

Wheeler (1983) conducted a similar study which provided supporting evidence for the Hackett and Betz findings. Wheeler found that differences in occupational preferences were related to the proportions of men and women in that occupation. In addition, differences in these preferences were found to be related to SE perceptions.

Clement (1987) makes a number of methodological criticisms of the work of both Hackett and Betz (1981) and Wheeler (1983). Both are criticized on the wording and format of their measures of SE, and on the grounds that neither study reported the reliability and validity of the measures used to test SE. Wheeler was also criticized for using very broad occupational categories which could have incorporated a wide range of jobs (e.g. banking). Clement concludes that 'The inadequacies of these previous studies mean that there is as yet no conclusive empirical evidence for a self-efficacy theory of women's careers.'

Clement then proceeded to conduct a study to provide such empirical evidence. In total, seventy-eight females and forty-three males took part. Of these subjects, fifty-three were prospective candidates for a psychology course and the remainder were university students following a variety of courses. These students were asked to rate their SE, their liking and their consideration of entering ten traditionally female jobs and ten traditionally male jobs. Again it was found that females had lower SE expectations with regard to traditionally male occupations. The males did not have lower SE in relation to traditionally female occupations. Clement questions whether this lower SE is really problematic for women, because the female sample in the study had considered entering seven of the traditionally male occupations and their reluctance to consider entering the remaining three occupations was not attributed to low SE expectations.

Clement's study is, however, based on a rather restricted sample of students, many of whom were subject to a selection procedure whereby bias due to 'demand characteristics' may have been operating. In addition, Clement discusses only *consideration* of entry to an occupation. It is possible that SE expectations may have a more powerful influence on the *actual* entry to an occupation. It is quite feasible that women who do enter male-dominated occupations and who succeed will require high levels of SE to overcome the obstacles which they may encounter.

Effort expenditure and persistence

Bandura (1986) suggests that it is partly on the basis of self-efficacy that people choose which challenges to undertake, how much effort to expend and how long to persevere in the light of problems. Cervone (1989) studied the bias on SE appraisal produced by differential cognitive focus on various aspects of the same task. Focusing on the difficult aspects lowered SE, while focusing on the easy aspects raised SE. It was also observed that the higher the perceived SE, the longer the individual would persevere on difficult or insolvable tasks before quitting.

Bandura claims that the diverse range of investigations which have been conducted with different modes of efficacy induction and varied populations in all sorts of domains of functioning support his statement that perceived self-efficacy contributes significantly to levels of motivation and performance accomplishments. The link between self-efficacy and successful performance is demonstrated by White (1982), who found that the striking characteristic of people who had achieved eminence was an inextinguishable sense of SE and a firm belief in the worth of what they were doing.

Thought patterns and emotional reactions

SE expectations influence people's thought and emotional reactions. Individuals who have low SE expectations for dealing with a particular activity tend to dwell on their deficiencies and to concentrate on the potential difficulties. Misgivings of this nature may deter people from effectively utilizing their skills because they are focusing their attention on their personal failings at the expense of looking for the most effective way to proceed.

Clement (1987) observed that women's lower SE in relation to traditionally male jobs has often been interpreted as women's misconstruction of their abilities compared to men's more accurate self-appraisal. Clement offers an alternative interpretation of this gender difference. She suggests that women have a more realistic awareness of their limitations than men, who tend to over-estimate their capabilities. In support of her argument, Clement cites Crandall (1969), who found that males tend to over-estimate their future successes relative to their ability levels. Bandura (1986) interprets this over-estimation of abilities as a benefit. He argues that if SE reflected only what people could routinely do, they would rarely fail, but they would not mount the extra effort needed to surpass ordinary performance. Evidence suggests that successful, innovative and sociable people take an optimistic view of their personal efficacy to exercise influence over events in their lives.

Bandura also notes that in the face of failure individuals with high SE perceptions tend to attribute their failures to insufficient effort, whereas those with lower perceived SE ascribe their failures to deficient ability. Langer (1979) points out that failure to attribute success to one's own ability can inhibit learning: 'Learned helpless individuals are not learning what they could be learning from the situations they are in, and reflections on these consequences will result in lowering of their self-esteem'.

The origins of self-efficacy

Bandura (1977) suggests that SE expectations are derived from four principal sources of information: performance attainment, vicarious experiences, verbal persuasion and emotional arousal/physiological state.

Performance attainment   Bandura (1982) states that personal empowerment through mastery experience is the most powerful means of creating a strong, resilient sense of efficacy. He claims that 'Enactive attainments provide the most influential source of efficacy information because it can be based on authentic mastery experiences'. Successes tend to increase perceived SE, whereas repeated failures lower it, especially if failure occurs early in the course of events and cannot be attributed to lack of effort or adverse external conditions. Once strong efficacy expectations are developed through repeated success, the negative impact of the occasional failure is likely to be reduced.

Vicarious experiences   The second most influential source of efficacy information is derived through observing others perform the task.

> Seeing similar others perform successfully can raise efficacy expectations in observers who then judge that they too possess the capabilites to master comparable activities. By the same token, observing others who are perceived to be of a similar competence fail despite high effort lowers observers' judgements of their own capabilities [Bandura, 1982].

Verbal persuasion   Verbal persuasion involves attempts to persuade people that they possess the capability to achieve their goals. Social persuasion will be most effective in creating enduring changes in SE if the heightened appraisal is within realistic bounds. Bandura (1982) suggests that 'Persuasive efficacy influences have their greatest impact on people who have some reason to believe that they can produce effects through their actions.'

Bandura (1986) also notes that perceptions of the communicator affect the impact of the suggestions: 'The impact of persuasory opinions on self-efficacy is apt to be only as strong as the recipient's confidence in the person who issues them. This is mediated through the perceived credibility and expertness of the persuaders.'

Emotional arousal/physiological state Information derived from the individual's internal physiological state may be used in judging capabilities. In situations which require strength and stamina, people take fatigue, aches and pains as signs of inefficacy. Bandura (1982) claims that:

> they read their visceral arousal in stressful and taxing situations as ominous signs of vulnerability to dysfunction. Because high arousal usually debilitates performance, people are more inclined to expect success when they are not beset by aversive arousal than if they are tense and viscerally agitated.

The origins of SE in women

Hackett and Betz (1981) suggest that socialization experiences, both during childhood and in organizational life, lead women to have lower SE expectations with respect to many career-related pursuits. They review the four sources of efficacy information outlined above and proceed to highlight the possible differences between males and females. The main tenets of their argument are presented in figure 4.2.

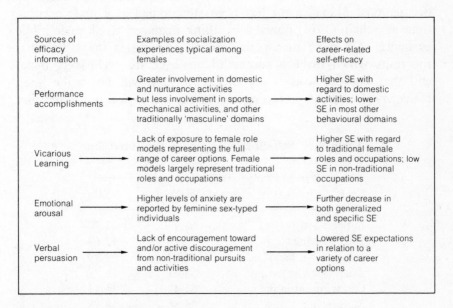

Figure 4.2 The origins of self-efficacy in women
Source: Hackett and Betz (1981)

The self-efficacy of successful women

Bandura (1977) suggests that the influence of self-efficacy operates in one of three different ways: through choice of behaviour, through one's persistence at a task and through one's thought and emotional reactions. The following discussion will consider how self-efficacy may have influenced the career choices of successful women and their persistence in achievement strivings.

Choice of behaviour

As previously mentioned, Hackett and Betz (1981) propose that self-efficacy theory represents a useful framework for explaining women's under-representation in traditionally male occupations. They point out that, due to external barriers such as discrimination and lack of support systems, women have numerous obstacles to overcome if they are to have successful careers in these domains. Therefore, it was predicted that women who choose to enter male-dominated occupations will have high self-efficacy beliefs.

Most of the women in the current study were engaged in some form of managerial activity simply as a function of their seniority. This was felt to be a common factor among the wide range of occupations. Management has been stereotyped as a male occupation; as Schein (1973) phrased it, 'think manager, think male'. The existence of a male managerial model perpetuates the belief that the traits which make a successful manager are exclusively male, and that because women are different, they will not make good managers. Given the preceding argument, it is logical to predict that

Table 4.5   Self-efficacy scores of the successful women

Scale	Mean	SD
Supervision	65.77	11.70
Harmonizing	70.20	12.69
Information handling	69.07	13.19
Analysing/evaluating	55.91	16.78
Changing/initiating	61.45	15.14
Monitoring	56.86	18.15
Total	62.89	12.58

women who enter the male-dominated world of management will have high managerial self-efficacy.

The scale employed to assess managerial self-efficacy was developed by Sadri (1988) and its structure is based on Allan's (1981) classification of managerial tasks. Allan's six dimensions incorporated Minzberg's (1973) ten roles and Mahoney et al.'s (1964) eight categories. Allan's classification was adopted because it explains the manager's role more succinctly than other classifications. Allan defined his six dimensions as follows:

1 *Supervision of employees.* Assigning work, developing, appraising and assisting subordinates with their work problems.
2 *Harmonizing.* Working with superiors, peers, representatives of other organizations, agencies and unions in integrating work activities or parts of the organization by smoothing, persuading or negotiating.
3 *Information handling.* Involves gathering, processing and supplying information inside and outside the organization.
4 *Analysing/evaluating.* Analysing and evaluating laws, problems, programmes, work procedures, processes and reports.
5 *Changing/initiating.* Activities aimed at changing the organization structure, tasks or procedures, or the behaviour of people.
6 *Monitoring.* Developing mechanisms for maintaining appropriate records and inspecting ongoing activities.

The scale produces six sub-scores and an overall measure of managerial self-efficacy. The scores of the successful women on each scale are shown in table 4.5.

Some comparative data are provided by Sadri, based on a sample of forty-eight management-science undergraduate students (twenty-seven male, twenty-one female) and a sample of 150 junior sales managers from a retail organization. When compared with the management-science undergraduates, the successful women in the main sample did not have significantly different levels of overall managerial self-efficacy (results are shown in table 4.6). It may be inferred from the choice of a BSc in management sciences that the undergraduates were committed to a career in management or related fields. According to Bandura (1986), choice of behaviour is influenced by levels of self-efficacy. If the undergraduates have chosen to pursue management, it may be assumed that they would have relatively high managerial self-efficacy.

Although no differences were observed in overall self-efficacy, the successful women were more self-efficacious on some of the sub-scales. The undergraduates had significantly lower self-efficacy

Table 4.6 Sample of 48 management science undergraduates compared with the successful women

Scale	Mean	SD	Min.	Max.	T-value	Significance
Supervision	60.2	10.6	57.7	92.3	2.39	0.05
Harmonizing	59.1	13.9	64.0	88.0	3.99	0.005
Information handling	61.3	11.0	48.0	89.7	3.10	0.005
Analysing/evaluating	54.1	11.3	45.7	74.0	0.35	n.s.
Changing/initiating	56.1	11.9	59.4	89.4	1.86	0.05
Monitoring	57.3	11.9	48.8	82.5	0.15	n.s.
Total	59.7	10.0	42.0	79.8	1.35	n.s.

in relation to supervision, changing/initiating, harmonizing and information handling. It is possible that the successful women have more efficacy information regarding their ability in these areas, resulting from a history of successes in their careers. The successful women have had more opportunities than the undergraduates to gather mastery information which Bandura (1982) suggests is the most powerful means of creating a strong sense of personal self-efficacy.

No significant differences were observed between the successful women and the undergraduates on the analysing/evaluating and monitoring scales. Both of these scales represent cognitive skills which may be taught and developed on an academic management course. This will give the students the opportunity to experience mastery of these skills and will, therefore, raise their levels of self-efficacy. The other scales relate to skills which require 'hands-on' experience in dealing with superiors and subordinates and of working within organization structures. Students are unlikely to gain such experience during their undergraduate degree. The development of SE in relation to practical managerial skills may lend weight to a case in favour of management degree courses which incorporate industrial experience.

When compared to 150 junior sales managers (forty-seven male, 103 female), the women in the main sample were significantly more self-efficacious on most of the scales at the 0.005 level of probability (the results are shown in table 4.7). It is not clear from the description of the sample precisely what was involved in the role of junior

Table 4.7 Sample of 150 junior sales managers in retail organization compared with the successful women

Scale	Mean	SD	Min.	Max.	T-value	Significance
Supervision	56.1	11.1	68.2	93.6	5.01	0.005
Harmonizing	50.1	13.1	69.1	89.0	9.01	0.005
Information handling	54.5	16.6	58.7	84.7	5.34	0.005
Analysing/evaluating	47.8	11.9	66.1	85.6	3.59	0.005
Changing/initiating	51.1	12.6	70.0	91.3	4.56	0.005
Monitoring	54.9	15.0	82.5	100.0	0.71	n.s.
Total	53.6	11.6	28.1	87.4	4.40	0.005

sales manager, but it is possible that it may have been equated with a supervisory role rather than management. The title 'junior manager' implies limited experience and, therefore, limited opportunity to acquire mastery information, which would explain the lower levels of self-efficacy.

Effort and persistence

Bandura states that it is partly on the basis of self-efficacy that people decide what challenges to take, how much effort to expend and how long to persevere in the face of difficulties. The successful women have high managerial self-efficacy which may have facilitated their decision to take on the challenge of a traditionally male managerial role. It is not possible to determine the order of cause and effect from the results of the questionnaire – that is, did high self-efficacy lead to the choice of management, or did successful performance in a management role raise self-efficacy. Longitudinal research tracing levels of self-efficacy throughout women's careers is required to resolve this issue.

When asked how they had achieved their success, many of the successful women said that they had tenacity and perseverance which had enabled them to work hard consistently throughout their careers. It is possible that their strong sense of self-efficacy may have contributed to this motivation. As one interviewee said, 'I achieved my success through determination, by putting myself up front, and by persevering.'

Gender differences in the origins of self-efficacy

Hackett and Betz (1981) suggest that the socialization experiences of men and women in childhood and organizational life result in different efficacy expectations in relation to careers. They point to sex differences in the four sources of efficacy information.

Performance accomplishments   Hackett and Betz claim that women have greater involvement in domestic and nurturing activities and lower involvement in traditionally masculine activities. This leads to high SE with regard to domestic activities, but to lower SE in most other domains. Several women in the current sample claimed that their families had an ethos of equity, independence, high standards and a belief that one could do anything one chose to do. This non-sexist socialization did not force the women into prescribed nurturing roles. Rather, 75 per cent of the women believed that their parents had been ambitious for them to achieve both in school and at work. This encouragement may have facilitated the exploration of non-traditional roles, so enhancing self-efficacy beliefs.

Thirty per cent of the successful women identified an early challenge as being a key event in their careers. This challenge provided the opportunity to prove their abilities. Successfully coping with the challenge was said to have raised their self-confidence. As Bandura (1982) suggests, performance accomplishments such as these should provide a powerful source of efficacy information.

Vicarious experience   Hackett and Betz suggest that the lack of female role models representing the full range of career options leads to low self-efficacy in non-traditional occupations. When talking about aspects of childhood which had made an impact upon their development, 21 per cent of the women talked of a person who had inspired them and had provided a model of success which they had imitated. An illustration is provided by one woman's account:

> I was very fortunate in the role models I had when I was young. I had a teacher who had been one of nine children, who had been very poor. She had become a teacher and she had succeeded and she wanted me to succeed. I saw her as someone who had achieved something because of who she was rather than because of where she came from and that made me realize that I could do it too.

Other than these models in childhood, there seems to be little mention of role models in the lives of the successful women. Therefore it seems that vicarious experience is not perceived to be an important source of efficacy information for the majority of successful women.

Verbal persuasion Hackett and Betz claim that lack of encouragement towards and active discouragement from non-traditional pursuits causes women to have lowered SE expectations in relation to a variety of career options. As mentioned earlier (chapter 2), the parents of the successful women actively encouraged achievement behaviour. Several of the successful women mentioned that the people who had acted as mentors during their careers had helped by demonstrating faith in their ability and offering encouragement and support. This faith was often reinforced by giving the women opportunities to demonstrate their talent and simultaneously to acquire mastery information. On the basis of these results, it might be suggested that an important role of mentors of aspiring women is to promote their self-efficacy beliefs.

Emotional arousal The final source of efficacy information is emotional arousal. Hackett and Betz claim that higher levels of anxiety are reported by feminine sex-typed individuals. This anxiety is said to lower general and specific SE. The sex-role beliefs and anxiety levels were beyond the scope of the current study, although they may warrant investigation in future studies of the SE beliefs of successful women.

Expectancy Theory: An Integrating Framework for the Components of Personality Relating to Success

It is possible that the three personality variables considered so far – locus of control, need for achievement and self-efficacy – have an influence on success through their impact on motivational processes. The following discussion will consider how these personality variables act to influence successful performance in terms of the expectancy theory of motivation.

The original formulation of expectancy theory was proposed by Vroom in 1964. Vroom's theory assumes that an individual's actions are based on the relationship between three factors, labelled 'valence', 'expectancy' and 'instrumentality'.

Valence This refers to the attractiveness or otherwise of a particular outcome. It is assumed that the most important feature of an individual's valences concerning work-related outcomes is that they refer to the level of satisfaction that the person expects to receive from them. People attribute positive and negative valences to outcomes depending on the level of satisfaction that they expect to receive.

Instrumentality Something is said to be instrumental if it is believed to lead to something else. Vroom suggests that instrumentality is the probability belief that one outcome will lead to other outcomes. Therefore, some outcomes are seen to be attractive because they lead to second-order outcomes which are positively valent. Vroom states that the valence of such second-order outcomes is determined by the nature of the individual's most salient needs and values.

Expectancy This is described as the subjective probability that one can perform successfully at a given level and that this will lead to desired outcomes. Vroom spoke of expectancy beliefs as action-outcome associations held in the mind of an individual.

In outline, Vroom's theory suggests that a person's actions will depend on a combination of the desirability (valence) of the perceived outcome of the action, and his/her expectation that the action will lead to the desired outcome. The valence of the outcome will be, at least partially, determined by its perceived instrumentality in relation to other consequent outcomes.

Vroom's model does, however, leave unanswered a number of questions concerning the origins of expectancy, valence and instrumentality. Porter and Lawler (1968) extended Vroom's work to provide an explanation of some of these issues. The model of motivation they developed is shown in figure 4.3. They suggest that an individual's performance depends on effort. This is influenced by two key factors: the value placed on outcomes and the degree to which the individual believes that effort will lead to those outcomes. They also point out that effort may not always lead to successful performance because of level of ability and role clarity (that is, understanding of what the task requires).

Intrinsic rewards are said to be closer to performance than

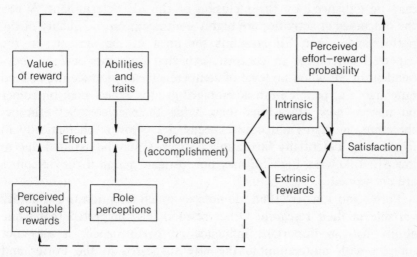

Figure 4.3 A revised model of expectancy theory
Source: Porter and Lawler (1986)

extrinsic rewards because the former result almost directly from performance whereas extrinsic rewards depend on outside sources. In addition, Porter and Lawler believe that rewards must be seen as equitable. The model incorporates a feedback learning process, in that satisfaction that is derived from outcomes will determine the valence placed on future outcomes. The strength of a person's belief that effort results in rewards is also said to be determined by experience of the relationship between effort performance and reward.

It is now possible to discuss the three main components (expectancy, valence and instrumentality) of expectancy theory in relation to personality and motivation.

Expectancy

It is suggested by Lawler (1973) that a person's beliefs about the strength of the connection between effort and reward can be broken down into two components: the strength of belief that effort will result in performance; and the strength of belief that performance will result in rewards.

The distinction between these two components of expectancy may be related to self-efficacy perceptions and locus of control. Wheeler (1983) has suggested that the predictiveness of expectancy theory may be enhanced by the inclusion of the SE determinant. When the outcomes of activities are highly contingent on the quality of the performance, then SE accounts for most of the variance in the expected outcomes. In contrast, expected outcomes will be independent of SE when no level of competency can produce the desired outcome (e.g. people in disadvantaged groups expect poor outcomes no matter how efficacious they judge themselves). Self-efficacy, therefore, mediates outcome expectancies (shown schematically in figure 4.4). Potentially favourable outcomes may be avoided due to low SE. Likewise, high SE may not instigate action if the outcomes are not valued.

Porter and Lawler (1968) do not pay much attention to the ability variable in their research. Other research has suggested that while ability has an important influence on performance, it may not interact with motivation in the way suggested in the Porter and Lawler model (Terborg, 1977). It is possible that the role of ability will be influenced by SE. Several studies have shown that SE expectations are partially independent of ability levels (Locke et al., 1984; Collins, 1982; Bandura, 1986; Betz and Hackett 1986). An individual may have high SE and, therefore, a potentially high expectancy of success regardless of his/her ability.

Locus of control can influence an individual's beliefs about the contingency between performance and outcomes. SE is of greater significance to people with an internal locus of control because they are able to link outcomes to behaviour. The perception of a contingency between action and outcome should spur the individual to action if the outcomes are valued and the efficacy expectations are high.

Bandura has emphasized the role of locus of control in determining the resilience of SE. Bandura and Wood (1989) found that managers who operated under the cognitive set that organizations are controllable displayed a strong sense of managerial efficacy. These managers exhibited high resiliency of SE under numerous difficulties.

Locus of control also has an impact on the learning process

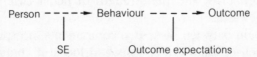

Figure 4.4   Self-efficacy and outcome

described in the expectancy model. If an individual does not attribute success to his/her own strengths, he/she is unlikely to learn very much about how the success was achieved. As a result, he/she is unlikely to raise his/her level of SE.

Valence

Vroom (1964) states that the valence placed on outcomes will be determined by the person's most salient needs and values. Need for achievement may be considered a salient need which has been associated with success. Individuals with a high need for achievement place valence on those intrinsic outcomes which allow a sense of pride to be derived from accomplishment (McClelland, 1951). They will engage in only those activities for which they have moderate expectancy of success and which offer the incentive value of success giving opportunities to excel self and others.

Instrumentality

In their study of women executives, Hennig and Jardim (1978) found that women made late career decisions. Up to the point of making the career decision, women tended to focus on the day-to-day aspects of doing a job well. As a result, they did not count present events as costs of a future career. Men, in contrast, were said to see their jobs as part of their career and were keen to act on the cues seen and heard. They strived to develop relationships and achieve visibility. This attention to being seen to do a good job rather than actually doing the job well was said to lead to promotion. Hennig and Jardim suggest that the women did not seem to realize that if one is not seen to be competent, then all the competence in the world will not get the job. It is possible to interpret these results as indicating unclear instrumentalities. It would seem that women's beliefs about the link between performance and desired outcomes (i.e. promotion) may be in error.

An alternative explanation could be couched in terms of locus of control. Women have traditionally had an unpredictable position within the labour market owing to changing domestic responsibilities and limited access to the structure of opportunity (Marshall, 1984). As a result, they may place greater valence on the more immediate intrinsic satisfaction of performing a task. As discussed earlier, locus of control has an impact upon the individual's willingness to defer gratification. Lefcourt (1982) has remarked that if the path from the initiation to the completion of plans is fraught with uncertainty, then one is more likely to opt for the certainty of immediate gratification. This explanation is consistent with Marshall's suggestion that men and women place different valence on outcomes. Women are said to want challenge and satisfaction from their work, rather than promotion for its own sake.

Personality Factors and Motivation for Success in Women

It has been argued here that the three components of personality, locus of control, SE and need for achievement have an influence on success through their impact on motivational processes. It is now possible to integrate these concepts into the Porter and Lawler (1968) model of motivation. This is shown diagrammatically in figure 4.5.

SE has an influence on the strength of belief that effort will result in performance. This represents one component of expectancy (Lawler, 1973). Wheeler (1983) has shown that when activities are highly contingent upon the quality of performance, then SE beliefs account for most of the variance in the expected outcomes. The women in the current sample had high managerial SE when compared with junior managers. High SE beliefs should enhance expectancy of success in a managerial role.

A second component of expectancy is the strength of belief that performance will result in rewards. Locus of control has an influence

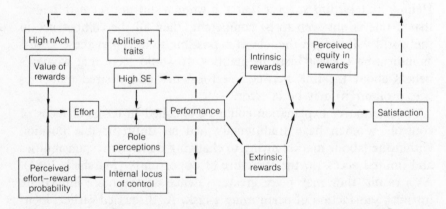

Figure 4.5 The role of personality factors in the motivation of successful women, considered within the revised model of expectancy theory

upon the beliefs about the contingencies between performance and reinforcements. The successful women demonstrated a high internal locus of control which should act to increase the expectancy that rewards are contingent upon behaviour rather than external factors such as luck.

The expectancy of success may not instigate action if the individual does not place value on the expected outcomes. Vroom (1964) has proposed that valence is determined by the individual's most salient needs. It was hypothesized that individuals with a high need for achievement would value outcomes from which they could derive a sense of accomplishment. The successful women desired to excel themselves and to attain high standards in their work. They also wanted recognition from others for doing good work. Therefore, it is possible to conclude that the successful women placed high valence on achievement.

The construct of need for achievement is mediated by SE beliefs. Individuals with a high need for achievement will be motivated to tackle only those goals for which there is a moderate probability of success. The high SE beliefs held by successful women will increase the expectancy of success for challenging goals.

5
Career Development

Introduction

Career choice is outlined by Hall (1976) as not just the choice of an occupation, but any choice affecting one's career. He claims that theories of occupational choice fall into two basic categories: 'matching theories', which describe what kinds of people enter what kinds of occupation, and 'process theories', which describe the manner in which people arrive at an occupational choice. It is the second category – i.e. the process of occupational choice – which is our main concern.

Much of the career-development literature is dominated by Erikson's (1968) view of development. Erikson formulated a theory of life-cycle development which attempted to account for changes in individual needs and capabilities, as well as changing societal rewards and demands. A series of genetically based factors in individual psychological and social growth are assumed to be approximately matched by a series of institutionalized social practices. These are cultural aspects of the environment within which each stage of self-concept development occurs. Aspects of the environment may also be forced to change as a result of individual action. Therefore individuals may be seen to produce their own development through behavioural intervention or behavioural agency. People can, for example, through their own efforts, overcome great obstacles within the environment to pursue successful careers. The life histories of many entrepreneurs have followed this pattern. Snyder (1981) suggests that this may be the most flexible way in which individuals can act as producers of their own development.

Identity statuses

Marcia (1966) developed an identity-status theory which is intended to allow measurement of Erikson's central concept of identity. An identity is described as a theory one has about oneself, an important aspect of which is that it influences how one feels about oneself. This theory of self is usually below the level of awareness unless it is brought into consciousness by being challenged by disconfirming evidence, at which point one becomes aware of one's identity. Erikson describes this state of heightened awareness as a 'crisis state'. Optimally, one then modifies the identity to accommodate the new experience. The identity statuses are said to represent the possible outcomes of the identity-crisis period. It is suggested that there are only four different modes of identity formation and that anyone over eighteen years of age should fall into one of the categories:

1 *Identity achievement*. Individuals experience a period of decision-making and are pursuing a self-chosen occupation and ideological goals.
2 *Foreclosure*. Individuals are committed to their occupation and ideological goals, but these have been parentally chosen. These people show no evidence of crisis.
3 *Identity diffusion*. Individuals who have no set occupation or ideological direction, regardless of whether or not they have experienced a decision-making crisis.
4 *Moratorium*. Individuals who are currently struggling with occupational and/or ideological issues – that is, they are in crisis.

Developing an identity status

Waterman (1982) points out that the normal formation of identity-status formation is characterized by progressive developmental shifts, leading ideally to the optimum identity status of achieved identity. Driver (1988) has criticized Erikson's model and its variants on the grounds that career choice has been viewed as a once-in-a-lifetime event. However, it is generally acknowledged by Marcia (1980) and other writers that identity statuses are not static and that they do not follow a uni-directional progression which stops when identity is achieved.

Marcia places emphasis on the formation of identity during adolescence. This is seen as a crucial period for the formation of the first full identity configuration. Successful solution in adolescence permits an openness to experience which will initiate subsequent periods of disequilibrium, identity crisis and resolution. Marcia claims that initial identity achievement in adolescence should guarantee a moratorium–achievement–moratorium–achievement cycle throughout life. This proposition is summarized by Grotevant and Thorbecke (1982), who suggest that 'the identity formation process should be viewed as a continually evolving self-structure . . . i.e. a spiral of cycles of exploration and commitment.'

Marcia expands on these ideas by discussing 'conferred' and 'constructed' identities. An identity can be said to 'happen' as one becomes increasingly aware of one's characteristics and one's position in the world. As such, the identity is said to be conferred. In contrast, identity is constructed when the individual begins to make decisions about who to be, with what groups to associate, what beliefs to adopt, what interpersonal values to espouse and what occupational direction to pursue. *Self-constructed identity involves superimposition of a decision-making process on a conferred identity.*

The origins of conferred or constructed identity

Waterman (1982) has proposed a number of antecedents of the four modes of identity formation leading to conferred or constructed identities.

1 Strong identification with parents before or during adolescence increases the likelihood of making commitment to parents' occupation – i.e. foreclosure.
2 Permissive, neglecting or rejecting parenting styles cause conflict and difficulty in adolescents trying to make vocational choices – i.e. identity diffusions. Kohut (1971) supports this view, suggesting that lack of integration and fragmentation of parental images result in developmental pattern leading to an absence of cohesive self, which then causes adaptation problems. These problems are said to lead to difficulties with career choice.
3 Democratic parenting is said to lead to consideration of a number of vocational alternatives, followed by a commitment to one – i.e. identity achievement.
4 The chance of experiencing identity crisis increases with the number of vocational identity alternatives the individual encounters.
5 The availability of role models facilitates the process of making of vocational commitment.
6 Social expectations of family, peers, and school will influence the pathway employed to achieve vocational identity.

7 Vocational identity will be established more successfully in those individuals in whom pre-adolescent personality provides a suitable foundation – e.g. autonomy, initiative.

Sex differences in vocational identity formation

Bakan (1966) claims that individuals have two basic stategies, 'agency' and 'communion', which constitute a fundamental orientation to life and may be used to deal the anxieties and uncertainties of living. The agentic strategy aims to reduce threat by changing the world around it, while the communion strategy looks to union and co-operation as ways to cope with uncertainty and threat.

Communion is the strategy associated with women. Their main strategy for dealing with the world is acceptance and personal adjustment. Understanding tends to be in terms of whole patterns of relations, seen to be embedded in their context. Women are said to be 'inner space'-oriented and interpersonal issues such as finding a suitable partner and having children are seen to be essential components of identity formation. In contrast, men are said to be 'outer space'-oriented and are associated with the agentic strategy. Finding an independent occupational role is a major issue in forming the male identity.

Although it would seem to follow that there should be sex differences in vocational-identity statuses, most empirical evidence suggests that there are more similarities than differences. However, this is not to deny that differences may exist in regard to concerns associated with identity development. As Archer (1985) suggests, 'If females are primarily interpersonal and male occupational in their orientations . . . then the findings of gender similarity with respect to occupational identity requires explanation. Perhaps the real issue for females is the potential conflict as they desire both roles'.

The desire to fulfil both occupational and interpersonal roles appears to be particularly true of successful women. Adams (1984) claims that high-achieving women have high expectations in both home and career, and therefore seek out occupations which will accommodate family life. Therefore, although males and females may be similar in their chances of achieving any one of the vocational-identity statuses, forging a vocational identity may be more complex for women due to the conflict between family and career.

Archer (1985) conducted a study of ninety-six high-school children to investigate the seriousness of female plans for career and the barriers which make identity development more complex. The areas investigated were occupation, sex-role preferences, family and career priorities, and orientations to social expectations. It was found that sex differences existed only in relation to family and career priorities. Women questioned these roles more than men. It is suggested that women may be attempting to define themselves in more life domains than men at this early point in their lives.

Kroger (unpublished, 1985), after studying the identity development of women in New Zealand, considers that identity formation may be protracted until other social roles are fulfilled. She states that 'support is obtained for the psychoanalytic view that identity formation is a lengthy and complex process, in fact it may not be until well past the 30s that the vocational, political and religious issues can be resolved.'

Vocational Identity Development among Successful Women

In our study of successful women we attempted to discover some of the main variables which may be linked to their individual differences in vocational identity development and the implications of this for successful career development.

Parental involvement in career decision-making

In an attempt to determine identity statuses of the successful women, parental involvement in career decision-making was examined, together with the extent of conscious decision-making. Only 21 per cent of the successful women said that their parents had been involved in their vocational decision-making. One of them recalled:

What they said and what was true were two entirely different things. They said that they wanted us to be happy. What they wanted was for us to have a profession which they could stick a label on and that was made very clear to us. They wanted my brother to be a doctor and me to go into the diplomatic service.

Waterman (1982) suggests that if occupations are prescribed by parents, then the individual is likely to experience foreclosure whereby he/she is committed to occupational goals which are not personally selected. To establish whether these women did have a foreclosed identity status, their early career patterns were examined. Six of these women did not show commitment to one occupation; rather they drifted between jobs with no obvious connections. Several of these women commented that they had rejected their parents' attempts to pressurize them, which had led to a period of identity diffusion – that is, they had no set occupational direction.

A large proportion (79 per cent) of the women claimed that their parents had no involvement in their career decision-making. Some felt that their parents were largely ignorant of potential career opportunities and were therefore not in a position to advise them. One woman explained, 'My parents couldn't advise me even on my choice of O- and A-levels because they hadn't been through it. They said it's your life so you choose.' Most of the women, however, said that their parents had simply allowed them to make their own decisions. For example, one woman said, 'My parents were not directing in any way. If I wanted advice, then I got it. They had ambitions for me to be happy and reasonably adjusted.'

Waterman claims that democratic parenting styles lead to a consideration of a number of occupational alternatives and hence to achieved identity. It is possible, however, that lack of parental direction in career decision-making could be attributed to permissive or neglecting parenting styles, which may lead to difficulty during adolescence in making vocational choices – i.e. identity diffusion. This issue was explored in more detail by looking at the association between parental expectations and conscious career decision-making. Table 5.1 shows the level of parental ambition in relation to women

Table 5.1 Parental ambitions and conscious decision-making

	Conscious decision	
Parental ambitious	*Yes*	*No*
Ambitious	5	5
Ambitious for education	4	3
Ambitious not pushy	15	2
Very ambitious	7	0
Ambitious but limited knowledge	5	2

who had or had not made conscious career decisions. The findings provide some support for the contention that women are less likely to make a conscious decision to have a career if parents are permissive or ambivalent towards their daughters' careers. It also seems that parents who are ambitious for their daughters to succeed but do not pressure them to follow a prescribed direction, facilitate conscious decision-making.

The relationship between parental ambitions and the stimuli for making a conscious decision to have a career was also examined. This revealed that the women who decided at a very early age that they would have a career were more likely to have ambitious parents who were supportive and encouraging in relation to their occupational pursuits. One of the successful women expressed this relationship between parental expectations and her decision to have a career very clearly:

> It was a conscious decision to have a career. I knew that I would have a career when I was at school. I think that it is because of the way I was brought up to believe that you don't live off your parents or anybody else, you make a career. I have two women friends who are fifteen years older than me and their attitude is totally different to mine. They were brought up to get married and depend on a man, while I never expected anybody to look after me and I wouldn't want that because I'm fiercely independent.

A smaller group of women whose parents had been ambivalent towards their career plans, or had expected them to follow traditional sex-role-appropriate career paths, had not always known they would have a career. One of them said:

> My parents were not ambitious for me in any formalized way. My father's ambition was for me to go to university to study something safe. My mother's ambition for me was not formalized. It was expected that I would marry.

Several of these women were prompted to make career decisions upon the realization that they did not want to be housewives. As one put it, 'I've always thought of myself as a working girl, I've never seen myself as a housewife. The thought of staying at home fills me with horror.' We are not clear what produced this realization, and so future research might look more closely at what leads to the rejection of the role of housewife. Others made a commitment to their careers when they separated from a partner, as this woman explained:

> I had to have a career when I was divorced. Otherwise I think that I would have been happy doing part-time jobs that interested me. I feel that I could easily have filled my time looking after the house, entertaining and looking after the kids which I've never had. The fact that I was divorced meant that I had to have a career to support myself. It was very tough and it has made me much more of a survivor than I would ever have been had I gone the conventional way.

Another woman also emphasized this point:

> When my marriage broke up I took a very dim view of men and I thought that from then onwards I would paddle my own canoe. At that point I decided that I would have to get more qualifications if I wanted to get anywhere, but I was going to do everything on my own.

The majority of successful women in our sample did make a conscious decision to have a career. Only 25 per cent of them said that they had never consciously decided to have a career and that it had crept up on them. These women had started in jobs which they enjoyed and they had become gradually more committed, as described by this one:

> I never made a conscious decision to have a career. I'm not ambitious in terms of status and I have never had a career plan. I have worked very long hours and once I reached a plateau I have needed another challenge. My inhibition is that I would reach my level of competence.

Early career patterns: timing of career commitments and resolution of role conflicts

It was thought that a greater understanding of vocational identity formation could be derived from analysis of early work history. The analysis of the work histories of the successful women in our sample revealed five basic career patterns which represented the order in which tasks associated with career devlopmental stages emerged. These five career patterns are shown schematically in figure 5.1.

The analysis of work histories showed that 54 per cent of successful women made a late commitment to their careers or had no coherent direction in their early working lives. A small number of

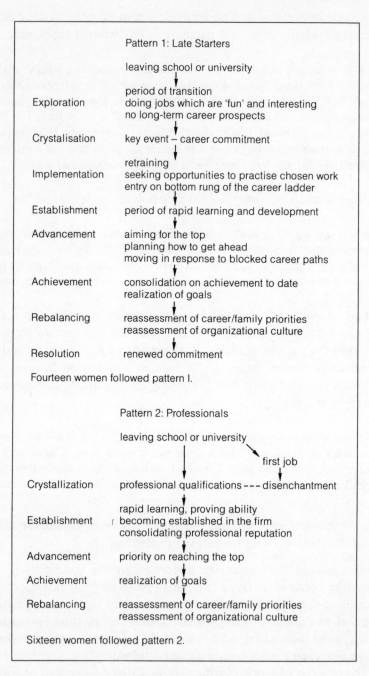

Figure 5.1 Five career patterns of successful women

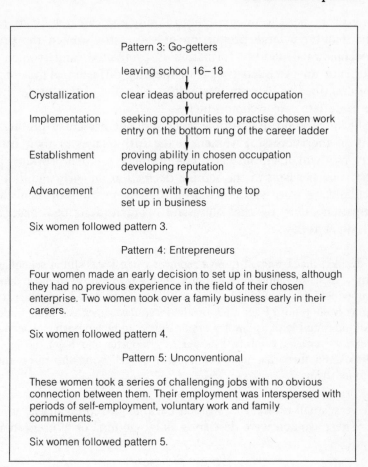

Pattern 3: Go-getters

leaving school 16–18

Crystallization — clear ideas about preferred occupation

Implementation — seeking opportunities to practise chosen work
entry on the bottom rung of the career ladder

Establishment — proving ability in chosen occupation
developing reputation

Advancement — concern with reaching the top
set up in business

Six women followed pattern 3.

Pattern 4: Entrepreneurs

Four women made an early decision to set up in business, although they had no previous experience in the field of their chosen enterprise. Two women took over a family business early in their careers.

Six women followed pattern 4.

Pattern 5: Unconventional

These women took a series of challenging jobs with no obvious connection between them. Their employment was interspersed with periods of self-employment, voluntary work and family commitments.

Six women followed pattern 5.

Figure 5.1 cont.

women felt that the commencement of their careers had been delayed by family issues. As one woman explains:

> I haven't found it difficult combining family and career because of the way that I have done it. If I had wanted to be a politician when the children were small it would have been impossible. Now we have a family house and I have a flat in London and I commute home at weekends. I give a hundred and ten per cent to work now, but I couldn't have done it with small children.

This finding supports the proposal put forward by Adams (1984) that forging a vocational identity may be more complex for women owing to the need to integrate both family and career roles. It would seem that for a large proportion of successful women the process of occupational identity formation is protracted, and women may experience an extended period of identity diffusion. These women were described as 'late starters', although some of the 'professionals' also made late career commitments.

The integration of multiple roles did not present a problem for many of the successful women in the early stages of their careers; many of them made an early commitment to their working lives. Thirty-one per cent of the sample decided at an early age that they would always work and entered on the bottom rung of their chosen occupation. One of the successful women described her career decision as follows:

> I decided that I wanted to be a reporter when I was still at school any my classmates found it very funny, which made me even more determined and single minded. I left school at sixteen and I worked in a grocery shop until I got a job on the local newspaper as a proofreader. All the time I kept asking for opportunities to be a reporter. After two years I went for a job as a junior boy reporter and I got the job. I discovered then that if you can't win by following the rules, then ignore them.

A very small number of women became entrepreneurs at an early age. These women were described as 'go-getters' or 'entrepreneurs'.

Career-planning

In their study of 100 senior women managers, Hennig and Jardim (1978) found that these women made late career decisions, approximately ten years into their working lives. This decision was attributed to the sudden realization that they would be working for the rest of their lives and that they enjoyed work.

Up to the point of making a late career decision, these women tended to concentrate on the day-to-day aspects of their job and career was seen as self-fulfilment in the far-distant future. This was said to have implications for career progress, as the women were unable to distance themselves from the problems of the present and count them as current costs of a future career. As a result, women talked of making the most of what developed, but they did not plan. Male managers, in contrast, were said to plan ahead and to have well-articulated long-term plans. This was not true, however, of the male managing directors interviewed by Cox and Cooper (1988). These men were ambitious, but they did not admit to an early desire to be managing directors or to have mapped out future plans in any detail. Therefore, the results on the career-planning behaviour of men is somewhat inconclusive.

Like the women in Hennig and Jardim's sample, many of the successful women had not planned their careers in any detail. Thirty-one per cent of the women had not planned at all. Several women were opposed to planning in principle. These women stressed the importance of being flexible and open to opportunities, a view summed up by the following remarks:

> I had a rough idea in the initial stages, but I think that if you are too rigid you will not be open to the opportunities that come up. I knew the career progression one would normally take in this field, but when opportunities came up elsewhere I would take them.

Although most of the women interviewed had engaged in some form of planning, 44 per cent felt that their planning could have been improved and, if so, they would have made faster career progress. When asked whether they had any regrets about their working lives, the most frequently mentioned regret was poor career management. Over 50 per cent of the women suggested that this lack of management and planning had caused them to make a slow start, to miss opportunities and had led to their spending too long in the same position. This regret is reflected in the words of one woman:

> I did not plan, and if I had known how to plan my career I would have put international experience in very early on and I would not have spent eight years in one place when my career wasn't moving fast enough.

Having mentioned these regrets, many of the women presented a positive outlook, suggesting that they had learnt from their mistakes. Some women felt that the lack of planning had allowed them to do jobs which, although not directly relevant to their current occupation, had given them the opportunity to develop a diverse range of skills which enhanced their current performance. As one said:

> I think that I would have been better off going in another direction because I wasted a lot of time drifting. Even so, the work that I did earlier which I believed was a waste of time is now coming into play

because the job I do now reflects the management consultancy skills I acquired earlier in my career.

As might be expected, it would seem that the women who made career decisions at an early age and then entered their chosen occupation on the bottom rung were goal directed and they planned their career moves to achieve that goal. Women who had no coherent direction in their early working lives were less likely to engage in career-planning at any stage.

Concepts of Career

Driver (1979) has extended Marcia's work on identity statuses by suggesting that one of the most crucial factors in understanding or developing careers is first to understand the concept each person has of his/her career. Research on career concepts has taken two directions: 'content' and 'structural'. Content refers to the field of choice and the possible underlying motives, interests or values lying behind vocational choices. Structural refers to the pattern within a concept. This involves factors such as differentiation (the number of parts in a concept), integration (modes of connection among the parts of a concept) and flexibility (the capacity of the relationship among the parts to change).

The structural component of career concepts

The structural variables in relation to career concepts include issues such as:

1 How much information is used to develop the career concept.
2 How many career directions the individual can forecast.
3 How open to change is the concept.
4 How pervasive is the career concept – i.e. does it pervade other life areas.

Driver suggests that individuals have characteristic decision-making styles which lead to the development of unique career-concept structures. The definitions of these styles and their resulting career concepts are outlined below.

Decisive style Just enough information is used to develop a workable stable concept which is then rarely re-examined. Individuals with a decisive style favour a career concept in which a profession is selected and held for life. It is probable that most decisive career concepts are formed early in life. This career concept is called the 'steady state'.

Flexible style   Just enough data are used to develop a concept, but it is constantly open to reinterpretation as new information becomes available. Individuals with a flexible style favour an open career concept which lacks any obvious pattern or focus and leads to a varied work history. This career concept is described as 'transitory'.

Hierarchic style   Elaborate concepts are formed based on maximum use of data and long-range planning. Tactical patterns may alter but the fundamental focus of the concept is fixed. This style lends itself to careful career-planning with long-term objectives of an impressive nature. This career concept is described as 'linear'.

Integrative style   This involves maximal use of information but is also open to constant change in structure. This style is said to be somewhat unusual. Although a lot of information is used, personal experience and trial and error are also important. A complex multi-dimensional plan tends to evolve with increased awareness on a variety of fronts, work and non-work. This career concept is described as 'spiral'.

Determining the structure of career concepts

As a guide to the investigation of the structure of career concepts, Driver (1979) has outlined a systematic approach employing issues discussed in relation to the four basic concepts. These are shown in figure 5.2. Driver also suggests that future researchers may attempt to elicit an individual's 'career decision-making story'. The analysis of such a career decision-making story would need to focus on:

1 work history to date;
2 planning, past and present;
3 integration of career concept with other life spheres.

The development of career concepts of successful women

We have clarified that career patterns of the successful women have been classified according to the structure of their career concepts. Twenty-five per cent of the group appeared to begin their working lives with a transitory career concept. They displayed no coherent

Career concept	Information use	Focus	Direction of change in pattern	Time of choice	Breadth of concept	Most likely decision style
Transitory	Minimal; contacts	Changing rapidly	Usually lateral	Continous	Work or other	Flexible
Steady-state	Minimal; authority	Constant for life	None	Youth	Work or other*	Decisive
Linear	Maximal research	For life	Upward	Youth	Work, hobbies, and family*	Hierarchic
Spiral	Maximal research and personal experience	Cyclic	Periodic lateral moves, inward building	5–7 year cycle	Work, hobbies, and family	Integrative

Figure 5.2   A systematic approach to analysing the structure of career concepts
Source: Driver (1979)

career pattern and they did not engage in career-planning. These women were passive transitory, drifting between jobs, placing value on freedom and independence. This career concept did not, however, persist throughout their careers. As Driver (1979) acknowledges, career concepts may undergo shifts as work or family situations change. These women appear to shift from transitory to spiral career concepts, a change prompted by a variety of events, most of which were specific to women. Many women developed a spiral concept when they were divorced or separated. Driver mentions that marital crisis is a route to the development of the spiral career concept. It is possible that separation raises women's awareness of their own needs. They may then undergo a period of withdrawal, during which they redefine their identity. They can no longer define themselves in relation to others – i.e. their family. It is feasible that at this point these women will begin to define themselves in terms of their own abilities and attributes. In Gilligan's (1982) terms, separation from a partner may stimulate the development of a spiral career concept through the convergence or perspectives of connected and separate selves. The *flexibility* of the transitory concept is maintained, but the women begin to integrate other aspects of their identity into their career concept. As one successful woman explained:

I did not make a conscious decision to have a career until I stopped motor racing and I joined the motor industry. Then I realized that I wasn't going to stop doing it for any other reason. Having said that, I had been separated from my husband and I do believe that while there was someone to lean on I was leaning. It was only when I was separated that I said to myself, 'What are you doing with your life?' and my plans began to firm up.

A small group of women who began their careers in the linear mode also shifted to a spiral career concept. These women were prompted to change by the desire to integrate aspects of their work and family lives. They encountered career and family conflicts which were largely attributed to working environments requiring them to work long hours in the office. This conflict caused the women to reconsider their earlier priorities and to strive for a balance between their work and non-work lives. As a result, the career concept becomes more *differentiated*. This experience was clearly described by one woman:

When I went back to work after having a baby the managing partner had changed and there was a change in the culture. The organization became more political and there was need to be seen in the office until late in the evening; good work was only seen as a bonus. This was the stimulus I needed to set up on my own.

Another stimulus for the spiral career concept was achieving a long-term linear career goal. These women were left with a feeling of emptiness, questioning what their next move should be, a factor which Driver also mentions as being a contributor to the development of a spiral career concept. For example, one woman said:

It is difficult to make plans for the future now because there is nowhere above where I am now. It's got to be a sideways move, for example a move to another company. Also, when you're on the fast track you've got to be prepared to have full mobility and I love where I live and I don't particularly want to be uprooted. If it is possible I will stay where I am.

Ten per cent of the successful women began their careers with an active steady-state career concept. These women did jobs with little prospect of promotion, but they invested their energy outside their work in their family lives. These women later developed a linear career concept when divorce or the realization that they needed financial security prompted them to strive for promotion, as one woman reported:

> The day that I went to train as an accountant I was determined that I was never going to be flat on my face with two children and no job or money. I have another husband now and we talked about starting another family when I was about thirty. I knew that even if we had chosen to go ahead I was going back to work. There was no way that I was going to be economically dependent on anyone else again.

Another woman emphasized this point: 'When my marriage broke up I had to get myself in gear and think, now I'm responsible for myself and three kids. Talk about motivation – there is no motivation like cutting off the retreat behind you.'

Later career patterns revealed that the successful women were evenly divided into two groups: those with linear concepts and those with spiral career concepts. Due to the diverse range of occupational pursuits in which these women had worked, it was difficult to assess whether career concept was related to occupation. It is feasible, however, that compatibility between career concept and occupational choice may be an important factor in determining success.

Future plans

The majority of the successful women did have plans for the future. Thirty-seven per cent talked in terms of expansion. These women were either planning the growth of their own businesses or they were looking for promotion. One woman described her plans: 'Having gone on an assessment programme, I have developed a fairly detailed development schedule with the company. This will involve several years of working abroad, but I will return to England as a general manager.'

In contrast, 35 per cent were consolidating their success to date. One woman reported:

> I have just made a big leap to director level and I wouldn't like to hurry on to the next job because I need to get to grips with this job. If you can't handle the volume of change, then your effectiveness starts to dive. Now I need to get conversant with personnel and it is a steep learning curve.

A similar need to consolidate recent progress was also expressed by women running their own enterprises. One of the female entrepreneurs made the following comments:

> We have done a lot in the last three years. We have moved from constricting premises to a purpose-built site. We have installed new technology and have gone completely computerized, gone open plan, non-smoking, non-union and now we have a woman chairman. We have got a lot to consolidate on. We can now settle in and develop. The move will enable us to expand and we are already starting to see it happen.

The above accounts of expansion followed by consolidation would suggest periods of disequilibrium followed by resolution or, in Marcia's (1980) terms, it is a cycle of moratorium–achievement–moratorium–achievement. The careers of the majority of successful women appear to evolve in *a spiral of cycles of exploration and commitment*.

Defining job and career

Hennig and Jardim (1978) reported that men and women have different conceptions of what constitutes job and career. These differences are said to have fundamental implications for their respective work behaviour. As described earlier, Hennig and Jardim report that men see their job as part of a career and, therefore, see the job in the contexts of now and later simultaneously. It is suggested that, as the job is seen as part of the career, the cues upon which men act, relationships they strive to develop and the visibility they seek to achieve have meaning in the present and in the future. In comparison, women were claimed to see the job as here and now, and a career was seen as self-fulfilment in the far and distant future. The implication was that women were unable to distance themselves from the problems of the present and count them as the current costs of a future career. The outcome was that these women tended not to plan, and they talked of waiting to see what developed.

Scase and Goffee (1989) offer an explanation for the phenomenon observed by Hennig and Jardim. They suggest that women may have been less inclined consciously to construct careers because they are more accustomed to unpredictable work experiences due to pregnancy, blocked career paths and moving with their spouse's career. As such, women have adapted to the limited opportunities by becoming job rather than career oriented, focusing on the immediate, intrinsic rewards rather than the long-term benefits.

The findings of the current study were not so clear cut. Several women had strong feelings about the terms job and career. Twenty-three per cent did not identify with the concept of a job. They felt that jobs were too constraining and unexciting, without scope for development. This view is illustrated by the following remarks:

> 'Job' doesn't mean much as a word because I don't think of myself as having a job. I have different problems to solve and I happen to have a job title. I don't mind being allocated areas of responsibility but I fight tooth and nail with personnel people who come up with job descriptions. I think that they are strait-jackets.

In contrast, 10 per cent of the women did not believe that they had a career. They perceived careers to be too inflexible and structured. This desire for flexibility could be the expression of a spiral career concept. One successful woman had the following conception of a career:

> I do not believe that I have had a career. I believe that a career involves working through the ranks. Other people may see my work as a career because it has progressed, but I have not taken on major responsibilities. I do not believe that creative people want to be administrators.

One third of the women did in fact see the job as part of a career. Unlike the women in Hennig and Jardim's sample, these women perceived career to be a planned route from A to B, incorporating direction and structure. This perception of career is reflected in the comments of one woman: 'A career is a ladder which you are aiming for the top of. There are steps along the way which you have got to attain. A career is a planned route from A to Z.' The jobs on route to the top were said to be progressively more challenging and satisfying. Therefore it would seem that these successful women incorporated both self-development and promotion into their concept of career.

A large proportion of the women felt that their career was an integral part of their lives from which they derived their identity. Several women said that their work was their main reason for existence. In the words of one: 'A career is an integral part of your life. A job is something that you do to earn a living. I see a career as a luxury and people are fortunate if they have one.'

Other successful women did not make a distinction between job and career. Many of these women also described their job as their main reason for existence. As one emphasized:

A job is a way of life for me, it's the thing that I spend most of my time doing. I think that jobs are interlinked with your personality and with personal ambitions. I don't look at a job as a way of making money.

This evidence provides further support for the proposition that many successful women have developed a positional identity.

Gilligan (1982) proposed that women reflect their sense of identity primarily in terms of their connection to others. The high-achieving women that she interviewed did not mention their achievements in describing themselves; rather they focused on career and family conflict. This was clearly not the case for many of the women in the current sample. Scase and Goffee (1989) also found that 30 per cent of the women in their survey ranked career achievement as their most important source of satisfaction. The centrality of career in identity has important implications for the integration of other social roles – an issue which will be returned to in relation to home – work interface.

Motivation and Career Development

One explanation given to account for the low proportion of women in top jobs is that women do not have the same motivations to work as men have. It is suggested that women are not as committed to work as men, and that they work for less serious reasons. In support of these contentions, Hunt (1968) presented the results of a survey of working women which suggested that women worked primarily to earn money to buy luxuries for the family, and for friendship.

More recent research has shown such stereotypes to be outdated. Crowley et al. (1973) carried out a review of studies that looked at assumptions about the motivations and aspirations of women workers. These assumptions include the notion that women would not work if economic reasons did not force them to; that women are more content to do intellectually undemanding jobs; that women are less concerned that their jobs should be self-actualizing; and, finally, that women are less concerned with getting ahead. The results of their review showed that the empirical data contradicted all these assumptions and that the motivations of both sexes were more similar than societal stereotypes would suggest. In support of these findings, Davidson and Cooper (1983) report no differences between male and female managers on achievement motivation, aspirations towards promotion and motivation to manage. Following a review of the literature, Brief and Oliver (1976) also concluded that studies show few differences between men and women in terms of motivation, especially when occupation, organizational level and education are held constant.

Factors intrinsic to the job

In agreement with the argument that there are more similarities than differences between men and women, there was a striking degree of similarity between the stated motivation of the successful women in the current study and the high flyers interviewed by Cox and Cooper (1988). As was the case among the male high flyers, most of the women were motivated by an intrinsic need to achieve and to excel in what they did. These women demanded interesting jobs which incorporated variety and provided them with a challenge. As one successful woman explained, 'I need variety and having more to do than there are hours in the day to do it. I need challenge and stimulus, I'm not a plodder. I find it hard to concentrate on doing one thing all day.'

This need for challenge was often felt to be stronger than the need for promotion. Only two women mentioned that they were striving to reach the top. Earlier research has also shown that women want challenge and satisfaction from their work rather than promotion for its own sake (Marshall, 1984). Cox and Cooper (1988) found that work was often the only real interest in the lives of the high flyers, amounting almost to an obsession. Similarly, the definitions of 'career' given by the successful women suggest that work plays a central role in their lives.

It is possible to interpret these findings within the framework of Farmer's (1985) three-factor model of achievement motivation. The tendency to prefer difficult and challenging tasks is indicative of strong mastery motivation. The women also display high career centrality, which is defined as the extent to which the individual sees involvement in a career as central to his/her adult life. Many successful women see their work as part of their own identity. A large proportion of the women made conscious decisions to advance their careers following the rejection of the traditional housewife role. This is consistent with Farmer's finding that low home-making commitment is related to high career centrality among young women.

The concept of career centrality could be crucial to the understanding of career success among women. Farmer notes that sex differences are greater for career centrality than for mastery and aspiration. This may be because long-range career motivation is more vulnerable to competing role priorities than mastery and aspiration. Therefore, we might infer that women will be in a stronger position to compete against men with high career centrality if they are able to resolve role conflicts and to give priority to their careers.

The fact that successful women do not mention the desire for promotion does not mean that they do not have high aspirations. Many of the women were already at the top of their career ladders and may, therefore, have temporarily satisfied their aspirations. When asked about their future plans, 35 per cent said that they were consolidating on a period of rapid expansion either in terms of their own company or their job. Another 37 per cent of the women did express aspirations for promotion or further expansion of the enterprise. Therefore, although promotion is not mentioned as a primary motivator by successful women, it does feature quite strongly in their plans.

It would appear that successful women have high aspirations, high mastery motivation and high career centrality, which in terms of Farmer's model indicates a high need for achievement. It is useful, however, to maintain the three-component structure of need for achievement when considering the role of motivations or the content of career concepts in the process of identity development. Marcia (1980) comments that the relationship between the content and structure of career concepts is unclear, but it is suggested that some content may preclude or foster subsequent identity development. Women with high career centrality may be viewed as having non-traditional views about the role of women in society. Weston and Stein (1977) observed that women with non-traditional views had a more highly developed identity than women with traditional views. This may be because they have resolved the identity diffusion associated with role conflict which will then facilitate achieved identity.

Some controversy may be raised concerning the timing of the

development of career centrality. Farmer found that age was not a significant influence on long-term career commitment, from which she concluded that career centrality was set early in life. This was true for 35 per cent of the successful women, who had known from an early age that they wanted to have a career. The development of career centrality occurred somewhat later among the other successful women, many of whom either rejected the role of housewife or embarked upon their careers following separation from a partner. The timing of the growth in the career sub-identity has implications for the stages observed in the career development of successful women which will be discussed in more detail later.

Self-development

Cox and Cooper (1988) state that closely related to personal ambition and drive for success is the woman's desire to improve and develop the organization, leaving it stronger than when she found it. It is proposed that for the high flyers this represents the organizational equivalent of immortality, in that the organization would go on after them. In the case of the successful women, the desire to develop their own companies was closely linked to their own development. This is well illustrated by the words of one:

> I did have a long-term plan for where my company went and I was involved in it. I knew where I wanted the company to go and I planned for that. The company and myself were absolutely entwined, we were one and the same. The aims for the company were the aims for me.

The theme of self-development was mentioned by 25 per cent of the sample, although this theme did not emerge among male high flyers. One successful woman claimed:

> Everything is about feeding into me and what I need to keep me going. So I read a lot and I study and educate myself daily. I go to the gym daily because I believe that physical fitness is important and I go to church because I feel that spiritual commitment is important. Everything has got to feed into me because at the end of the day I'm all I've got.

The women executives interviewed by Hennig and Jardim (1978) also emphasized the role of self-development in their careers. These women had implicit faith in the formal organization and, based upon the assumption of a meritocracy, self-development was the most obvious route to promotion. The promotion strategies of the successful women in the current study is examined in more detail in relation to power and politics in chapter 7.

It is possible that the desire for self-development could be a symptom of creative discontent. This is defined as discontent with the present situation which takes expression in positive attempts to do something about it. Creative discontent could be an artefact of high ego ideals. In Freudian terms, this high ego ideal is the conscience which directs our 'should behaviour'. The ego ideal is formed early in childhood and represents a state towards which the ego is continually striving. There is always a gap between the ego and the ego ideal; the larger the gap the more energy that is expended to close it. Therefore, this gap between ego and ego ideal may represent an internal source of motivation. The successful women are constantly striving to achieve high standards which are self-imposed. Like the change makers interviewed by Cooper and Hingley (1983), successful women seem to be in pursuit of excellence, striving for an ideal which they never fully achieve. As one woman put it, 'I am highly self-motivated to succeed, not at anything specific but at whatever I do. I have a need to achieve.'

Feedback and recognition

Concrete results providing external evidence of achievement were important for a large proportion of the women. Several women also mentioned that they were motivated to obtain the recognition of others for doing a good job. For example, one said:

> I need to be seen to do things well. I want to be compared favourably with the next person. Maybe it's because I'm a woman in an all-male environment, but I would hate for someone to say, 'Oh well, I didn't expect her to do well because she's a woman.' I feel that I have to perform so that people can't say that I haven't.

In this sense payment was important to these women, as it provided recognition of their worth. One woman summed up this point:

> Money is important to me these days because I believe that you should be paid for what you do. I have had years of being under-paid because I enjoyed the work. Fortunately, those days seem to be going because

of a change in attitudes. I think people should be paid well for what they do, if they do it well.

Both the desire to excel and to attain high standards, and the need for concrete feedback on results are suggestive of a high need for achievement as outlined by McClelland et al. (1953).

Autonomy

Twenty-five per cent of the successful women said that they valued autonomy. They enjoyed power and freedom to make their own decisions, as one explained: 'I like having the power to make decisions and to stand by them. My definition of success is being in control and taking the responsibility for that.'

When asked whether they had any complaints about their work, the most commonly mentioned negative aspect was the bureaucracy which they felt stifled creativity and reduced the amount of control that they had over their work. This view is summarized by the remarks of one woman:

> One of the negative aspects of my work is the management inter-ference. The need for reports, having to explain yourself every two minutes, having to fight with commercial people who want you to do something that you don't want to do. There's a lot of time-wasting. All management structure that is imposed on you tends to stop you in your creative work.

Several of the high flyers also mentioned the importance of the level of control and power that they had. This power was not associated with influencing people; rather it was concerned with influencing events. The desire expressed by successful women to have control over events in their working lives could be a reflection of the poor parent–daughter relations experienced by many of the women during childhood. Lack of control over relationships in childhood may result in the desire to have control over a tangible entity in later life, symbolized by the working environment.

A small group of the successful women claimed that they needed to feel that their work was worthwhile. This need was clearly expressed by one of them: 'If think that I can change the system, then I will challenge it. I need the satisfaction of knowing that I'm doing some-thing in the organization that makes it better and more effective.'

Twenty-five per cent of the women mentioned that they valued the social contacts they derived from their work, although for most women this was not their primary motivation – from which we may infer that need for affiliation was not a fundamental motivation among successful women.

The content of career concepts

It is now appropriate to draw attention to the content of the career concepts. Driver (1979) has used the notion of 'career anchors' developed by Schein (1977) to explain the content of career concepts. Schein started work on career diversity in the 1960s, beginning with a study of forty-four Massachusetts Institute of Technology (MIT) Masters degree graduates whom he interviewed six months and one year after their graduation. These interviews were then followed up by questionnaires after a five- and then a ten-year interval. Schein found that the careers of these graduates were quite diverse after ten years, although they had all started with enthusiasm to climb the corporate ladder.

Career anchors

On the basis of his research, Schein sorted individuals into five groups:

1 *Managers*. Climbed the corporate ladder with undiminished enthusiasm.
2 *Technicians and specialists*. Content to concentrate on the details of their profession.
3 *Security oriented*. These individuals found promotion rewarding because it meant that the company valued them and so wanted to keep them.
4 *High autonomy needs*. Found ways to carve out their own niche in the organization.
5 *Entrepreneurs*. Started up their own ventures to meet creative and autonomy needs.

Schein (1982) later identified other basic career orientations which he termed career anchors. A career anchor is defined as a basic value or motive which plays a significant role in forming the direction of a career. They include:

1 Dedication to an ideology, a cause or a group.
2 Pure challenge – individuals thriving on competition, adventure and risk.
3 Maintaining a balance between professional and private life.

It is proposed that career anchors suggest sub-divisions within the career concepts. The transitory concept is divided along a passive/

active dimension. The passive transitory drifts from job to job, valuing freedom and independence. The active transitory is entre- preneurial, valuing innovation, but moving out when stabilization sets in.

The steady-state concept may also be divided along the active/ passive dimension. The passive steady-state is a security seeker, motivated by fear, hedonism or duty. Such people may have invested their energy outside their work, in family or social life. The active steady-state is decisive and energetic. These individuals achieve a desired level and then aim to maintain it by constant update of skills.

The linear career concept could also be divided along the active/ passive dimension, but Driver (1979) suggests that the technical/ people orientation is a more appropriate distinction. Technical linears seek recognition of their competence from their peers, while people linears seek power and organizational scope.

Driver suggests that these sub-divisions provide a detailed map- ping of career patterns which should enable individuals to determine where they are and where they want to go. Driver does not deny that career concepts may change. It is possible that systematic shifts in patterns of events may result in decision style shifts. Therefore, it is feasible that career concepts may undergo systematic shifts as work or family situations change. This is particularly relevant to women, as changing family and social environment appears to have greater impact on the working lives of women than upon those of men. Research might, therefore, focus specifically on the shifts in women's career concepts as family conditions change.

Career orientations

Driver (1988) suggests that a promising direction for career theory might be to attempt to integrate career concepts and motives into a minimum set of categories for describing career orientations. Such a set would have to do justice to human complexity and at the same time avoid proliferation of sets. A prototype of such a set might be that outlined by Derr (1986). Derr claims that five distinct career orientations have been identified among organizational employees:

1 *Getting ahead*. Making it to the top of the hierarchy or status system. This orientation represents a fusion of the linear concept and the managerial anchor.
2 *Getting secure*. Involves achieving recognition, security, respect and insider status. This is fusion of the steady-state concept and the security anchor.

3 *Getting high*. Getting excitement, challenge, adventure and cutting-edge opportunities. This equates to the spiral concept.
4 *Getting free*. Involves getting the maximum control over one's working life. This represents a fusion of the transitory concept and autonomy anchor.
5 *Getting balanced*. Involves achieving a meaningful balance among work and self-development so that work becomes neither too absorbing nor boring.

The career orientations of successful women

The current research was entirely exploratory in the sense that there is no published research evidence concerning the predominant career orientations of successful women. It was anticipated that the issues associated with each orientation would vary over the life cycle with shifts in career concepts and motivations. The aim of the study, however, was to establish the current career orientations of the successful women.

The women were asked to state what they demanded from their work. The responses to this question were taken to represent the value which the women placed on elements of their work, or, in Schein's terminology, the demands could be equated to career anchors. To assess the career orientation of successful women, the relationship between career concept (as defined by work history and planning behaviour) and characteristics demanded from work were explored. Many of the women mentioned more than one demand, but only the primary demands were used in the analysis.

Getting ahead   None of the women placed priority on getting to the top of an organizational hierarchy or status system. It was noted, however, in relation to the aspirations of successful women, that many were already at the top of their career ladder. It is possible that during earlier stages of their working lives getting ahead may have accurately described their career orientation, but on arriving at the top, their career orientation shifted to include other values.

Getting secure   Thirty-one per cent of the women did mention that they wanted recognition for their achievements. However, this desire was rooted in a personal need for achievement rather than in the need to be reassured that the organization valued them.

The argument that the successful women do not have a strong security anchor is further supported by their attitudes towards risk-taking. The majority of women perceived themselves as risk-takers;

several felt that risk-taking was an essential ingredient for career and business success. Twenty per cent of the women said that they had taken career moves which appeared risky but had paid dividends. A large proportion of the successful women claimed that they had taken moderate or calculated risks, which is consistent with the reports of male high flyers (Cox and Cooper, 1988).

Getting high   Derr (1986) claims that this orientation represents a combination of the spiral concept and the challenge anchor. Several of the successful women do, in fact, display this combination of the concept and anchor (i.e. demanding challenge, variety and interest from their work). It is possible that this orientation may also include successful women with a linear career path. In striving to achieve their long-term goals, they seek constant challenge. In addition, women with a linear career concept demand intrinsic interest and variety in their work. It is possible that these women represent what Driver (1988) descibes as 'active, technical linears', who strive for the top but at the same time seek challenge, achievement and recognition for their expertise. In total, 48 per cent of the women had a getting-high orientation.

Getting free   Getting free in this sense implies a strong need for freedom and independence. Fifteen per cent of the successful women, with both linear and spiral career concepts, valued autonomy in their work. These women rejected the constraints of a job description, preferring to carve out their own niche, either within an organization or via self-employment. In reaching the top, successful women obtain a degree of autonomy which allows them to pursue their own development.

Getting balanced   The evidence presented thus far indicates that successful women do not place priority on getting balanced, as work plays a very central role in their early and mid-careers. The issue of getting balanced is explored in more depth in chapter 8 in relation to the home–work interface.

Career Stages

The careers of the successful women were classified in five basic patterns representing the order in which tasks associated with career developmental stages emerge. The rationale behind the search for patterns of adjustment to life in general and career in particular is that we might identify issues associated with ages or stages that might help our understanding of individual behaviour in organizations, which may lead to more effective planning.

Most of the work on career stages has focused almost exclusively on males and has been largely condemned on the grounds that it fails to take account of the experiences of women. Perun and Beilby (1981) suggest that the age structures of some stage theories are inappropriate when applied to women. They also point out that the determinants of occupational behaviour are different from those of men, and that the trajectory of the work cycle of women is less predictable than that of men. Larwood and Gutek (1987) propose that, owing to the unpredictable nature of women's career paths, it might be better to conceptualize women's careers as a network, or tree, of possible alternatives, each combination of which has a potentially different outcome. Such a conceptualization was thought to be preferable because it overcame the need to incorporate the elements of timing and age.

For the purposes of the current discussion, ideas have been borrowed from both stage theories and the notion of a network of alternatives. The issues observed in each of the five career patterns have been integrated with the issues associated with combining career and family roles to create a model of career development for successful women (shown in figure 5.3).

It is proposed that no matter what their occupation, successful women will grow through specific life stages. The nature, duration and exact timing of certain events may differ, but certain development tasks are thought to be predictable. This premise is borrowed from stage theory (e.g. Levinson et al., 1978). Certain issues did appear to emerge in chronological order and therefore the mean age of women dealing with this developmental task is given. The ages of transition are best perceived as being very flexible. Further research is definitely required to test the validity of this age-linked structure. In accordance with the notion of career as a network of alternatives, the options considered by the successful women in each developmental stage are presented.

The model of career-stage development of successful women compared with earlier career-stage models

The model of career development of successful women outlined above bears a strong resemblance to the career stages described by

Early Adult Transition, 17–25 (Exploration)
- early commitment to an occupation
- testing of initial choices about preferences for living
- identity diffusion caused by role conflict

Entering the Adult World, mid-twenties (Crystallization and Implementation)
- development of sense of personal identity in relation to work and non-work
- rejection of the housewife role/separation from partner, resulting in growth of career sub-identity among late starters
- high career centrality among early starters (go-getters)
- seek opportunities to practise chosen occupation/profession

Establishment, 25–33
- period of rapid learning and development
- establishing a reputation as a high achiever

Early-thirties Transition, 33–5
- raised awareness of biological clock – decision whether to have children

Settling Down, 35 (Advancement)
- decision about motherhood resolved
- minimum maternity leave
- strive toward the achievement of personal goals

Late-thirties Transition, 38–40
- regret lack of children
- family–career conflict
- move in response to glass ceiling

Achievement, 40–50 (Rebalancing)
- resolution of career–family conflict
- rationalize decision not to have children
- realization of personal goals
- develop greater stability and consolidate of achievements to date

Maintenance, fifties onwards
- continued growth and success
- cycle of expansion and consolidation

Figure 5.3   A stage model of the careers of successful women

Levinson et al. (shown in figure 5.4), although Levinson's model was based on in-depth interviews with forty men. This was not thought to be entirely surprising, given that these women had succeeded in a world of business which is structured to accommodate male lives. Like the men interviewed by Levinson, the successful women experienced periods of stability followed by periods of questioning

Early adulthood
Early-adult transition, 17–22
- start thinking about place in the world separate from parents and educational institutions
- test intitial preferences for living

Entering Adult World, 22–8
- develop sense of personal identity in work and non-work

Thirties Transition, 29–33
- evaluate accomplishments of thirties and make adjustments

Settling Down, 34–9
- strive towards achieving personal goals
- make commitments to family and work

Middle adulthood
Mid-life Transition, 40–45
- review life structure adopted in thirties
- recognize mortality limits on achievement

Entering Middle Adulthood, 46–50
- developing greater stability as questions raised in mid-life transition are answered

Fifties Transition, 51–5
- raise questions about life structure previously adopted

Culmination of Middle Adulthood, 50–60
- answer questions raised and adjust life choices

late adulthood (over 60)

Figure 5.4 Levinson's model of life development

and change. This contradicts Super's (1984) contention that people have relatively stable attitudes towards their careers across all stages. The main points of departure from the Levinson model relate to the timing of relationship and family events.

The model is based largely on the career paths of the younger women in the sample. Only 10 per cent of the successful women had taken career breaks, the mean length of which was 9.4 years. These women were among the older members of the sample, their average age being fifty-six years. They had followed what have been labelled unconventional career paths, as they are less apparent among successful women today. The early career stages – i.e. early-adult transition, entering the adult world and establishment – were discussed at some length in relation to strategy formulation.

Early-thirties transition

A more common pattern among the women was to wait until their career was well established before contemplating a family. A number of the women in the sample were going through this period of contemplation; the mean age of this group was 33.1 years. This transitional period was followed by a decision to have a child and to take minimum maternity leave, or to remain childless.

Setting down – late-thirties transition

Following approximately four years of renewed commitment to their careers, the women entered another transitional phase. Some women who had decided to remain childless began to express regrets about their decision. The women who had decided to have children in their early thirties began to feel the strain of career and family conflict. This conflict was often resolved by a change of organization or by becoming self-employed. It was often during this period of transition that the successful women encountered the 'glass ceiling' described in the report by the Hansard Society (1990); that is, they could see the top but they were prevented from getting there. These women made out-spiralling moves, changing organizations to gain promotion.

Achievement – maintenance

The resolution of issues in the late-thirties transition leads to a period of achievement and rebalancing. During this stage, childless women rationalize their decision not to have children, stating that they could not have achieved their current career success if they had children. This change of attitude may be explained in terms of Festinger's (1957) concept of cognitive dissonance. Dissonance is created in the thirties transition because women start to feel that the sacrifices they have made were too great. Dissonance theory suggests that people are motivated to reduce this inconsistency in cognitions; therefore women begin to place greater importance on their career achievements. These women are convinced that for them career and family are mutually exclusive. The average age of this group is 46.8 years. Having reached the achievement stage, the women enter a maintenance stage. No evidence of further periods of transition was observed. The women nearing retirement age were still involved in their work, although some women mentioned that they worked fewer hours, which might be viewed as the beginning of a decline stage. Because of the small number of women in this age group, it was not possible to draw any conclusions on the dynamics of the decline stage.

6

Aspects of Successful Careers

Introduction

Handy (1987) suggests that there are two main routes into top management: accountancy, or working one's way up through a large corporation. The chief executives studied by Cox and Cooper (1988) generally conformed to this pattern, although there was an equal representation of engineers and accountants, together with quite a wide range of other backgrounds. In this study we were interested in finding out whether the careers of successful women follow a similar route to that of their male counterparts, or whether there are significant differences. In chapter 5 we looked at successful women's perceptions of their careers. In this chapter we look at some of the key events which contribute to their success.

Early Challenge

Cox and Cooper (1988) report that many studies have shown that successful people often achieve positions of responsibility at an early age. In their study of high flyers they observed that many of the managing directors mentioned a make-or-break experience when they were given complete responsibility with very little outside support. This was perceived as a key developmental experience.

A possible explanation for the importance of such events may be derived from Hall's (1976) notion of career growth. As individuals acquire competence relevant to their career role, their career sub-identity is said to grow. Sub-identity extension in relation to career role is described as career growth. As the career sub-identity expands, proportionately more of the total identity is invested in the career role. A person is claimed to experience career sub-identity growth when he has feelings of success. Hall identifies four conditions under which career growth may be achieved:

1 The person sets challenging goals for him/herself.
2 The person determines his/her own means of achieving goals.
3 The goal is important to the self-concept.
4 The person actually attains the goals.

An increased sense of personal success leads to increased self-esteem. A person's orientation towards a given task situation is partly a function of his present level of self-esteem. If self-esteem is high, the individual will seek success to develop competence. If self-esteem is low, the individual will attempt to avoid challenging situations in order to avoid failure.

Early challenge for the successful women

Almost all the successful women were able to identify a significant event or turning-point which they felt had made an impact upon their working lives. Thirty per cent of the women said that they had been given a challenge early in their careers which had offered them the opportunity to prove their abilities. These women described this experience as being thrown in at the deep end and then managing to stay afloat. Successfully coping with this challenge was claimed to have raised self-confidence, which led the women to seek further challenge. One woman gave the following example:

I took a job as a management-services officer and I worked on non-computer projects. Then the company decided to computerize all of its outlets, so I got thrown in at the deep end deciding what they should have, designing the system and installing it.

Another woman reported a similar experience:

I was told that if I was serious about banking I would have to get credit experience, so I went to a financial-analysis department. I was placed in a team with others who had degrees, MBAs and accountancy qualifications. I felt inferior and I assumed that the others were better than me. As time went by, I was persuaded that I could do the job and I learnt a lot from the others in the group.

As mentioned earlier, the male high flyers interviewed by Cox and Cooper (1988) also recounted memories of make-or-break experiences. What Cox and Cooper found to be significant was that all the MDs had coped successfully. An interesting issue for future research might be to investigate what happens to those individuals who do not cope successfully with early career challenges.

As the women acquired evidence of their competence and gained experience of psychological success, it is possible that their career sub-identity began to expand, which may explain the development of career centrality among the successful women. Consistent with Hall's (1976) suggests that a sense of personal success will lead to increased self-esteem, the women in our sample reported raised self-confidence. Given high self-esteem the individual will seek further success to develop competence.

The notion of career growth is closely linked with the concept of self-efficacy. Bandura (1982) states that success and mastery experience is the most powerful means of creating a strong, resilient sense of self-efficacy. In addition, once a strong sense of self-efficacy has been developed through repeated success, the negative impact of the occasional failure is likely to be reduced. Lewin (1951) also comments that success generates success. He suggests that a person is most likely to set a new higher level of aspiration following a successfully attained goal if he/she has a history of previous successes. The person accustomed to failure is likely to quit while ahead.

Several of the successful women credited open-minded bosses for giving them the opportunity to demonstrate their abilities and for having faith in their competence regardless of their gender. As one woman commented: 'A chap that I worked for was prepared to encourage me, where other people would have seen being female as a disincentive.' This finding coincides with the reports of Hennig and Jardim (1978), who found that female managers had mentors who helped them to develop the confidence to take on extra responsibilities and to test new competencies. Missirian (1982) also found that the mentors of female executives provided an environment conducive to experimentation with new behaviours. The women in the current study suggested that their bosses' confidence in their ability was demonstrated in the provision of concrete opportunities to show their talent. Taking advantage of the opportunities gained, the women heightened exposure and visibility.

Nine of the women mentioned that they had achieved a position of responsibility at an unusually young age, or that they had achieved a position which was unusual for a woman. This early achievement provided challenge and heightened visibility. It is likely, however, that these women would be subject to the effects of being a 'token woman'. This was illustrated by one woman talking of her early career in the police force:

> I was promoted at twenty-two and won the record for the youngest person to be promoted to sergeant. I gained experience in the vice squad and then as detective sergeant in the CID. I passed my inspector's exams, but in those days the police force didn't really know that to do with women. I was made acting inspector and then back to sergeant. At that point I got really fed up, so I decided to transfer out of that force.

Centrality and Women's Careers

Women may disadvantage themselves by making early career choices which do not readily lead to senior positions. Women are concentrated in jobs which have poor promotion prospects – e.g. clerical, retail and catering. Even when women enter higher-status occupations they make different entry choices. Alston (1987) found that fewer female lawyers go into private practice, which makes them less likely to become partners.

Women tend to follow different functional careers within organizations. For example, Hirsh and Jackson (1990) report that women in insurance are more likely to be in personnel than to be actuaries; in retail they are in staff management rather than store management; and in manufacturing women tend to be located in sales and not production. Ryecroft (1989) showed that women are more likely than men to be in administration, personnel and accounts. This finding is supported by the results of the survey conducted by Nicholson and West (1988), which found that women were more likely to be in personnel and less likely to be line managers.

The majority of women are concentrated in support functions. They are in positions which are not generally considered to be central to the functioning of the business, which leads to the assumption that they do not have the real business understanding required for senior management. Successful people might, therefore, be expected to prefer situations which have a higher degree of centrality, allowing them to obtain and use power. Some power may be obtained in staff positions such as human-resource management, but staff positions are usually viewed as more peripheral, supporting line positions that have authority over what the organization considers to be its primary activity. Staff positions are less important to the work flow of the organization and are likely to accumulate less power.

There are some contradictions surrounding the issue of centrality. Accountancy may be viewed as a support function, yet it is commonly viewed as a route to senior management. In a study of nurse managers, Hutt (1985) found that men were promoted more rapidly than women. This was partly explained by the fact that the men were younger and careers in nursing may have developed more quickly in recent years. It was observed, however, that the majority of the female nurse managers started in general nursing, while 60 per cent of the men started nursing in mental illness, which is less central. It is therefore not entirely clear whether we should always expect movement towards line positions by successful women.

Career Progression

Movement into senior positions requires one to have a wide range of experience. In managerial careers individuals are expected to have experience of more than one function. This was found to be the case for the high flyers interviewed by Cox and Cooper (1988). All the MDs had moved around a lot in their early careers, spending approximately two or three years in each job. Most of the MDs had experience of more than one company. Cox and Cooper comment that whatever the pattern of moves, whether within one organization or between organizations, all the managers had a breadth of experience involving many functions. In some cases experience was gained by working in a small company, which gave experience of top management.

McCall and Lombardo (1983) noted that one of the differentiating factors between those managers who made it to the top and those who derailed was their track record. Derailed managers had a series of successes, but usually in similar situations; for instance, they had managed progressively larger jobs but in the same function. The arrivers had more diversity in their successes. They showed a breadth of experience and interest that, over twenty years, had resulted in detailed knowledge of many parts of the business, as well as first-hand experience with different kinds of challenges.

It would seem that moving between functions is vital preparation for successful careers, yet much of the research suggests that women stay longer as specialists within one function. Nicholson and West (1988) concluded that women tend to describe themselves as functional specialists. Where women achieve equivalent status to men, they do so through specialist routes. Hennig and Jardim (1978) reported that American female executives changed jobs in their first two years because their original companies refused to accept women in anything other than routine work. Having found a suitable organization, none of the women worked for any other firm. Hennig and Jardim commented that this was less than typical of highly motivated success-oriented male managers. Male managers were said to be on the watch for every reasonable opportunity to get ahead and would regularly progress up the executive ladder through company moves. In contrast, the women in their sample felt that women would only move up if they were competent at their jobs. They also felt that it was more difficult for a woman to establish good working relationships than it was for a man, and that once she had established these relationships it would be unproductive to move to another company where she would have to develop them again.

Nicholson and West did find some evidence that younger women were changing organizations. They suggest that women are more likely than men to make an out-spiralling move, changing employer and function, accompanied by an upward move. They note that the women adopting this pattern are younger specialists. This finding might mean that women's ambitions for promotion are thwarted and the only way to progress is to move organization.

Mobility is often seen as a requirement of a successful career because it demonstrates commitment and it gives greater experience than can be gained at a single location. Fast-track programmes often expect frequent changes which may involve relocation worldwide. Cox and Cooper (1988) found that many of the high flyers had experience of working abroad. However, the real need for mobility may be less than is commonly supposed. Atkinson et al. (1987) found that in a sample of managers and professionals, only 40 per cent had relocated in the last ten years and only 16 per cent had moved more than once in that time. Although Nicholson and West (1988) portray job changes as becoming more frequent, the changes did not always involve a change of location.

Breadth of experience among successful women

As expected, most of the successful women had a wide range of experience. This experience was gained by moving between functions within the same organization, moving between key positions in different organizations or from experience in an 'incubator' organization. Incubator organizations are small firms where the individual has good opportunities to learn a range of functions. This was illustrated by one successful woman's description of her early experience:

> I worked on a little magazine as a copy-taster and I did everything. There were a lot of top-heavy people who took long lunches, drank a lot and didn't do much work. I was the 'girl Friday' who ended up doing everything. I fell in at the deep end and I learnt a lot. It was an all-round dogsbody job, but it was useful.

Another woman described a similar experience:

> I've been fortunate in the people that I've worked for. I joined a small organization where nobody had the skills that I had and I worked for people who were confident in their own right and they let me get on with it. In a larger organization I wouldn't have had the freedom to develop. I would encourage others to work in a small organization, learn the business inside out and then move on.

Twenty-seven per cent of the women also mentioned that they had been responsible for turning round a failing company or establishing a new department. For example, one woman said:

> I was asked to go to London to set up a new business-development and marketing department. I went believing that it would be for two years. In fact the work was very stimulating and challenging and I found that I did not want to go back to my previous support role, and so I became the first female manager to be appointed. The next move was when the company decided to overhaul its communications and marketing as a result of a new strategic direction. I then became responsible for communications within the whole group. I was responsible for one of the most radical changes of image this century in terms of this sector. From there I was head-hunted to a merchant investment banking group.

As noted before, this breadth of experience has been found to be a differentiating factor between those executives who make it to the top and those who derail. Arrivers are said to have diversity in their successes (McCall and Lombardo, 1983). Cox and Cooper (1988) also reported that male high flyers had experience involving many functions.

Nineteen per cent of the women interviewed did not change organizations or functions; rather they followed a career track. This pattern was most common among the professional women. It is possible that the career path required for success in the professions differs from that required of organizational careers. It may be speculated that professional firms place higher value on loyalty than evidence of breadth of experience.

Prompts for movement

The most commonly mentioned stimulus for a career move was a blocked career path. Upon realizing that the potential for promotion was limited, 23 per cent of the women made what are described as 'out-spiralling' moves, changing employer or function to gain an upward move. As previously noted, Nicholson and West (1988) have observed an increasing occurrence of out-spiralling moves among younger female specialists. They suggest that this pattern could be a response to the glass ceiling over women's aspirations. However, this pattern was observed by Hennig and Jardim (1978) as being characteristic of male managers. It was found that men were on the watch for every reasonable opportunity to get ahead and would regularly progress through company moves. In contrast, the women in their sample felt that they would move up the ladder only if they were competent at their jobs. It is possible that over the last decade women have become more accustomed to careers and they have begun to adopt the career strategies which men have always employed to get ahead. The strategy of making out-spiralling moves cannot, therefore, be viewed as proof that women must move to circumvent the glass ceiling.

A small proportion of the women had been head-hunted. It is possible that this is a reflection of passivity on the part of the successful women, in that they waited to be chosen. This explanation seems rather implausible, however, given the level of the jobs for which they were head-hunted. Most of the women did seem to be pro-active concerning the direction of their careers. Twenty-five per cent claimed that they had made false moves in their careers which they had quickly rectified. Only two women felt that they had stayed too long in a particular position.

Cox and Cooper (1988) found that many of the high flyers had experience of working abroad. Twenty-three per cent of the successful women had also spent time working in another country, although not in very senior positions. These women travelled abroad during the early exploratory stages of their careers and they did not think that foreign travel had made a significant impact upon their careers. Those who did view their experience of working overseas as being important felt that it had given them a more detached perspective. They believed that this perspective enabled them to perceive situations at home more objectively, as one woman said:

> My years in America totally changed my outlook. The philosophy was that you didn't have to worry about who you were or what your background was; if you wanted to do something then you could do it. When I started working there was no work for me. I had an idea that I would set up a nutrition unit in a health authority for pregnant women. There was nothing like it at the time so the idea was very pioneering. I had these elevated ideas, which were implanted in me from America, that if I could do the job then I should go for it. Otherwise I wouldn't have had the nerve.

Mentoring

Kram (1985) defines a mentor as 'An experienced, productive manager who relates well to a less experienced employee and facilitates his/her personal development for the benefit of the individual as well as that of the organisation.'

Mentoring can be either formal – that is, part of the formal organizational policy – or informal, a private arrangement between two individuals, which does not necessarily have organizational approval. Most mentoring relationships are informal, although Klauss (1981) suggested that formal mentoring schemes which match mentors and protégés are becoming increasingly popular in both public and private sectors.

The benefits of mentoring

Few rigorous quantitative studies have been conducted to investigate the antecedents and outcomes of mentoring. Much of the literature comes from America, where the main focus has been on the male experience of mentoring. Initial work conducted by Kram (1983, 1985) and Burke (1984) suggests that mentors provide both career and psychosocial benefits to their protégés. They claim that, in career terms, a mentor may advance a career by nominating the protégé for promotion (sponsorship), by providing the protégé with opportunities to show talent (exposure and visibility), by suggesting strategies for achieving work objectives (coaching), by minimizing involvement in controversial issues (protection) and by the assignment of challenging work. In psychosocial terms, the mentor may enhance the protégé's sense of competence and identity by giving performance feedback; mentors may serve as role models and they may encourage protégés to experiment with new behaviours.

The benefits of a mentoring relationship are not limited to the protégé, as Clutterbuck and Devine (1985) have pointed out. The mentor is said to achieve increased job satisfaction, increased peer recognition and potential career advancement. The organization may also benefit in areas of recruitment and selection, in the motivation of employees, in the stabilization of corporate cultures, in leadership development and by improved communication.

The findings of a recent comparative study of male and female junior managers revealed that gender difference exists in terms of the benefits which men and women derive from mentoring relationships (Arnold and Davidson, 1990). Some of the roles performed by the mentors were viewed as being equally important by the men and women. Both the male and female managers found that their mentors were important for introducing them to the informal network of power relations which existed in the organization. A large difference was found, however, between the women, who felt that their mentors had been important in teaching them the appropriate corporate image, and the men, who said that they learnt through observation when they felt it necessary. Encouragement was the psychosocial role considered important by the largest percentage of the managers. The other psychosocial roles mentioned were self-confidence, legitimacy, role-model counselling and emotional support. Many of the women managers referred to their lack of confidence, their invisibility and their feelings of anxiety about their jobs. These problems they believed had been resolved to a large extent by the help and support given to them by their mentors. A higher percentage of women than men considered each of the psychosocial roles to be important, which Arnold suggests may reflect women's greater need for affirmation psychological support. In contrast, for men the role of the mentor is associated with career benefits. Further support for this distinction between male and female managers was found in their identification of the main beenfits derived from mentoring. Forty per cent of the women and 20 per cent of the men identified building self-confidence; 20 per cent of the women and none of the men named friendship as a beneficial outcome. More of the men named a beneficial career-development outcome (60 per cent) than a psychosocial one (40 per cent), whereas women were as likely to name both.

The women in the survey who did not have a mentor felt that their career progress would have been improved if they had been able to develop a mentoring relationship. They highlighted certain areas where they thought that a mentor's support would have been an advantage. These included company politics, access to information, career development and emotional support. These findings are replicated in other research (e.g. George and Kumnerow, 1981; Bishop and Bresser, 1986; Stewart and Gudykunst, 1982). It is claimed that without a mentor women are often unable to understand the reality of the male-dominated business culture. They fail to obtain the sponsorship needed to identify them as highly talented and to direct them in their career advancement.

Mentoring and career success

Ilgen and Youltz (1986) suggest that the career and psychosocial benefits of mentoring increase the likelihood that women will receive co-operation of peers and their subordinates which may enhance their probability of success. In addition, it has been found that women who had one or more mentors reported greater job success and satisfaction than women who did not (Riley and Wrench, 1985). Interviews with women executives revealed that mentors had created opportunities for them to operate outside the organizational norms; they had set high standards and stimulated personal motivation, publicized achievements and provided an environment which was conducive to experimentation with new behaviours (Missirian, 1982).

Research which has focused on successful men and women shows that these individuals can identify people who have acted as mentors. In their study of high flyers, Cox and Cooper (1988) found that all the managing directors had a mentor who was often an immediate boss at some earlier period of their careers. This was not generally a formal mentoring arrangement; rather it was a good boss who had given guidance. The positive attitude of this group of high flyers towards mentoring was reflected in their own companies where they had frequently implemented formal mentoring programmes to make the benefits which they had received more widely available.

Hennig and Jardim (1978) claim that the women executives in their sample identified a 'good boss' as a critical make-or-break factor. A typical woman maintained a distant and solely work-based relationship with her peers and subordinates. In contrast, she developed a deep and abiding friendship with the man for whom she worked. As he moved upwards, she moved with him. When asked to describe her boss and her relationship with him, she likened him to her father. As discussed in the section on childhood, the fathers of these women encouraged them to achieve what they wanted to do, regardless of their gender. In a similar way, the boss acted as a supporter, adviser and was the woman's strength in the company. He was said to admire her competence and believed that women should be in business. The boss acted as salesperson for the woman wherever he went inside and outside the company. He used his reputation to develop hers and his respect from others to gain acceptance for her. His support helped provide her with the confidence to take on extra responsibilities and new tests of her competence. Only with her boss, as with her father earlier, did she feel that her gender was taken for granted and primary emphasis was placed on her intelligence and ability. As her career developed, the woman became more autonomous and her relationship with her mentor became a friendship between equals.

The role of the mentor in the careers of the women executives in Hennig and Jardim's sample could be explained in terms of need for achievement. According to McClelland and Burnham (1976), the need for power is one of the most important motivational forces for a successful manager. Research indicates that women managers possess greater needs for achievement, power and motivation to manage than men (Chusmir, 1985; Stahl, 1983). However, the influence of needs for achievement and power may be inhibited by women's lack of confidence in their ability to perform successfully in male-dominated roles owing to their socialization experiences (Lenney, 1977). Women's lack of confidence in achievement situations may be alleviated by the use of positive feedback (McCarthy, 1988). Mentors may, therefore, reinforce achievement-oriented behaviours by giving specific task feedback.

Women's expectancy of success in male-dominated environments may also be increased by direct and observational learning (Bandura, 1977). If a mentor is available to act as a role model, it is likely that women's aspiration levels and self-efficacy regarding traditionally male work will be raised (Barclay, 1982; Hackett and Betz, 1981).

In an interview conducted as part of a study of change makers (Cooper and Hingley, 1983), Sara Morrison, a director of GEC, also emphasized that women need mentors who can act as role models. She suggests that women may miss out on the climb to the top because they lack female role models and they therefore have little idea about how to go about the search for success. Their response is simply to mirror the behaviour of the successful male executive, which Sara Morrison believes will further isolate women because their lifestyle doesn't lend itself to the male managerial model.

It is possible that, because of the lack of women in senior management, those women who do have a mentor will have a male mentor. Warihay (1980), in a survey of 2000 female managers, found that as they advanced to upper management the absence of female mentors was felt acutely. A factor inhibiting the use of female mentors is that men hold more centralized and critical positions, which gives them access to valuable information concerning job openings, pending projects and managerial decision (Barnier, 1982; Smith and Grenier, 1982). Therefore, a male mentor may have a wider power base, may help to set realistic goals, may provide greater visibility to important organizational members and may have access to more valuable resources than a female mentor (Woodlands Group, 1980). Although it may be true that male mentors have a wider power base, both men and women tend to prefer to work with others of their own gender (Larwood and Blackmore, 1978). Whereas male mentors provide women with legitimate access to power, female mentors can also bring a better understanding of the stress and problems which may arise for women.

In the absence of a female mentor, it is possible that successful women may seek alternative sources of support. Kram and Isabella (1985) argue that peers may provide some functions of the mentor when no mentor is available. Arnold and Davidson (1990) also point out that the junior managers in their sample emphasized the importance of support from partners, peers and colleagues inside and outside the organization. Also, women's networks were mentioned by some of the female managers as being sources of emotional support and career development in addition to their mentors.

Successful women and their mentors

None of the successful women in our sample had been involved in a formal mentoring program; however, the majority could identify a person who had been influential in their careers or who had acted as a mentor. Only 12.5 per cent of the women in the our sample said that they had not had a mentor. Some of these women actually felt that having a mentor was a symptom of weakness, as the relationship was inherently one of dependency on the part of the protégé. These women believed that strength should come from within oneself, as one explained:

> Mentors are not that important; the mentor should be oneself. You can look to other people for pointers but mentors can be dangerous. I think that there is too much dependency involved and too much control that you're putting in someone else's hands, and in my opinion that is not the wisest thing to be doing.

In contrast, a large majority of the women felt that their success could in part be attributed to another person. Previous research has shown that the benefits derived from mentoring relationships can be roughly divided into psychosocial benefits and career benefits. Both were mentioned by the successful women. Thirty-eight per cent in our sample said that their confidence had been increased because their mentor had shown faith in their abilities. This faith had been reinforced with encouragement and support. One woman emphasized the importance of her mentor in her self-development: 'I worked for a man who was my mentor. He believed in me and gave me a tremendous opportunity to grow. He made me discover abilities that I didn't know I had got.'

Arnold and Davidson (1990) found a similar proportion of the women in their sample felt that the main benefit derived from mentoring was in building self-confidence. It seems, however, that this is less important to developing male managers, as only 20 per cent considered confidence-building to be the main benefit. The results of the current study appear to support Arnold and Davidson's conclusion that women express greater need than men for psychological affirmation from their mentors.

In addition to psychological support, the successful women also thought that their mentor had given practical help in advancing their careers. Having raised their self-confidence, 29 per cent of the women said that their mentors demonstrated their faith by giving them opportunities to demonstrate their abilities and to acquire a good reputation. In proving their talents, these women became more visible to senior management. One woman described the process as follows:

> The director of the organization has been very supportive and encouraging. I gained a reputation for achieving targets within tight timetables and for getting things done to a high standard. So, whenever he has a problem he has looked to me for a solution. It has been give and take: he has given me the opportunity and I have done the task and so have been given other opportunities.

The women reported two other ways in which their mentors had helped them. Twenty-one per cent of the successful women said that their mentor had helped them to clarify their career plans. The mentor had offered advice concerning career direction and prospects. Several of the women valued their mentor's objectivity about their strengths and weaknesses. For example:

> The director who appointed me in the north-west was a mentor. I got to know him well personally. He was keen for me to succeed and he gave me advice from time to time. I always felt that if I got into a corner I could call him. He knows the company and can be objective about me.

None of the successful women in our sample mentioned that their mentor had acted as a role model. This does not necessarily imply that acting as a role model is not an important function of the mentors of young women. The result may be a reflection of the fact that the majority of the women had male mentors. Sara Morrison (Cooper and Hingley, 1983) warned that a danger for women who do not have female mentors is that they may mirror the behaviour of successful male executives and in doing so they may mute their feminine traits. This does not appear to be the case among successful women. It is possible that successful women look to other organizations, such as women's networks, for their role models.

The findings of the current study are almost an exact replication of the results obtained by Clutterbuck and Devine (1987) following a survey of ninety-eight randomly selected women managers and entrepreneurs. Almost all of their sample (94 per cent) said that a mentor had a significantly beneficial impact upon their careers.

Improved self-confidence and self-image were the most commonly cited benefits, mentioned by 34 per cent of the women. Another frequently given reason was that the mentors made the women more visible to senior management and supplied them with opportunities to prove themselves. Twenty-five per cent of their sample said that mentors helped them to focus their aspirations and 18 per cent said that they acted as role models. This consistency among research findings would suggest that formal programmes designed to facilitate the careers of young women should focus on these primary needs.

Conclusions

The factors which influence the careers of successful women are surprisingly similar to those reported for successful men. One important factor seems to be overcoming challenges in early work life. Another important influence is gaining wide experience in a range of jobs and functions. Successful men and women both record the value of mentors. Almost invariably this is an informal relationship, usually with a male boss or more senior manager.

7
Power and Politics

Introduction

In this chapter we identify the fundamental processes which underlie the under-representation of women in positions of authority within the public world of work. It is intended that this research will enhance our understanding of how women can achieve power and influence, and how in the future it may be possible to reverse Rendel's (1980) view that 'where women are power is not'.

Power and Influence in Organizations

The dominant–muted framework

Marshall (1984) claims that men are ascribed dominant status at birth, and then use overt power to maintain this inequality between the sexes. Dominant members are punished if they support a member of the sub-dominant group. The sub-dominant group is kept in place by being labelled sub-standard and being ascribed appropriate sex roles. The sub-dominant are said to be preoccupied with survival and adopt a strategy of accommodation, whereby they accept the dominant group's definition of the relative status of each group. Members of the muted group accommodate to the extent that they define their own aspirations in terms of the dominant group goals. This has the effect of reducing identification with their own group.

The underlying dynamic of the dominant–muted framework is threat; that is, the muted group is suppressed because it represents a challenge to the dominant group. There exists a form of latent conflict: 'There would be a conflict of wants or preferences between those exercising power and those subject to it if the latter were to become aware of their interests' (Lukes, 1980). What is strange is why the conflict remains submerged and why women appear to act to support existing values.

The normative nature of power

Davies (1985) suggests that one explanation of why the conflict remains latent is the normative nature of power. The greatest strength of any existing power order is that those who have power present it as the normal way of being, and they never consider that there is an alternative rational view. The natural order of society, which Coser (1982) suggests has been internalized by men and women, is for men to be involved in activities outside the home and to look for external status and rewards. Women's core concern is to care for the family and the home, and their involvement in working life is contingent upon that. No conspiracy, therefore, exists between those with power to exclude the others. Part of the strength of the normative nature of power is that it relies heavily on the powerless supporting and defending the status quo. For example, some of the most vigorous opposition to women's liberation movements has come from women (Novarra, 1980). Self-interest, experience, culture and socialization are said to define what is the normal way of behaving and seeing the world. Alternative ways of seeing the world can raise severe conflict for the individual.

Marshall (1984) also points out that the proponents of the dominant–muted framework fail to recognize that women do not see men as oppressors. Marshall claims that the intimate relations existing between men and women act to prevent these latent conflicts from surfacing. Male domination is moderated in the private arena, because within the family women establish their identity, skills and influence and they are positively valued. It is only when women enter the public arena that they are devalued. This contradicts the propositions of the dominant–muted framework, which would predict that women would be muted in all spheres. In selectively concentrating on the public sphere, the dominant–muted framework devalues female arenas and in doing so confirms male values. Women must have values and experiences of their own so that they can interpret the world independently of male values.

Communion and agency

Marshall (1984) offers an alternative theoretical framework for understanding why inequalities are perpetuated, which attempts to avoid devaluing women's experience. Individuals are said to have two basic coping strategies which were originally described by Bakan (1966) as 'communion' and 'agency', which may be used to cope with the anxieties and uncertainties of living. The agentic strategy aims to reduce threat by changing the world around it, while the communion strategy looks to union and co-operation as ways to cope with uncertainty and threat.

Communion is the strategy associated with women. Their main strategy for dealing with the world is acceptance and personal adjustment. Understanding tends to be in whole patterns of relations which are seen to be embedded in their context. Therefore, action based on communion may be highly appropriate to the situation. In contrast, the agentic strategy associated with men tries to change the environment to match preconceived ideas. Agency creates a world of competition, seeking control and dominance, whereas communion involves co-operation and, therefore, is destined for submission, not equality. These differences in life strategy are said to account for a large part of the inequalities which exist between men and women in society.

Marshall (1984) points out that the labels 'agency' and 'communion' may represent a false agentic distinction. It is plausible that individuals have the potential to use both strategies, but men actively suppress the communion strategy while women have agency and communion in an undifferentiated whole.

Why Do Women Fail to Make the Formal–Informal Distinction?

Communion as a life strategy

A consequence of communion as a dominant life strategy is that women's understanding tends to be in whole patterns. This argument is supported by neuro-physiological evidence which shows that women are dominated by the right hemisphere of the brain, in contrast to men, who are left-hemisphere dominated. The right brain has a holistic mode of operation, while the left brain is logical, analytic and abstract. Given this mode of operation, it is plausible that women will not make a clear distinction between formal and informal systems within organizations. Reif et al. (1975) showed that women do tend to see the organization as an interrelated whole, and that they also have a more positive view than men of formal organization and its ability to satisfy their needs. Although women may perceive the informal system, they continue to place priority on the formal.

Hennig and Jardim (1978), in their study of 100 senior women managers, concluded that women often do not recognize the difference between the formal organization and its informal communication networks. In talking about their success, women tend to suggest that 'they were lucky', that 'it just happened' or that 'somebody did it for them'. This passivity is reflected in women's strategy of doing a good job and 'waiting to be chosen' as means of achieving success. This approach depends upon an implicit belief in the formal structure's definition of roles and policies about the way things should be done. Mitigating against this strategy is an informal system of relations and information sharing, ties of loyalty, dependence upon favours granted and owed, and mutual benefit and protection. Men, unlike women, generally take these aspects of informal networks into account.

Childhood socialization

Hennig and Jardim (1978) hypothesize that childhood socialization and the games children play lead to women's failure to account for the informal system, while men take advantage of it. Small boys are said to learn about teams, about being members of teams and about winning and losing. A team makes it possible to become a star, to share in the star's lustre by association, and it may even be a place to hide and to be given a second chance. On the basis of this childhood experience, it is suggested that men already have the ground rules for interpersonal relations among other men and they acknowledge that co-operation is needed to get the job done. Girls, by comparison, are claimed to have no parallel experience. It is suggested that most of women's sports are one-to-one and that whether you win or lose is less important than how you play the game.

Men and women vary in the style they adopt towards superiors. Men look for what the boss expects of them, because the chances are that the boss can give them the promotion they desire. Women's attitude is, 'This is who I am, take it or leave it.' These differences in style are again related to team experiences. Boys learn how to tolerate each other to a degree that women rarely find necessary (i.e. you need eleven for a team). As a result, men's behaviour towards their superiors may seem to a woman to be hypocritical, but it is justified in the internal male logic of 'Why make enemies deliberately when making friends is a means to one's end?'

Hennig and Jardim's argument that women fail to learn the rules of interpersonal relations because they do not have the childhood experience of team games seems difficult to accept in its entirety. Many women do play team games, such as netball and hockey, in which interpersonal relations operate. Also, it does not seem fair to say that women do not play team games to win, as some women are clearly competitive. What we may hypothesize is that those women who do not have the experience of team games are less likely to engage in organizational politics.

Hennig and Jardim's approach has been criticized on the grounds that it represents an androcentric perspective, which encourages women to become more like men if they want to succeed in a male-dominated world. The burden of inequality is placed entirely on the individual.

Lifestyle

Women's lifestyles can act to prevent them taking part in informal networks. Many networks are maintained by mixing socially, staying late for a drink or playing sport. Because of domestic responsibilities, women tend to keep to official working hours. Women are also deliberately excluded from informal systems, because many of the informal network norms are developed in exclusively male territories, such as private clubs.

Group processes

Women may also be excluded from informal networks by more subtle group processes. Kanter (1977) suggests that organizational structure has been constructed to exacerbate and exploit gender differences. The existence of formal and informal systems influences what Kanter has identified as 'opportunity and power' – that is, the individual's ability to move up the organizational hierarchy, to get things done and to achieve goals. Kanter suggests that entry into the informal system of an organization, and hence access to power and opportunity, is determined by the relative numbers of men and women in the organization. Groups which vary in the proportion of people of different gender differ qualitatively in their dynamics and processes.

Kanter identifies four group types:

1 *Uniform*, in which all members are male or female.
2 *Skewed*, whereby one type predominates (85:15).
3 *Tilted*, in which the minority is more likely to effect the culture of the group as a whole (65:35).
4 *Balanced groups*, in which there is an equal number of men and women.

Successful women as a skewed group

Successful women are a skewed group and the experience of being a token woman in male-dominated work environments results in skewed group processes. To maintain the boundaries between the minority and majority group members, the dominant members exaggerate the differences between the groups. This process is called polarization. The informal system operates partly to control uncertainty and risk, and those who are perceived as different introduce risk. People who are on the margins of an organization often have a different perspective from those more centrally placed, and outsiders need to be controlled by those managing performance. Women experience the powerlessness of the outsider as they move into the public domain. Their own view and experience of what is happening is constantly denied. The experience of women can be likened to that of Griffin (1962). In the cause of journalism, Griffin transformed himself into a black in the Southern states of the USA. He found that his own view of himself as a person, and his con-structs in life, were denied by the way in which the white power élite perceived and interpreted his actions.

Epstein (1981) observes that all élite structures have mechanisms that provide channels of mobility for members of the in-group and close them to the out-group. She comments that women are tolerated only to the extent that their participation is not threatening to those in power and to those who are defined as being within the group.

As there are too few tokens to form a counter-culture, women react by becoming isolates or by trying to become insiders. To become insiders, women must adopt male values and norms towards other women. The implication of this is that any development of joint women's consciousness, with potential to impact upon the existing system, will be inhibited, despite the number of women spread throughout the organization. Kanter (1977) suggests that a solution would be for a quantum number of women to be employed by the organization and to cluster them rather than spread them across it. In this way it is hoped that women may influence the organizational culture.

This solution does not, however, address the root of the female demise in the workplace. The underlying premise of Kanter's work is that organizations can be fundamentally changed by internal reform. Little attention is given to the embedded institutional mechanisms reproducing sex-segregation which are reinforced by external structural constraints (Roos and Reskin, 1987). Kanter does not acknowledge that most American and British organizations are structured on a division of labour, authority and expertise that excludes most employees from genuine power. Blum and Smith (1988) suggest that proposals for empowerment of workers are often only symbolic gestures toward actual empowerment. Boecker et al. (1985) claim that many women managers are critical of the 'window-dressing' policies which don't fundamentally increase opportunities for advancement.

Women will have little lasting impact on the culture of an organization unless the value systems incorporated in the informal networks of organizations are changed. Many women entering an organization identify to some extent with the prevalent male norms and values, and in doing so they limit their own sense of themselves as females. What needs to be addressed is 'how women can have the right to be women and to be valued'. How can women gain respect for their female qualities, which can make a significant contribution to organizational life in their own right?

Successful women's view of politics

As noted above, Hennig and Jardim (1978) reported that the senior women executives in their study did not recognize the difference between the formal organization and its informal communication networks. When they asked these women how they had achieved their success, they suggested that they were 'lucky', that it 'just happened' or that 'somebody did it for them'. Hennig and Jardim suggest that this passivity was reflected in women's strategy of doing a good job and waiting to be chosen.

A remarkably similar pattern of responses was obtained from the successful women in the current sample when they were asked about how they had achieved their success. Fifty-four per cent felt their success could be attributed to a combination of hard work, tenacity and determination, while 15 per cent thought that they had been lucky.

On first appearances, therefore, the results seem to confirm the findings of Hennig and Jardim – that is, that women passively believe that hard work should lead to success. Further exploration of the issue, however, revealed some significant differences. When asked how people get promoted, the successful women suggested a strategy which involved the use of the informal system and political behaviour. Rather than waiting to be chosen, the successful women recommended that people should actively sell themselves. They advocated that people should show competence and simultaneously make others aware of their contribution, particularly those with the power to promote. In addition, several women mentioned the importance of making one's ambitions well known; for example:

> You need to make it known that you are looking for promotion and then do what you are currently doing very well. It is important to look out for opportunities and to build good relationships with the people who you are reporting to so that the people who can help you know what you want.

Another woman gave emphasis to the need to promote yourself: 'Just working hard isn't enough – that's a fallacy. You need to sell yourself. If you just work hard an organization will leave you there because they like a little workhorse'. Only 15 per cent of the women felt that good work alone was enough to get promotion. Further evidence of the women's acknowledgement of informal systems may be derived from their recognition of politics at work. Only two of the women in the sample said that they were not aware of it.

As noted before, Hennig and Jardim (1978) suggested that women's failure to learn the rules of interpersonal relations at work could be attributed to their experience of childhood games. Young boys are said to play team games which teach them the ground rules for interpersonal relations among other men, and they acknowledge that co-operation is needed to get a job done. Hennig and Jardim claimed that women did not have a parallel experience. It was argued, however, that many women do play team games in which interpersonal relations operate. Sixty-two per cent of our sample of successful women did play team games while they were at school, which may have facilitated their apparent recognition of the informal system of influence. It is unlikely that participation in team games represents a full explanation of an individual's acknowledgement of the distinction between the formal and informal system, as approximately 30 per cent of the successful women in the study did not play team sports, although they were clearly aware of organizational politics. It is likely that there are individual differences in ability to read the organizational lines of influence, which may be reflected in political style.

Women's distaste for politics

Arroba and James (1987) claim that women are reluctant to engage in politics, and propose three factors to account for this reluctance. First, women feel that they lack competence in relation to their political skills. As a result, women lack confidence in their skills. Third, women are said to feel distaste for politics. They view the political arena as foreign and, therefore, avoid getting involved. Marshall (1984) has observed that women believe in honesty, authenticity and co-operation, and they consistently reject superficiality, putting on false appearances and aggression. Marshall goes on to say that 'Many women's reluctance to work at making the right impression and to engage in politics holds them back'. Arroba and James consider that women's distaste for politics could be based on a misguided view. Politics is seen as devious manipulation, ambitious achievement at any cost, back-biting, 'put-downs' and nastiness.

The Lighter Side of Politics

Schein (1977) has described the political aspect of organizational behaviour as an inadequately explored reality. It is claimed that power struggles, alliance formation and strategic manoeuvring are as endemic to organizational life as planning, directing and controlling. Kakabadse (1986) shares the view that politics are an integral part of organizational life, based on the premise that differences rather than similarities between people form the basis of life in organizations. Kakabadse states that 'Politics in organisations are ever present. No matter who you are or what you do, it is impossible to escape the power/political interactions that take place between people at work.'

Hayes (1984) comments that individuals in organizations who do not acknowledge the informal system will become politically incompetent. He suggests that many managers are less effective than they might be because they assume that choices are made rationally with the aim of maximizing shared goals. Hayes proposes that a more realistic view of organizations is to see them as political organisms, within which individuals and groups attempt to influence each other in pursuit of self-interest. Derr (1986), in her book describing the 'new careerist', confirms this view of organizations. She points out that the perceived gap between actual and ideal states may lead many careerists to resort to politics to reduce the tension between what *they want* and what the organization *will allow*. Skilled political behaviour involves understanding how the organization works and mobilizing resources to achieve organizational purposes, without subordinating personal needs or exploiting others.

Arroba and James (1987) emphasize that, although politics in organizations does have connotations of immorality and deviousness, this is not necessarily the case. Jones (1987) claims:

> Organisational politics as the 'darker side' is indeed part of the story in some organisations. But acknowledging this does not then require us to hold a narrow view of politics which consigns notions of trust, sensitivity to others and negotiated collaboration to that nice but naive category.

Kakabadse also believes that politics are not all bad. Politics, in his opinion, are nothing more than getting what you want done, preferably with the full permission and approval of others around you.

Implications of the neglect of the informal system

Arroba and James (1987) stress that, although politics may have a lighter side, it is still tough. Not getting involved, however, means staying put. Women who acknowledge only the formal system may feel that the system gets in their way and constrains their freedom to act. These constraints may be proving too great for many women, as Devine and Clutterbuck (1985) have noted: 'Advancement to senior management is still a tortuous process in large organisations . . . more women are circumventing these barriers and setting up their own ventures'.

For those who are not willing to give up, Hayes (1984) emphasizes the need for individuals to be pro-active and to develop the ability to behave strategically to overcome barriers to goal achievement. Playing by the book and reacting to situations using traditional practices does not guarantee survival. Kakabadse (1986) states that to achieve high office rapidly requires skills in negotiating and bargaining with people who have different goals. When a conflict of interest arises, it is the power of the individuals involved that determines the outcome. Organizational politics is the activity associated with the acquisition of this power. As discussed earlier, Kanter (1977) has suggested that 'opportunity and power' determine the individual's ability to move up the organizational hierarchy, to get things done and to achieve goals. Kanter proposes that entry to the informal system is necessary to gain access to power and opportunity, and hence to success.

Women's refusal to take part in informal systems, and their denial of or exclusion from them, has important implications for their career advancement. Hennig and Jardim (1978) found that women were preoccupied with self-development, and tended not to make known what they want to the people with the power to promote them. They failed to recognize that if one is not seen to be competent, then all the competence in the world will not get the job.

Exclusion from informal networks means that women are less likely to be noticed for promotion. The informal system is the organization's main mechanism for coping with uncertainty. This helps individuals to evaluate each other, and to establish relations through which official work can be achieved. Within the informal system, signs of suitability develop to supplement official criteria of performance and trustworthiness. This informal behaviour contributes to senior personnel's assessment of suitability for promotion. Women outside the informal network are less likely to be noticed. In addition, because women do not engage in the informal network, they do not share others' base for handling potentially difficult face-to-face situations. For instance, they may receive less accurate feedback on their performance because their superiors do not know how they will react.

Individuals who cannot draw on a base of 'knowing and being known' may be deprived of others' co-operation in achieving objectives. Informal channels are also an important means of transmitting information. Exclusion from informal networks can lead to failure to understand how organizational norms are translated into practice.

Women will often have to learn for themselves what is considered 'heroic' in the organization and what is 'taboo'.

Successful women's attitude towards politics at work

Although the successful women were aware of the existence of politics, 63 per cent felt that these politics had negative connotations. Several women said that the politics had been one of the hardest things for them to accept on their way up the organization. The higher up the career ladder they climbed, the tougher they found the politics. As one woman said:

> I'm aware of politics although I wouldn't climb over bodies to get on in an organization. I think that a lot of women are too naive about politics and it's the hardest part of the job to accept. The higher you get the more politics there are. You also have to accept that a lot of . people will be very nasty about you. I think the most difficult thing when you're climbing the ladder is coping with the politics.

This negative perception of politics was also reflected in the descriptions given by the successful women of the political strategies that people employ. A third of the women in the sample said that strategies were frequently used to further personal goals at the expense of the organization. They described political strategies such as secretiveness, controlling resources, stealing ideas, blackmail and back-stabbing. These views are expressed in the following remarks made by one of the women:

> Secretiveness, depending on a position of power in an organization, refusal to delegate, maintaining personal control over the budget and making staff compete openly for resources are all strategies that I have seen employed. People may further their own causes at the expense of the organization.

Seventeen per cent of the women felt that politics was a male domain, and that women were more direct by nature. As a female executive commented:

> I am aware of politics. It is denied, but it is there. It is awful, lots of hidden agendas, etc. I sometimes wonder at how naive I have been in the past in not being more aware of it. I think it's because women are more direct. I can't cope with politics very well, I get impatient with

it. Experience tells me that you need to be a bit political to achieve what you have got to do, but rather than being used selectively I find that it is used all the time and I don't like it.

This is consistent with Marshall's (1984) observation that women tend to believe in honesty, authenticity and co-operation. Marshall suggests that women's reluctance to get involved in politics may hold them back. However, 17 per cent of the successful women actually felt that their honesty and integrity were the secret of their success. In their study of male high flyers, Cox and Cooper (1988) also found that many placed emphasis on the importance of honesty and integrity. McCall and Lombardo (1983) found that among the fatal flaws that lead to the derailment of executives were insensitivity to others, betrayal of trust and being overly ambitious, thinking of the next job and playing politics.

As previously mentioned, Arroba and James (1987) suggest that there is a lighter side to politics. The women who express a distaste for politics may be reacting to the strategies employed by individuals to enhance their own power at the expense of others, and to the connotations of immorality. Derr (1986) points out, however, that skilled political behaviour involves understanding how the organization works and mobilizing resources to achieve organizational purposes without subordinating personal needs or exploiting others. Seventy-five per cent of the successful women described political strategies in terms of understanding the organization, its climate and its systems of influence. They talked of influencing the right people with the power to promote. As one successful woman put it, 'A major political skill is to know where the buck stops. In an organization you need to know whom to impress and who stands between you and success'.

The successful women also suggested that people need to be aware of key organizational values. Having established the limitations, they believed that one could operate according to one's own values. Fifty-two per cent of the women claimed that they were aware of the need to be sensitive to politics, but they tried to minimize the negative aspects of politics by generating an open working atmosphere.

A small proportion (21 per cent) of the successful women did not perceive politics to be negative. These women claimed that they were not above using informal contacts and that they would employ politics to protect their own interests. Cox and Cooper (1988) found that a small proportion of male chief executives were involved in politics at work. It is possible that more male and female high flyers employ politics, but refrain from admitting it in an interview because of the negative connotations.

Political competence

Women must be encouraged to question established norms and practices and to think about their organization in new ways. Awareness that they are constrained by the system is not sufficient. Women need to think about ways of achieving a more desirable state. Hayes (1984) has pointed to a need for political competence – women need to acquire and exercise power to improve their contribution.

The acquisition and exercise of power

Organizational politics is the activity associated with acquisition and exercise of power. Arroba and James (1987) postulate two dimensions that affect political behaviour:

1 Awareness or understanding of the organization – that is, ability to 'read' the organizational world.
2 Awareness of one's predisposition to behave in certain ways – that is, understanding of what one 'carries' into a situation.

To understand the organization, women need a knowledge of how it works, its processes, procedures and systems. It is important to have an understanding of the power bases and informal systems. Arroba and James warn that an inability to read between the lines of the formal organizational chart, or an unwillingness to become organizationally literate, will leave women at a disadvantage when trying to mobilize resources.

The second dimension is concerned with the orientation of behaviour. At one end of the dimension, personal needs are of prime importance: they shape action, with little concern for organizational or other people's needs; behaviour is 'self-oriented'. At the other end of the continuum, individuals carry awareness of organizational and their own personal needs. The issue is how to achieve organizational purposes without compromising personal needs. These two dimensions result in four styles of behaviour (shown in figure 7.1).

Political styles

Individuals with an 'innocent' political style are said to be blind to power and organizational issues. They place emphasis on rationality

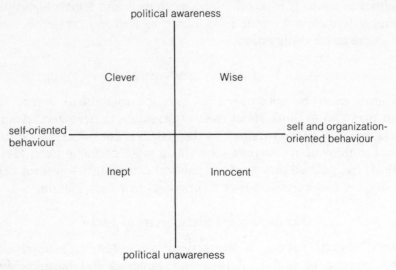

Figure 7.1   Four styles of political behaviour
Source: Arroba and James (1987)

and the formal organization, and all politics are seen as unpleasant. These people assume that they can mobilize resources through formal channels. The senior executive women interviewed by Hennig and Jardim in the late 1970s would seem to fall into this category. There is a small contingent among the successful women interviewed in the current study who also appear to be 'innocent'. These women believed promotion could be gained by working hard, without the need to influence others. They felt that politics simply interfered with the process of getting the job done. This view was expressed by one of them in this way:

> I have been aware of politics and it was the aspect of the job I liked least because I felt it was unnecessary and had nothing to do with the greater good. To me there seemed to be one aim, to do the job as well as we possibly could and to get paid appropriately, and the politics got in the way of that.

This innocent style does, however, seem to be less common among the successful women of the late 1980s. It is possible that during the last decade women have become more familiar with the work environment and, as a result, have learnt to read the organization more effectively.

None of the successful women could be described as 'inept'. Such individuals have a selfish orientation and an inability to read the organization. It is possible that some of the women may have been 'clever' politicians. These women acknowledge the informal system and will use politics to achieve their own ends. Whether they are clever or wise is not clear from the data. It is difficult to obtain the truth concerning an individual's deployment of politics and his/her objectives. As Schein (1977) suggests, an individual using covert or political means to bring about personal intents will have an overt set of intents and means, which give the impression that he/she is in accordance with organizational goals.

The majority of the successful women appear to be wise politicians. They are aware of what is happening within the organization. This skill is said to require intuition which stems from sensitivity to others, awareness of personal values and an intimate knowledge of the context. As discussed earlier, 75 per cent of the successful women emphasized that politics required sensitivity to the organizational climate and its systems of influence, although they stressed that one should not become too entrenched in political games. As one woman explained:

> The company has certain things that you can and cannot do – that is, there are norms for behaviour. You can get away with challenging these up to a point, but you need to be sensitive to the line that you can't cross. I tend to be fairly outspoken and it has paid off. I can be controversial, but I'm not stupid enough to think that I could demolish a senior person in public and continue to be seen in a reasonable light in the company. I don't have a lot of time for politics. It would be naive to say that I never use them, but I'm not an overtly political animal. People who are overtly political eventually come unstuck because they get to a position where they aren't competent to do the job that they had aspirations to do.

Similarly, the high flyers interviewed by Cox and Cooper (1988) demonstrated what could be described as wise political behaviour. A number of the high flyers claimed to be motivated by the level of control and power that they had. This power was not totally self-oriented. It was said to be unrelated to being in a position of exercising power over others, but was associated with influencing events. These high flyers spoke of the pleasure gained from knowing they were in a position to influence the company's success.

Some of the high flyers did acknowledge that they enjoyed the political aspect of their work. Cox and Cooper propose that possibly more of their sample may have employed politics but they were not prepared to admit it. They suggest that a strong negative feeling about organizational politics leads to denial.

As Gilligan (1982) has pointed out, women need to incorporate themselves among those that they care for. To achieve success in the public domain, women should not be self-effacing. They should avoid the 'communion-based' tendency to discount self. Women need to accept the legitimacy of personal rights so that they can begin to be pro-active, taking control of what happens in their working lives. Marshall (1984) indicates that a positive direction for women is to adopt a strategy of communion enhanced, supported and focused with agency. By employing communal and agentic resources women should be able to use the wise behaviour advocated by Arroba and James (1987).

Women are already well placed to be politically skilled. In the discussion of childhood development, it was noted that women develop empathy which enables them to understand the viewpoint of others. Also, the dominant female strategy of 'communion' means that women see patterns embedded in their context which could be useful in reading the situation. Women may be more in tune with organizational events, so that action based in communion can be highly appropriate to the situation.

How can women develop their political skills?

Several authors have listed ways in which individuals can enhance their political skills (Kakabadse, 1983; Hunt, 1979; Hayes, 1984). Two important variables which will determine an individual's power are resource and dependence. Therefore, a simple strategy would be to maximize these two variables.

Maximizing the resource   The resource is something possessed by the individual (e.g. knowledge, expertise, skill, past performance). It is important to be professionally competent, as it is difficult to influence others if one is seen to be obsolete. In addition, one must not only be seen to be competent, but must also maintain high visibility.

Maximizing dependence   Others must be aware of their dependence on you within a climate of mutual support and co-operation. Individuals must also be aware of their dependence on others. It is necessary to identify who the significant others are and who can help or hinder the achievement of personal goals. Recruiting the support of others is encouraged, although Hayes warns that sponsorship inevitably involves some dependency. Networking is also said to be useful in the search for alternative resources and it reduces dependence on any one individual. If women are excluded from male networks, Arroba and James encourage women to form their own networks. Women can work together to overcome some of the effect of tokenism.

Organizational Socialization and the Implications for Political Competence

Organizational socialization is the process of learning the ropes – that is, being indoctrinated and trained in what is important to the organization. The speed and effectiveness of this socialization determines employee loyalty, commitment, productivity and turnover. Therefore, the stability of an organization depends upon its ability to socialize its new members. Learning the organization's values, norms and required behaviour patterns is said to be the price of organizational membership.

When an individual has correctly anticipated the norms and values of the organization, then the socialization process will simply mean reaffirmation of these norms. If the individual enters the organization with incongruent norms, however, then the person must undergo an unfreezing phase during which the individual is detached from his/ her former values so that the self may be redefined in terms of the role allocated by the organization.

Marshall (1984) claims that women have different values from men and that they don't want the same things from work as men do. They want challenge and satisfaction from their work rather than promotion for its own sake. In addition, work does not take priority over all other life areas. This hypothesized clash of values could be seen as a limiting factor in women's career development, in that women may be less amenable to organizational socialization.

On entering an organization, women have to go through the initial identification stage to be proved acceptable. Women may feel they have to adopt the male-valued traits which are consistent with the prevalent male models of success. In doing so, they may preclude the development and/or expression of traits highly valued in females.

Indirect support for this line of reasoning is derived from a study by Campbell (1971). Using the 'Strong Vocational Interest Blank', it was shown that women working in traditionally male roles, such as mathematics or chemistry, failed to select items which were endorsed by women in traditionally female roles, such as air hostesses or fashion models.

Within an organization, some values are 'pivotal' – that is, if members do not accept them, they will not survive long (e.g. value of getting a job done, belief in free enterprise and competition). There are also other values which are 'relevant', but they are not absolutely necessary (e.g. standards of dress and decorum). The process of socialization will reinforce compliance with these values.

Responses to socialization

Schein (1979) claims that individuals will respond in basically three different ways to the pressures of socialization: by conforming, rebelling or creatively.

The conformist Schein claims that conformity is most limiting to an individual's potential. Some of the pioneer women who have made it to the top appear to have responded in this way to organizational socialization. Women have a different time period for occupational decisions compared with those espoused by Schein (1978). In order to accommodate the organizational pattern and to acquire insider status, women have adapted to the male norms. Successful women managers tend to marry later, have fewer children, have them later in life and return to work soon after the birth (Hennig and Jardim, 1978). Gutek et al. (1981) found that many women who opted for careers in management chose to avoid the conflict of the dual career relationship by remaining single. This has led to the stereotype of the dedicated single and single-minded career woman.

A surprising outcome of conforming to male organizational norms is that successful women are no more tolerant of other women than men and, therefore, do not pave the way for other women by helping them to climb the ladder. Staines et al. (1974) described this as the 'queen bee syndrome', whereby women who have had to fight their way through the organization actively guard their uniqueness by discouraging prospective challengers for their power. Being part of the élite as a minority raises their own power. Having achieved success through the present system, they have the same vested interest in maintaining it as men do. The justification is in terms of commitment, ability and a belief that the present system is open to all those with ability.

The rebel People may rebel, in which case they will reject all organizational norms and values. It is possible that this reaction could be an explanation for the low proportion of women in senior positions – that is, they basically do not accept the male values which they are required to adopt.

The creative individualist Many successful women, it seems, have succumbed to the pressure to deny female qualities which may have enriched themselves and the organization. Blum and Smith (1988) have noted that management consultants are becoming critical of traditional organizational practices which reflect extreme masculine behaviour – being overly rational, instrumental and, therefore, rigidly bureaucratic. There is a call for a broader acceptance of women and feminine personality traits. Reeves (1984) states that 'Women should be favoured as personnel, not to promote equality, but because their gender socialisation has come to have corporate significance'.

Possibly the preferable response to organizational socialization which would allow women to express their feminine qualities is what Schein (1979) describes as 'creative individualism'. This response accepts pivotal values, but may reject relevant ones and by doing so maintains the potential for creativity.

The link between responses to organizational socialization and gender identity

Marshall (1984) has hypothesized that there is a sequence of increasing awareness of gender which some women follow as they integrate 'being female' more fully into their sense of identity. This sequence is conceptualized as a continuum of gender awareness.

Marshall found that women managers as a group were against identifying themselves as disadvantaged because they were women. Marshall questioned whether the majority of women could really believe that being a woman was not an important factor in career development, when so few women occupy senior positions.

What Marshall found was a conflict between levels of expression. Half the women who were interviewed appeared to have little awareness of their gender and indicated that being a woman was irrelevant to their experience of work. They felt that both sexes have their problems. The conflict of expression arose because all either identified disadvantages of being female by identifying negative consequences for their personal and social lives, or they believed that women were at a disadvantage in organizational life. Many of these women acknowledged that it is a man's world and they warned other women to beware of it. They also commented that achieving a satisfying working life is harder for married women with children.

Marshall explained this 'balancing act' as a strategy for managing the potential stress of being a woman in a man's world. Women 'mute' their own awareness of being different to men. They distinguish themselves as particular cases separate from the general population of women. Some try to minimize contacts with other women to preserve their individualistic status. As long as their own private strategy works, they have no need to raise their visibility by identifying with a larger group of women. By muting their awareness of their femininity, it seems that these women felt they decreased the likelihood of the potential disadvantages of being a woman becoming significant.

The women who mute their awareness of their femininity are in a sense adopting a conformist response to organizational socialization. Individuals who perceive the system and the organizational norm as inflexible suppress divergent thought and creative action. Denial of the feminine aspect of one's identity leads to an inability to contribute to one's full potential. Women must take the initiative to break the organizational mould if it presents a barrier to their effectiveness.

Marshall identified a second and much smaller group of women managers who appeared to be going through a period of 'painful turmoil' because of perceived or actual discrimination against them because they were women. This group had arrived at an acute consciousness of themselves as women, which had shattered previous perspectives. Marshall claims that this period of changing attitudes and perspectives is extremely stressful and these women are very sensitive to prejudice. They are undergoing the process of evolving new values which acknowledge their gender, but, as yet, it is not welcomed.

The third group of female managers whom Marshall observed had gone through this period of turmoil after which, she claims, there is no going back to muted awareness. This group had developed a clear sense of themselves as women; they realized that they were different and had been treated differently and that these are truths which cannot be avoided. These women had greater concern about women as a group. This group of women could be seen as 'creative individualists'.

Responses to organizational socialization among the successful women

In an attempt to explore Marshall's continuum of gender awareness, our successful women were asked questions which focused on the key characteristics which Marshall attributes to women in each of the three groups. The first category muted their awareness of being female. The indicators of this strategy were that the women did not feel that gender was relevant to their experience of work. This group of women distinguished themselves as being different from the general population of women. To maintain this individualistic status, they attempted to minimize contacts with other women. Marshall found that the majority of the women managers that she interviewed fell into this category.

Marshall's findings were not replicated in the current study. A much smaller proportion of the successful women fell into the category of muted-gender identity. Although 44 per cent of the women claimed that they would not describe themselves as feminists, only 21 per cent felt that feminism had outlived its usefulness. Like the women in Marshall's study, these women believed that gender was irrelevant to their work experience. They felt that people could succeed if they were prepared to use their ability, regardless of their gender. As one women said:

> I'm not a feminist. I've always felt that women who emphasize the importance of female development were paddling a canoe that I didn't want to know about. I've succeeded because I'm me – it has nothing to do with being female. The fact that I'm female has never concerned me; I've always expected people to take me at face value.

The remaining women who did not classify themselves as feminists, and considered the movement to be too radical and extremist, which they thought was damaging to the cause of working women. One of this group said:

I'm not a feminist, I find the movement unattractive and too aggressive. I think that feminism is counter-productive and it didn't do anything for me as a working woman. I found that people made judgements about me on the basis of other more strident women and I resented that.

Fifty-six per cent of the women said that they would describe themselves as feminists. A large proportion of these women commented that they were concerned about the definition of feminism. They felt that the title had negative connotations which denied their femininity. These women did not want to be like men, but they supported women's rights and they believed in equality of opportunity. This view is illustrated by the following comment:

It depends on the definition of feminism. I'm not a member of the bra-burning brigade. I believe that women have had a rough ride in terms of society and their place in it, and if we can do something about that then yes, I am a feminist. I'm not the militant type because I don't think that's the way. I think that those times are over. You achieve far more by being a charming business woman rather than being a ruthless man-aping feminist. It's all a question of degree.

Similarly, there was little evidence that successful women aimed to maintain their individualistic status. A large proportion of women expressed no preference for working with men or women. Several women actually preferred to work with women, who in they perceived to be less political and more industrious. Thirty per cent of the women said that they preferred to work with men. In many cases, this preference was qualified by the comment that in their position they had little experience of working with women.

Further evidence of the integration of femininity into a broader sense of identity may be derived from their concern for women as a group. The majority of the women were members of women's networks. Nineteen per cent of these women did not find the network useful, because they felt that it didn't address the issues of women at work. Overall, the successful women gave positive reports of the networks. Among the benefits derived were opportunities to meet other professional women, so reducing their isolation. As one woman manager remarked: 'I have found the network a tremendous outlet. I have met some very good fiends and have developed a good social life through that. It has widened my horizons because I've met people outside my field.'

Some women felt that they had made valuable business contacts through the network which had advanced their careers. Twelve per cent of the successful women said that it was too late in their careers for the network to be useful. They maintained their membership of a network because they wanted to help its younger members. This was expressed by one woman as follows: 'Networks came too late for me. I belong to them more for what I can give than for what I can get. I would have appreciated networks when I was younger because I was moving in a man's world.'

Marshall (1984) noted that women who tend to mute their gender awareness demonstrate a conflict between levels of expression. Although the women that she interviewed stated that gender was irrelevant to their work experience, they did identify negative con- sequences that working had for their personal and social lives. They warned other women to beware that it is a man's world. Only 25 per cent of the women in the current sample expressed this contra- diction. They pointed out that it would be harder for women, but they advised that women should not let their gender become an issue.

The majority of successful women recommended that aspiring young women should be very single-minded. They described career striving as a constant battle to achieve objectives which required total commitment. This single-mindedness is reflected in the continuous career patterns of the majority of the successful women. It was argued in the discussion of the literature that adapting to male time schedules for careers is a conformist response to socialization. It may be speculated, however, that a continuous career pattern is perceived by women as a pivotal value in most organizations which is a pre- requisite for career success. As one woman said:

Life's about choices and if you take a choice about having a serious career then you've got to be honest with yourself and say you can't have everything and do it well. Those who think that they can are fooling themselves and they are going to come to grief. If you look at how men get on it's because they're focused on their career and their wives assist them in getting on. Women have got to be as focused as that and if we're not going to take ourselves seriously we won't get on. Women have too many self-doubts. Once you make a choice, stick

with it. I'm a strong believer that the stayers win. The race is for
stayers and it's all about delivering excellence. Mediocrity does not
count.

Accepting this career structure as a pivotal value does not necessarily preclude the expression of feminine qualities. The discussion
of attitudes towards feminism, preferences for working with men or
women and membership of women's networks seems to indicate that
the majority of the successful women have developed a clear sense of
themselves as women, as illustrated by the following remark: 'What
we have got wrong is that too many women have cloned to join, but I
would say above all don't clone because you don't bring your own
skills to the table, you bring a copy of other people's.'

The majority of the successful women acknowledged that the fight
for success would be harder for a woman, but they took a pragmatic
approach, striving to find ways around the obstacle that they encountered, as the following respondent indicated: 'You have to
recognize that it will be harder for a woman than a fella. It's no good
fighting against that – it's a fact of life. You need to look for ways of
getting around it.'

On the grounds of the previous discussion, it would seem that
there is some evidence to support the validity of Marshall's continuum of gender identity. The groups who occupy both ends of the
continuum were evident, although a larger proportion of the successful women had integrated their femininity into their sense of
identity; that is, they were operating as 'creative individualists'.

Marshall suggests that such individuals may be described as
having an inner power based on an awareness of their feminine
identity. It appears that these women have recognized their own
power to be themselves and have learnt to combine this internal
power with the present structural constraints. Davies (1985) sets a
challenge for management development courses to develop a strategy
which will facilitate this combination of individual power and
structural constraints. In other words, how can we help more women
to become 'creative individualists'?

There was little evidence of the group of women whom Marshall
suggests are located between the two extremes. These women were
said to be undergoing a process of evolving new values which
acknowledge their gender, during which time they are highly sensitive to prejudice. It is possible that women in this stage will find
the male organizational norms unacceptable and they may rebel by

leaving the organization. This may explain why women belonging to this group were not observed among the successful women in the present study.

Creative Style

The notion that the successful women might be what Schein (1979) describes as creative individualists was explored further by looking at their 'creative style'. In 1966 Rokeach first put forward the proposition that an individual's creativity depended upon his/her position on a continuum ranging from open-mindedness to closed-mindedness. Ten years later, Kirton (1976) developed this idea based on his observations of the progress of management initiatives within organizations. Kirton noted that there were two crude groups of managers, 'adaptors' and 'innovators'. The refinement of these observations led Kirton to suggest that everyone could be located along a continuum ranging from an adaptive style to an innovative style of decision-making. Adaptors are described as individuals who 'Characteristically produce a sufficiency of ideas based on but stretching existing ideas and definitions of the problem and likely solutions. Much of their effort in change is in improving and doing better'. In contrast, the innovator is 'more likely to reconstrue the problem, separating it from its enveloping accepted thought, paradigms and customary viewpoints to emerge with less expected and probably less acceptable solutions. Their effort in change is concerned with doing things differently'.

Kirton is at pains to emphasize that his theory is one of style (i.e. what manner), separated from cognitive capacity (i.e. how much) and also distinct from learned techniques of creativity (i.e. how can). Given that creative style is said to be a manner of thinking, the theory incorporates concepts of decision-making and problem-solving. Kirton suggests that creative style is formed in early childhood, and it is described as a relatively stable dimension of personality.

Kirton suggested that because the adaptor works within existing cognitive systems, he or she is also at home in bureaucratic ones. Adaptive solutions to problems depend directly on agreed paradigms, and as such ideas derived in this manner are more readily acceptable to the organization. The failure of ideas is less damaging to the adaptor than to the innovator, because the false assumptions and paradigms upon which the ideas were based are also shared by colleagues. In contrast, because the innovator's ideas are not related directly to the prevailing paradigms, they are more strongly resisted and treated with suspicion. Rejection of the individual tends to persist even after an idea has been accepted. This rejection, and possible isolation, occurs largely because the innovator tends to disregard convention in pursuing his/her ideas, and so introduces threat in the form of risk and uncertainty. In this way, the innovator bears resemblance to the creative person described by Rodgers (1959). Creative people were said to

1 have little awe of traditional knowledge or practice;
2 compulsively toy with ideas;
3 display a high need for social recognition, without regard for the challenge they present to the consensus.

Kirton designed an 'adaptation–innovation inventory' (KAI) to assess an individual's position on the continuum of creative style. Where an individual is placed on the continuum from extreme adaptor to extreme innovator depends on the balance of three factors. 'Originality' (O) is defined as the proliferation of ideas; 'efficiency' (E) is defined as the extent to which the person is precise and disciplined; and 'rule/group conformity' (R) is described as the extent to which an individual is constrained by the rules of the norms. The adaptor can be quite original, but will also tend to be high on efficiency and conformity so that his/her creativity will be constrained within the system. In contrast, the innovator is high on originality but low on conformity and efficiency. As such, the innovator is less constrained by existing systems.

Creativity and success

Superficially, adaptors would appear to be at an advantage within organizations. The adaptor has in fact been likened to the 'organizationally socialized manager'. Drucker (1969) argued that the aim of a large organization is the efficient accomplishment of defined tasks, set in approved ways. Bureaucracy looks for managers who, when confronted by problems, 'have the ability to do things better rather than the courage to do things differently'. Bureaucratic structures put pressure on officials to be disciplined and to conform with the existing paradigm. These are qualities of the adaptor, and what Merton (1957) has termed the 'organizational man'.

The logic of the above argument is not supported by evidence. Kirton (1976) has found that there is an even distribution of adaptors and innovators within the management population as a whole. Cox and Jennings (1990) conducted a comparative study of three groups of male high flyers:

1 *Élite independent entrepreneurs*. Individuals who had started their own companies and had built them into very large corporations in which they still had a very large holding. They were usually major shareholders, holding the controlling interest. They were all multi-millionaires.
2 *Élite modal entrepreneurs*. Chief executives of highly successful companies. They had been responsible for the development and expansion of the organization, although they did not contribute to its foundation. They were essentially employees of the company, although they were members of the original founding family. They too were multi-millionaires.
3 *Ubiquitous modal entrepreneurs*. Also chief executives of successful companies, but they started with no family advantages. They started at low levels in the organization and worked their way up. In most cases, they changed employers several times during their careers. They were all very successful, but were not millionaires.

Cox and Jennings found that the ubiquitous modal entrapreneurs were markedly the most innovative (as measured by the KAI). They suggest that one of the implications of their findings is that chief executives do not reach the top of their organizations by following the rules and accepting authority. They are more likely to challenge the existing system and find novel solutions to problems. The explanation offered for the differences observed in their sample is that the entrepreneurs may not need to be as innovative as highly successful intrapreneurs. They are said to be less likely to be constrained by an imposed organizational structure, and so do not need to challenge an existing system. Cox and Jennings point out, however, that their results may be due to a cohort effect. At the time when the data were collected, British industry had just come through a period of major reconstruction. Many of the top managers had spent two or three years reorganizing their companies, and many of them had been specifically recruited for this purpose. They suggest that it is possible that more adaptive top managers would be found during times of economic stability.

Occupational variations

Kirton (1984) has stated that innovators can succeed within organizations, but it depends on the ethos of the organization. Every organization is said to have its own particular climate and at any given time most of its key employees will reflect a general outlook.

Kirton hypothesized that an individual who chooses to work in a very stable environment will incline towards adaptation, while those who operate in a turbulent environment will incline towards innovation. Support for this suggestion was provided by Holland (1982), who found that employees of research and development-oriented companies tended to be innovators, while employees who worked in relatively stable environments, such as banks and local government, tended to be adaptors.

Successful women and innovation

Kirton (1984) also speculated that people who are most willing to cross boundaries of any sort are likely to be innovators. The more boundaries there are, and the more rigidly they are held, the more innovative the individual must be to cross them. This speculation has relevance to women working in male-dominated realms of work. It is plausible to suggest that women will need the ability to look beyond the existing paradigm which dominates thinking about the role of women in society. As such, we would expect women who succeed in the world of work to be highly innovative. Evidence to support this hypothesis may be drawn from a small-scale study of female managers and entrepreneurs (White, 1989). The results showed that, while the entrepreneurs were more innovative than the managers, both groups of women were more innovative than the general population (as measured by the KAI).

Creative style of successful women

The current research also employed the KAI to assess creative style. This showed that the successful women were more innovative than any group of male high flyers studied to date. Cox and Jennings (1990) reported that 51 per cent of the male chief executives scored in the eightieth percentile on the overall measure of creative style; in comparison, 57 per cent of the successful women scored in the top tenth percentile (see table 7.1).

The majority of people fall within the range of 80–112 on the scores of the KAI (as shown in figure 7.2). The mean score of the main sample of successful women (shown in table 7.1, p. 173) is much closer to the innovator end of the continuum. Where the individual is placed on the continuum depends on the balance of the three factors: the degree of originality, efficiency and rule/group conformity. The Kirton adaptation–innovation inventory is organized

Table 7.1 Creative style of successful women

Scale	Mean	S.D.	Min.	Max.
R	45.84	6.67	61	61
O	49.18	8.12	27	63
E	22.39	6.48	10	37
Total	117.43	17.24	73	158

Table 7.2 Normative data for KAI

Scale	Mean	S.D.	Min.	Max.
R	35	8.6	14	56
O	41	8.9	17	63
E	19	5.6	7	33
Total	95	17.9	45	145

Source: Kirton (1987)

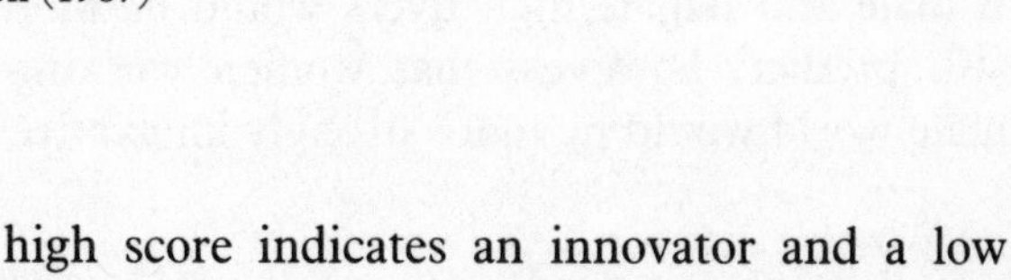

```
32 . . . 48 . . . 64 . . . 80 . . . 96 . . . 112 . . . 128 . . . 144 . . . 160

   adaptors              _____/              innovators
                   67% of people fall
                   within this range
```

Figure 7.2 Range of KAI scores
Source: Kirton (1987)

so that a high score indicates an innovator and a low score indicates an adaptor. In order for this to occur, the sub-scales are arranged so that a high O score indicates high originality, but a high E and R score indicate low efficiency and low rule conformity.

Comparison with the normative data (shown in table 7.2) shows the main sample to be outside the normal range of scores on the KAI. The successful women are highly innovative. The above-average scores on each sub-scale indicates a preference for a proliferation of ideas, an ability to cope with uncertainty and imprecision and a willingness and ability to resist rules and group pressure.

Comparison with the élite entrepreneurs and the ubiquitous modal entrepreneurs studied by Cox and Jennings (table 7.3) shows that, on the overall scale of creative style, the successful women are more innovative. The élite modal entrepreneurs and the ubiquitous modal entrepreneurs score lower than the successful women on all the sub-scales. The élite independent entrepreneurs have higher scores on the originality and efficiency scales than the successful women, although they score much lower on the scale of rule conformity. Therefore, it would seem that the élite independent entrepreneurs have a slightly higher proficiency of ideas and are more willing to accept imprecision, but they are less willing to resist rule conformity than the successful women.

As noted above, Kirton has suggested that people who are most willing to cross boundaries of any sort are more likely to be inno-vators. It may be argued that women who reach the top in business, commerce or industry occupy positions which have traditionally been the exclusive preserve of men. In taking senior positions, these women have crossed a significant boundary into a male domain. The highly innovative score of the successful women indicates that they have the ability to think beyond existing paradigms, which may enable them to question the traditional role of women in society. This ability to work outside the existing paradigm concerning appropriate sex-role behaviour may have facilitated the investment of identity in the work role rather than the home-maker role. In addition, it must be remembered that the successful women were operating in a similar economic climate to the male chief executives studied by Cox and Jennings. It is possible that in a period of greater stability both male and female high flyers would be more adaptive. We would still predict, however, that women working in a pre-dominantly male world would be more strongly innovative than men.

Table 7.3 Comparative data for KAI

	Means scores			
Sample	*O*	*E*	*R*	*Total*
Elite independent entrepreneurs	51.0	25.6	26.8	104.4
Elite modal entrepreneurs	42.3	21.4	30.9	94.1
Ubiquitous modal entrepreneurs	48.5	20.4	41.9	110.8

Source: Cox and Jennings (1990)

The trait sub-scores provided further support for the above explanation, in particular the scale of rule conformity. Cox and Jennings found that the chief executives with no family ties to the organization were very non-conforming. What they found surprising was that people who had set up their own organizations were more conforming than those who had chosen to work within organizations. Cox and Jennings suggest that a possible explanation is the role of the chief executives as agents of change. An alternative explanation may be derived from the work of Kets de Vries (1980). Within Ket de Vries's framework, the enterprise represents a cathectic entity which acts as an active part of the individual's fantasy life. As a result, the entrepreneur has limited ability to distance himself from the venture. The entrepreneur is said to have a tendency to run the organization in a very personal and autocratic way. This management style is believed to be a symptom of a childhood background which has proved unreliable. In early life, the individual suffered lack of control over his/her environment. On becoming an entrepreneur, the individual gains control over a tangible entity symbolized by the enterprise. The rules of the company determine the level of control that the entrepreneur can exert. Therefore, the entrepreneur has a personal investment in conforming to the rules which he/she has introduced.

The successful women in the current sample were less concerned with conforming to the rules than any of the groups of male high flyers reported by Cox and Jennings. This supports the hypothesis that women must defy what is considered to be normative behaviour if they are to work successfully in the male-dominated world of work.

On the scale of efficiency, the successful women were slightly more efficient than the self-made entrepreneurs and less efficient than the male chief executives. Cox and Jennings suggest that it is likely that people working within an organization have to be more precise and methodical. The current sample consisted of both female entrepreneurs and women employed within organizations. It is not surprising, therefore, that their efficiency score falls between the group of male entrepreneurs and the group of male chief executives.

On the scale of originality there was little difference between the male entrepreneurs and chief executives and the successful women. All groups score well above the norm, indicating that all these successful people have a preference for producing a sufficiency of ideas.

Political Style

It is possible that the women who were studied by Hennig and Jardim in the 1970s were only just beginning to encounter careers and were unfamiliar with certain aspects of the work environment. As a result, they tended to neglect the distinction between the formal and informal organizational systems. During the fifteen years since that study, it is feasible that women may have adapted to working in a male-dominated world. We hypothesized that successful women of the late 1980s may have learnt to operate the political systems within the workplace in their favour. We speculated that women who succeed within organizations would have a characteristic political style. This hypothesis was tested using Kakabadse's (1986) operationalization of the concept of political styles.

Kakabadse has outlined four stereotyped political styles based on a model of the formation of mental maps. He states that we structure our experience to form a map and that two fundamental drives lead to the formation of this map: one's perceptions and one's actions. Kakabadse's perception–action model is shown in figure 7.3. The horizontal axis represents the determinants of a person's perceptions – i.e. values and beliefs. The two extremes are inner-directedness and outer-directedness. Individuals who are inner-directed develop

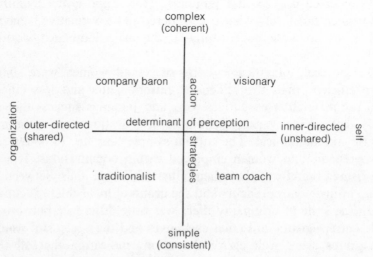

Figure 7.3   Perception action model
Source: Kakabadse (1986)

perceptions and views with little reference to the outside world. Individuals who are outer-directed need to comply with perceived attitudes and behaviour that others exhibit in that situation. Complying with the norms of the situation is said to lead to 'shared meaning'. People who need conditions of shared meaning adhere to the values of the organization. People who generate their own values of life are self-dependent – that is, they live with unshared meaning. They appreciate that the people with whom they interact may feel differently to themselves, but see no need to adapt to suit others.

The vertical axis represents the determinants of people's actions – their ability to put their views and values into practice. Kakabadse proposes two alternative strategies, simple and complex.

Those who adopt a simple strategy, aim for consistency. Irrespective of whether the people in the situation work on shared or unshared meaning, the behaviours they feel they should adopt are predictable, commonly recognized and probably previously practised. In this way, individuals are seen to be consistent and previous experience of those behaviours reduces the degree of felt threat, and it does not involve any original thought. The key point for a person practising this strategy is to behave in a manner acceptable to all others in the situation.

Those who adopt a complex strategy behave in ways which they consider suitable to meet only their needs in the situation. To the outsider, the individual may appear to exhibit no consistent pattern of behaviour. The behaviour may be inconsistent, but it is coherent with the individual's desired objectives. Complex action does involve new and original ideas and actions and possibly risk-taking.

To clarify the concept of politics, Kakabadse has analysed the four stereotyped characters, based on the perception–action model: traditionalist, team coach, company baron and visionary.

Traditionalist Traditionalists wish to fit in with the rest of the organization. They accept the fact that they are dependent on objectives set by others. They accept the way things are done, even if it is detrimental to their own interests. If things have been done in a particular way in the past, then that is the way things should continue. Traditionalist people will ensure that their group's identity and prevailing attitudes are not threatened with change, for they pay particular attention to the way that new members interact with established members. If someone is seen to misbehave, then some form of reprimand will follow. Despite their group orientation, traditionalists do not like warm, friendly relations. Their main concern is with their role. They strive to be 'top dog' over others.

Team coach The team coach develops his/her own ideas and beliefs about how to conduct his/her life and affairs. However, independence of thought is not matched by independence of action. The team coach does need to belong to a group of like-minded people and may spend some time searching for the group with whom he/she wishes to associate.

A group of bright team coaches can make for an innovative team. They do have capacity for independent thinking and generating new ideas. Team coaches seek a task orientation to their work. Rather than being concerned with their personal status, team coaches would aim to produce goods or services of high quality – that is, they are concerned with doing their job well.

Company baron The company baron has two dominant characteristics: an ability to see the total organization as it really is; and a continuous strong drive to enhance his position, if need be at the expense of others.

The company baron and the visionary (see below) share one strong characteristic: the insight to develop an overview of their organization. This skill enables them to recognize who has power and, therefore, whom to influence to get what they want. They also know which are the unspoken norms and values in the organization which should never be challenged.

Although the company baron has insight into how things are done and why, what he/she finds difficult is to become separate from the majority in the organization. Hence the company baron would be unlikely to introduce changes which would result in a shift of organizational values. One thing is certain – the company baron would never do anything unless it suited his/her purposes.

Visionary The visionary is similar to the company baron in his/her ability to see the organization in total; however, the visionary does not see the same need for loyalty to the company. Not only can the visionary question the way things are done in the organization and explore what might be suitable alternatives, but he/she can stand back from the values, views and stereotypes held by the rest of the organization.

Visionary people develop their own personalized visions and

beliefs about the future, and their own philosophies about work and strategies for action. As a result, they tend to operate in relative isolation. Sharing personal values is difficult. It is hard to co-operate with someone who has equally well-formed ideas, but which stem from separate shared values. Conflict may arise and may ultimately mean that one of the warring parties will have to leave the organization. They may also feel constrained by the systems in the organization, which may lead them to be critical of the management or to leave.

The application of political styles to successful women

The characteristics of the traditionalist seem to reflect a number of the traits associated with what Schein (1973) describes as the conformist response to organizational socialization. Many women who do achieve success within organizations do so by conforming to the predominant male norms. This may not be in their best interests as they try to mute their feminine traits and their potential for creativity. In a similar way to the traditionalist, those women who have climbed the organizational ladder often aim to maintain their position of superiority over other women, creating the phenomenon described as the 'queen bee syndrome' (Staines et al., 1974).

The attributes associated with the team coach also bear resemblance to the proposed characteristics of many women managers. The main similarity is their orientation to a task rather than concern with their own personal status (Marshall, 1984). As Hennig and Jardim (1978) have discussed at some length, women pay attention to doing the job well, as opposed to being seen to do a good job.

The visionary style may place women in a position to be politically competent. A clear understanding of the organizational norms and values enables one to 'read' situations. Operating on a system of unshared meaning enables women to question established practices. This awareness of organizational constraints may lead women to expect resistance. Therefore visionaries may take initiatives to acquire personal power which can be employed to reduce their frustration with the system.

The political styles of successful women

Kakabadse (1986) has developed a questionnaire to identify an individual's dominant and back-up political styles. This questionnaire revealed that our sample of successful women could be predominantly classified as having a team-coach or visionary political style (table 7.4 shows the distribution of political styles among the successful women). Forty-one per cent of the women were visionaries; this would suggest that these women have the insight to develop an overview of the organization. This skill enables them to recognize who has power and, therefore, whom to influence to get what they want. They also know which are the pivotal norms of the organization. In the terms of Arroba and James (1987) mentioned earlier, these women have the ability to *read* the organization, a component of *wise* political behaviour.

The visionary has independence of thought which enables him/her to stand back from the values, views and norms held by the rest of the organization and so develop personalized beliefs about the future and the way things should be. The team coach also operates on a system of unshared meaning. Fifty-two per cent of the successful women were classified as team coaches. Both the visionaries and the team coaches are inner-directed and therefore, develop their perceptions and views with little reference to the outside world. Inner-directed individuals generate their own values in life. (A total of 93 per cent of our sample successful women were either team coaches or visionaries).

The characteristic described as independence of thought was also reflected in the KAI scores of the successful women. The successful women were shown to be highly innovative with a low concern for rule conformity. This was said to show that they had the ability to think beyond existing paradigms and to do things differently. The theme which emerges from both the measure of political and creative style is the potential to generate one's own values, giving the ability to think beyond the constraints of the position traditionally allocated

Table 7.4 Political styles of successful women

Political Style	
Visionary	18
Team coach	23
Traditionalist	0
Company baron	0
Team coach/visionary	2

Source: Kakabadse (1986)

to women at work. This was also apparent in the discussion of gender identity. The majority of the successful women were classified as 'creative individualists' who accepted the 'pivotal' values of the organization but rejected the 'relevant' ones. Rather than conforming to the 'male model of success', these women had integrated their femininity into the sense of identity while operating within the structural constraints of the organization. These women have the ability to challenge the normative nature of power which has been postulated as one of the fundamental processes underlying women's under-representation in positions of authority. It is possible that this may be a vital characteristic for women entering the male-dominated worlds of business, commerce and industry.

8
Work and Family

Introduction

Fitzgerald and Betz (1983) claimed that the lack of attention to women's careers could be attributed largely to two assumptions. First, it has been assumed that the theories and concepts developed to describe and explain male career development would generalize to the description and explanation of women's career development. The second assumption was that women's primary roles were those of housewife and mother. Conventionally, the concept of career has been reserved for men. If women worked, it was expected that it would be a secondary activity – that is, they would have a 'job' rather than a 'career'. When working outside the home, women occupied primarily low-level, low-status positions providing little or no opportunity for advancement or social recognition. A career, as distinct from a job, represents a sequence in which there is a relatively high personal commitment; it has a developmental character and the assumption is that career takes precedence over private life. Rapoport and Rapoport (1980) comment that career was seen to be legitimate for men, but if a woman wanted a career it was assumed that she would forego marriage or at least children. Much of the early work in vocational psychology considered that the important things to know about women were their marital and maternal status, and how these interfaced with work behaviour.

Women's career patterns

Zytowski (1969) attempted to characterize female patterns of occupational behaviour. His central proposal was that the modal life role for women is the 'home-maker'. He postulated that vocational and home-maker participation are largely mutually exclusive. Zytowski then went on to suggest that vocational participation could be characterized in terms of three dimensions: age of entry, span of participation and degree of participation (i.e. traditional versus non-traditional). Based on these dimensions, Zytowski described three resulting patterns:

1 *Mild vocational pattern:* early or late entry and brief participation.
2 *Moderate pattern:* early and lengthy span, but low degree of participation.
3 *Unusual career pattern:* early entry, lengthy and uninterrupted span and high degree of participation.

Fitzgerald and Betz (1983) criticize Zytowski's description of women's career patterns on the grounds that it is inadequate in terms of many women who enter male-dominated occupations, unless they enter early and work continuously.

Wolfson (1976) added to Zytowski's formulation, introducing two new categories: 'never worked' and a 'high-moderate pattern' (that is, women whose span of participation was eighteen years or more). Wolfson looked at the differences among women in the five different categories. College graduation, attendance in graduate school and unmarried status were predictive of membership in the high-moderate or unusual groups. All the women in the other three groups were or had been married, while half of the women in the high-moderate or unusual groups were single. The largest number of women in Wolfson's sample were classifed in the mild pattern (49 per cent) and the smallest number in the unusual pattern (0.05 per cent).

Super's (1957) work on the career patterns of women also embodied assumptions about the primacy of marriage and children in relation to work. Super described seven career patterns for women:

1 *Stable home-making:* marry while in or shortly after leaving school and have no significant work experience.
2 *Conventional career pattern:* work outside the home until marriage.
3 *Stable working pattern:* work continuously – i.e. have a career.
4 *Double track:* combine work and home.
5 *Interrupted:* women returners.
6 *Unstable:* irregular and repeated pattern of home or work involvement.
7 *Multiple trial:* unstable job history.

Vetter (1973) looked at the frequency of these patterns in a cross-sectional national sample of women. The findings shown in table 8.1 demonstrate that the conventional and stable home-making patterns were most common at that time. It is unlikely, however, that these

Table 8.1 Women's career patterns

Pattern	Percentage
stable home-making	22
conventional	27
stable working	3
double track	14
interrupted	16
unstable	18
multiple trial	not used

Source: Vetter (1973)

patterns would be evident in the same proportions in the 1990s. Social Trends (1989) summarizes some of the key changes that have been taking place in relation to patterns of marriage and cohabitation, although there is no breakdown by occupation. There is a trend towards later first marriage (the average age in 1986 was 24.1 years, compared with 23.1 years in 1981). There has been a increase in cohabitation (11.5 per cent of women aged between eighteen and twenty-four, which is more than double the rate in 1981). This is linked to the increase in the number of children born outside marriage, which accounted for 23 per cent of all live births in 1987, almost double the rate in 1981. The divorce rate in the UK has also increased and is now the highest in the European Community. The major impact of later marriage, increased cohabitation and later childbirth is that women spend longer in employment, and have greater expectations of and opportunities to develop their careers (Rajan and Bevan, 1990).

Even more recently, Warr and Parry (1982) focused on the priority of the maternal role over the vocational role in women's lives:

[We assume] the greater proportion of women with children at home are emotionally involved in the parenting role . . . and that in general this takes priority for them over paid employment. Overall, we expect this group to be of relatively low occupational involvement, especially when their children are young.

Fuchs (1988) suggests that childcare and women's economic equality are inextricably intertwined. Yet again, the role of mother and home-maker is said to have priority. Fuchs states that, on average, women want children more than men do and that they feel greater concern for their well-being. This statement is supported by recourse to biology and the early bonding between mother and child. Fuchs draws his conclusion primarily from statistics which show that in the USA women over the age of twenty account for two thirds of the births to single-parent families, and that half of these births are intended at conception. Fuchs claims that in order to accommodate their desire for children women have to make choices that curtail their economic activity.

The Effect of Female Employment on the Family

One outcome of the focus on the priority of the biological over the vocational role is that research has tended to investigate the effects of female employment on the family, rather than looking at the effects of family on women's career development. Female employment was thought to produce conflict for women between their families and their careers, and this in turn was considered to produce a destructive effect on the husband and the family. This notion has its roots in psychoanalytic psychology, which views women's nature as intrinsically passive, nurturant and unaggressive. Parsonian sociology of functionalism (Parsons, 1965) also proposes that female employment generates familial conflict and confuses status lines. Both these schools of thought serve to perpetuate the status quo, one by appealing to 'natural order' philosophy, and the other by arguing that 'what is, should be', otherwise it would not have survived so long in the social order.

Despite these arguments, there is little evidence that women's employment has a deleterious effect on the family. Following a review of the literature, Nye (1974) claimed that, up to this point, 'the research is not completely consistent, but provides predominant support for the thesis that differences favouring the housewife occur mostly in the lower social classes'.

Richardson (1979) tested the hypothesis that greater marital unhappiness would exist for both husband and wife when wives achieved greater occupational status, but found no support for this thesis. Wright (1978) also found that women's employment had little or no effect on middle-class marriages.

Research findings are inconclusive about the impact of maternal employment on the children of working women. Hoffman (1980) found that maternal employment was related to strain in father–son relations among lower socio-economic class families, and to lower academic performance in middle-class families. Maternal employment did, however, have a positive influence on adolescents, especially daughters. Among infant and pre-school children, the nature and quality of day-care are important in determining the adjustment. When the quality is high, there are no negative effects on emotional adjustment or relations with the mother. In a study of female entrepreneurs, Carter and Cannon (1988) actually found that proprietorship improved their relationship with their children.

Changes in the structure of opportunity

In her model of career choice and work behaviour, Astin (1985) introduces the concept of 'structure of opportunity' to depict how social forces shape and reshape occupational decisions. Astin proposes that individuals strive to satisfy three basic needs:

1 *Survival needs*. Employment provides an income which is essential to physical health and well-being. The home-maker has an implicit agreement with the breadwinner and satisfies survival needs indirectly.
2 *Pleasure needs*. Intrinsic pleasure is derived from various work or home-making activities.
3 *Contribution needs*. Humans need to feel that they are contributing to the well-being of others.

Working on the assumption that home-making is a woman's primary role, we might expect that women would satisfy their needs in the private sphere. However, Astin points out that, owing to the changing structure of opportunity, women may find alternative means of satisfying their needs in the public sphere.

Increased longevity means that individuals have more years to fill with meaningful activity. Astin suggests that planning for work over the lifespan is now imperative. In the past, having a family and caring for it satisfied women's contribution needs. The declining birth rate, associated with the higher educational level of women, means that women now seek other sources of need gratification in paid employment. Medical advances in reproductive technology have given women greater control over their lives. They now have the freedom to plan and prepare for their working lives. The increase in the divorce rate means that women can no longer be sure that their survival needs will be satisfied by someone else. In addition, the rise in inflation has meant that many women now work out of financial necessity (West, 1982). The codification of women's rights has lead to a reduction in overt sex discrimination at work. Women now have access to careers which have been traditionally the reserve of men.

These social trends have reduced the barriers facing women so that they now have more options available. There has been, therefore, a proliferation of non-traditional lifestyles. Rapoport and Rapoport (1980) comment that more women are combining work and family. More men are said to be adopting a family-oriented approach to life, sometimes at the expense of career advancement. Astin (1985) suggests that 'The multiplicity of social roles open to both sexes means that men and women will be able to transcend gender differentiated occupational boundaries and choose from a wider range of careers'.

The Effect of Family on Women's Career Development

Laws (1979) contends that family and children affect career to a greater extent than career affects the family. The literature in vocational psychology has tended to assert that the major difficulty in women's career development is the uncertainty of marriage plans, and the difficulty in participating simultaneously in two systems, the claims of which are practically incompatible (e.g. Osipow, 1975; Fitzgerald and Betz, 1983; Davidson and Cooper, 1987; Gilligan, 1982). The absence of family demands appears to be beneficial for career advancement. Frieze et al. (1978) noted that single professional women tend to be more productive and successful than married professional women.

Tinsley and Faunce (1980) employed Sobol's (1963) classification of variables which influence the decisions of married women to work outside the home:

1 *Enabling conditions:* family characteristics, including spouse's salary and satisfaction with the marriage.
2 *Facilitating conditions:* educational level and work experience.
3 *Precipitating conditions:* attitudinal factors – i.e. self-concept and sex-role beliefs.

The research focused on the conditions of women who were classified as 'career oriented' or 'home-makers'. Their findings showed that the variables which best differentiated the career oriented and the home-makers were the enabling conditions. This was said to be consistent with earlier findings. Astin and Myint (1971) found that marital status and familial status are among the best predictors of women choosing careers in sciences, professions and teaching, as opposed to housewives and office workers.

Tinsley and Faunce (1980) offer two explanations. Women may decide in advance that they do not want a career outside the home. Alternatively, women may take the decision to have children without clearly appreciating the long-term implications for their careers.

Role conflict

Hawley (1971) found that women's perceptions of the sex-role stereotypes held by men were strongly related to their own role expectations. These perceptions place home and the family primarily in the domain of the feminine role and may place pressure on women to sacrifice their career for their family. It appears that, although women can add the role of career woman, they have difficulty in shedding the roles of housewife and mother. This can lead to role conflict. O'Leary (1977) described three types of role conflict:

1 *Intra-role conflict:* incompatibilty of multiple demands within a single role.
2 *Inter-role conflict:* incompatibility of the demands associated with two or more roles, conceptualized as being primarily psychological in nature.
3 *Role overload:* inability to satisfy all role expectations in the time available, despite recognizing the legitimacy of all the demands.

Inter-role conflict and role overload have particular significance for women's career development.

Inter-role conflict   In discussing inter-role conflict resulting from family and work roles, Coser and Rokoff (1971) remarked:

> The conflict derives from the fact that values underlying these demands are contradictory; professional women are expected to be committed to their work 'just like men are'. At the same time they are normatively required to give priority to their family. The conflict is one of allegiance, and it does not stem from the mere fact of involvement in more than one social system. It is a conflict of normative priorities.

Following a review of the literature, Gray (1980) identified three sources of psychological pressure resulting from inter-role conflict:

1 Lack of support or disapproval of significant others.

2 Supposed incompatibility of career success in non-traditional domains with feminine role.
3 Guilt of combining the role of mother and worker (Johnson and Johnson, 1977).

Role overload   Role overload is primarily related to the finite nature of time. As Fitzgerald and Betz (1983) quite eloquently point out, 'Married career women are faced every day with the regrettable fact that Parkinson's law does not have an inverse; time does not expand to encompass the work available!'

Division of domestic labour

Research clearly shows that wives, even those with full-time careers, still perform the overwhelming majority of domestic tasks (Bird, 1979; Hall and Hall, 1980). Studies reported at the American Psychological Association's conference suggest that, even if their wives work, most men do no more than one third of the household tasks (Cunningham, 1981). Reed and Fanslow (1984) report a similar pattern for self-employed women. Time management was found to be crucial to women entrepreneurs, because they still bear the major responsibility for household chores.

Hochschild (1989) interviewed and observed ten working couples with children over a period of ten years. She found that struggles over the second shift were part of every marriage. Hochschild found little evidence of 'fifty–fifty' accommodation. The wife, willing or not, consciously or not, does most of the second shift. This is consistent with the findings of Berk and Berk (1979). In a sample of urban families, they found that two thirds of the husbands of working wives made no more contribution to 'after-dinner' chores than did husbands of full-time housewives.

Hochschild divides couples into three broad categories on the basis of their attitude towards home and work:

1 *Traditional couples*. The husband works and the wife stays at home. Both agree where each should be and how their work should be valued.
2 *The transitional couple*. He does less than she thinks that he should (he may be willing to do more than she will allow). Spouses are often 'divided within themselves' – that is, their images of men and women clash with the reality of their lives. What they say they want – a career and to share the responsibilities at home – does not mesh with what they feel they ought to do.

3 *Egalitarian couple.* Based on the equal-commitment model, husbands and wives spend equal amounts of time on their families and careers.

Haas (1978) studied marriages in which both partners shared in the areas of breadwinning, decision-making and domestic chores. These couples reported four types of difficulty which resemble those observed in transitional couples:

1 Lack of skills on the part of one of the spouses.
2 Lack of inclination to do some of the non-traditional tasks.
3 Wives reluctant to give up authority over domestic chores.
4 Different standards of housekeeping – i.e. wives had higher standards of cleanliness.

Childcare

Bird (1979) reports that the working wife retains almost sole responsibility for the care and well-being of the children. Moss (1988) provides a detailed review of childcare provisions in the European Community. The report is based on national reports prepared for each of the national representatives on the childcare network. As regards the position of the UK, the report notes: 'a high proportion of employed women with children under five use family based childcare [and] the use of formal institutional care such as crèches, day care and nurseries is relatively rare, reflecting their limited availability.'

Highly successful women are likely to require geographical mobility and are, therefore, likely to live some distance from their parents and siblings. It is probable that they will rely on paid childcare. Similarly, Longstreth et al. (1986) found that the majority of self-employed women do employ childcare, although only 8 per cent hired others to clean their homes.

Children and Career Breaks

Only a minority of women continue to work full-time throughout their childrearing years. However, the differences between men and women should not be exaggerated. Recent statistics show that in the UK most women between the ages of twenty and fifty-nine are in continuous employment, with an average break of only five years while raising a family (Equal Opportunities Commission, 1984). Long (1984), in a study of Institute of Personnel Management (UK) members, showed that one third of women had a career break, in comparison with 13 per cent of men. The average length of the career break for all his respondents was less than one year, and only 16 per cent of the women took a break to get married or to have children. Thirty per cent of these women had at least ten years' work experience before the birth of their first child, lending support to the trend that managerial women are having children later in life than is the norm.

Rix and Stone (1984) point out that as long as women step off the fast track to meet family responsibilities, they will be at a competitive disadvantage given the current structure of career advancement within the majority of organizations. The thirties is a make-or-break time in most careers. The pacing of modern managerial careers could not be worse for women seeking to combine work and family. It is claimed that it takes twenty years to reach general management level at General Motors in the USA. Even allowing for a small range of variation, it would seem logical to employ aspiring managers at twenty-five rather than at forty-five years of age. If women have their children early, they are too old to be trainees in their late twenties, even though they may have the appropriate credentials. If they have their children in their thirties, this is the most critical time in the struggle for career success. When women are ready to commit themselves to their careers in their forties, they are too old. Research is needed to assess whether women feel that they would be better advised to start their careers before leaving briefly to have children, as opposed to having their children first. Bernard (1981) has emphasized that timing and age are particularly important elements in women's career development. They are not key issues for men, because it is assumed that men are in continuous employment with a constant level of opportunity.

Davidson and Cooper (1987) feel that women are unfairly penalized by the majority of employers for taking a career break. Povall (1983) claims that maternity leave is viewed in a different light to those breaks initiated by the employer, such as study breaks or transfer to another discipline, which are viewed as inevitable. Women who do become pregnant are often victims of die-hard stereotypical attitudes (Adams, 1984). They may be removed from the fast track, excluded from important meetings and reduced to a lesser role. Dex (1987) found that downward mobility was more common among women with children than those without. Gutek et al. (1981) found that many women in managerial roles choose to avoid the conflict between family and career by remaining single. Having said that, Adams (1984) claims that high-achieving women have high expectations in both home and career and, therefore, seek out occupations which will accommodate family life.

The Integration of Professional and Private Lives

Coping mechanisms

Epstein (1970) has identified nine mechanisms that women might employ to cope with the conflicting demands of their multiple roles:

1 The elimination of social relations: women are more selective in their choice of relations, eliminating those whose expectations cause strain.
2 Reduction of the total amount of contacts involved in the total set of relations – e.g. limiting size of family and number of friends.
3 Reducing the number of roles in the role set.
4 Redefinition of roles – e.g. a woman working with her husband may define it as helping to relieve the guilt of leaving her children.
5 Intermittent activation of roles.
6 Compartmentalization by scheduling: careful timing to avoid the intrusion of one role into another.
7 Delegation of tasks and roles.
8 Increasing observability of role demand.
9 Reliance on rules for the legitimation of behaviour: appeal to deadlines and organizational schedules to legitimize non-participation in family activities.

Hall (1972) has condensed this list of coping mechanisms into three coping strategies:

1 *Changing the demands of the role:* e.g. employing a nanny to ease the demands of childcare. This strategy is described as structural role redefinition.
2 *Setting priorities on certain role demands:* learning to live with the added conflict. This strategy is described as personal role redefinition.
3 *Attempting to meet the demands of all multiple roles:* this strategy is described as reactive role behaviour.

It would be interesting to observe the coping strategies employed by successful women. It is possible that they may eliminate roles and forego marriage and children. Alternatively, they may, as Adams (1984) suggests, have high expectations in both home and career and must, therefore, employ coping mechanisms which enable them to pursue their careers successfully.

Effectiveness of coping mechanisms

Hall (1972) suggests that, in general, structural role redefinition is positively related to satisfaction with one's career, while reactive role behaviour is negatively related to career satisfaction. Kroeker (1963) claims that attempts to meet all the demands of multiple roles is maladaptive and reflects defensiveness rather than coping. Gray (1983) studied 232 married professional women and found a strong positive association between satisfaction and strategies of sharing household tasks with family members (role delegation), reducing standards within certain roles (personal role redefinition) and considering personal interests important (prioritizing). Other strategies were negatively associated with satisfaction. These included overlapping roles, keeping roles totally separate, attempting to meet all expectations, eliminating entire roles and the absence of a conscious strategy for dealing with role conflict.

Role conflict or role diversification

Valdez and Gutek (1987) discuss whether family roles are a help or a hindrance to working women. The role-conflict theory would appear to suggest that the added demands of family roles are a hindrance to a woman's career. As stated in the earlier discussion, one of the major obstacles to women's career development is the pressure to fulfil the domestic roles of home-maker and mother.

In contrast, the role accumulation theory proposed by Sieber (1974) suggests that the conflict and overload resulting from a multiplicity of roles can be overshadowed by the rewards of role accumulation. Role strain may be compensated for by the buffers against failure that multiple roles provide. The net effect is positive.

Crosby (1982) found support for role accumulation with respect to the effect of family roles on job satisfaction. Single people were found to be less satisfied with their jobs than married people or parents. It was concluded that, 'For married workers and especially parents, the joys of home may wash away the disgruntlements of the office, factory or shop. Perhaps, too, some of the woes of parenthood . . . may put difficulties into a new rather soft light.' Crosby did not distinguish, however, between men and women. For men, marriage is an asset, but for women it may result in role conflict.

Valdez and Gutek (1987) conducted a study to test the role conflict and role accumulation theories. Their sample included women across a range of different occupational groups. On the basis of the role-conflict theory, they predicted that professional and managerial women who had jobs requiring above-average commitment were more likely to be single and childless. This represents a strategy to reduce role conflict by eliminating roles (Goode, 1960). In addition, those women experiencing role overload were expected to be least satisfied. In contrast, role accumulation theory predicts that the added strain of multiple roles is compensated for by added rewards. On the basis of this theory, therefore, it was predicted that professional and managerial women would have the same family circumstances as other women and that they would have equal satisfaction.

Valdez and Guteik's findings provided partial support for both theories. In accordance with role elimination theory, they found a higher rate of divorce and separation among professional and managerial women. They also found that, 'As the level of commitment and preparation required for a job rises, there is a general decrease in the proportion of women with three or more children and a general increase in the proportion of childless women'.

However, women who had the potential for greater role conflict (i.e. married professional and managerial women with children) did not report lower job satisfaction. Role accumulation theory explains why the lowest levels of job satisfaction were found among single women. Based on the findings of their research, Valdez and Gutek suggest that a positive way forward for women is to combine the roles of wife, mother and careerist. They draw on the advice of Gutek et al. (1986): 'The most satisfactory lifestyle may be one where a person can accumulate many new roles without expending great quantities of energy on any of them'.

The balancing careerist

Many authors are calling for a reassessment of the balance between work and family life spheres. Foster (1988) noted that many young graduates in the UK, both male and female, are demanding quality of life as well as a vocational career. A workaholic man or woman who neglects other aspects of his/her life is no longer a viable role model. Foster draws on Derr's (1986) concept of the 'balancing careerist' to describe the emerging roles.

Stone (1989) argues that achieving this balance is feasible, and she suggests that it is time to rethink the logic that equates long hours with superior performance and workaholism with commitment.

Stone believes that the concept of quality time spent with children should be transferred to the workplace. She encourages people to think less about the number of hours spent in the workplace and more about what they do there.

One way in which women may balance family life with a career is to work part time. Part-time jobs are, however, overwhelmingly lower skilled and lower paid. For those women who occupy more senior positions, part-time work does not offer a viable option. Statistics indicate that there is a neglible number of women working part time in managerial jobs (New Earnings Survey, 1988). Bevan, Buchan and Hayday (1990) did a study of women working in a hospital pharmacy. They found that two thirds of a sample of 550 managers agreed with the statement 'part-time status and managerial work do not mix'.

Ryecroft (1989) has pointed out the fallacy that managerial roles cannot be performed part time. Ryecroft notes that many managers, especially senior managers, fulfil multi-faceted responsibilities. They are, therefore, managing each function part time. Also, many company directorships are part time.

Alban Metcalfe (1987) presents her hopes for the future:

> Might it be that we could use the opportunity created by the increasing numbers of women entering management, with the possibly different approach that they may bring to the organisational culture, to reassess the nature and balance of the work and non-work spheres of our lives, to produce a healthier society?

Processes linking work and family

Following a review of the literature, Lambert (1990) concludes that research has not adequately explored the processes through which job and family characteristics intrude across the work–family nexus (or how a balance is achieved). Lambert describes four theories of work and family linkage:

1 *Segmentation.* Home and work are seen to segmented and independent. Seeman (1967) studied Swedish workers with alienating jobs. The alienated workers were found to be the same as non-alienated workers in terms of their attitudes about leisure and society. Seeman proposed that workers come to terms with their work life rather than let it influence their non-work life. Other research suggests that if segmentation occurs it is not 'natural'. Workers are said 'actively' to separate work and family life in order to deal with work-related stresses (Piotrkowski, 1979).

2 *Compensation*. Workers respond actively by trying to compensate for the lack of satisfaction in one sphere through finding more in another sphere. For example, Parker (1972) found that British miners and deep-sea fishermen saw their leisure time as compensation for their dangerous lives and difficult work.

3 *Spill-over*. The feelings, attitudes and behaviours created by work spill over into leisure. Bartolome (1972) argues that executives whose jobs demand that they adopt tough roles have difficulty in expressing feelings of dependence and tenderness towards their wives and children.

4 *Accommodation*. Lambert (1990) suggests that this process typifies the experience of women. Workers limit their work involvement or their family involvement to accommodate the demands of the other sphere. The causal order of this process is the reverse of compensation – that is, high involvement in one sphere results in low involvement in the other.

Lambert considers that there is a possibility that all four processes operate simultaneously. In the case of successful women, it may be that certain jobs and family characteristics are limited to one sphere and some spill over. A study of female managers and entrepreneurs showed that, although these women made an effort not to bring work physically into their homes, they did think about work while at home (White, 1989). It is possible that, by examining the relationship between home and work, we may be able to identify circumstances in which particular processes operate and why. By investigating the links between the jobs and family histories of successful women, we might gain an insight into how they manage the home–work interface.

Modelling the careers of successful women

An assumption behind the 'spill-over' hypothesis is that work is central to a person's identity and, therefore, what happens at work permeates the rest of life. In contrast, the 'compensatory' hypothesis assumes that work is only one part of identity, not necessarily central. These two hypotheses may be reconciled by introducing Hall's (1976) concept of sub-identities. Hall proposed that an individual's identity can be conceptualized as consisting of several sub-identities, representing various aspects of the individual and engaged when behaving in different social roles. The career sub-identity is defined as that aspect of the person's identity which is engaged in working in a given occupation. Career involvement may be seen as the importance of the career sub-identity in relation to

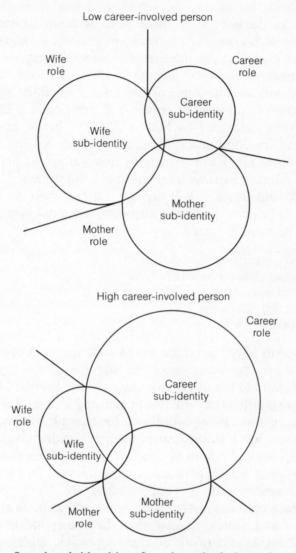

Figure 8.1 Sample sub-identities of two hypothetical people, one with low career involvement and one with high career involvement
Source: adapted from Hall (1976)

other sub-identities. This relationship is represented diagramatically in figure 8.1.

As the individual acquires competencies relevant to the career role, which is comprised of the expectancies people hold for individuals in that career, the sub-identity will grow. Sub-identity extension, in the context of career role, is termed career growth. Career growth can consist of increases in motivation, knowledge and career-related ability. As the career sub-identity expands, proportionately more of the total identity is invested in the career role. Choice, growth and involvement can form a spiralling combination of career choice, sub-identity growth and commitment. This process equates to that described by Marcia (1966) – that is, moratorium–achievement–moratorium–achievement. What is interesting to speculate on is whether any patterns may emerge in the timing of career sub-identity expansion among successful women.

Larwood and Gutek (1987) suggest that five concerns need to be added, or to be given particular attention, when discussing women's careers as opposed to men's:

1 career preparedness;
2 opportunities available in society;
3 influence of marriage;
4 pregnancy and childbirth;
5 age and timing.

These concerns have been discussed at some length in this review. It is not possible, however, simply to add the elements specific to women's careers to the more basic male model. Larwood and Gutek claim that two differences still divide men and women. First, women feel the tug of alternative possibilities; for example, if a woman finds that her career has plateaued early, she may decide to begin a family and give up work. Such an option is less viable for a man. Second, although women legally have equal opportunities, they are still discriminated against. As the opportunities are fewer, progress is slower, which may make other alternatives appear more attractive.

Larwood and Gutek suggest that the theory might be better conceptualized as a network or tree of possible alternatives, each combination of which has a potentially different outcome. Such a conceptualization is preferable to an 'age-linked' stage theory, because it overcomes the problem of incorporating the elements of timing and age. Using the network idea, it may be possible to gain a perspective on the effect of time-lags on career development in different situations – that is, in the careers of successful women.

Alternatively, Rapoport and Rapoport (1980) suggest that an appropriate model for thinking about career behaviour is a triple helix. At each turning-point in the developmental process one

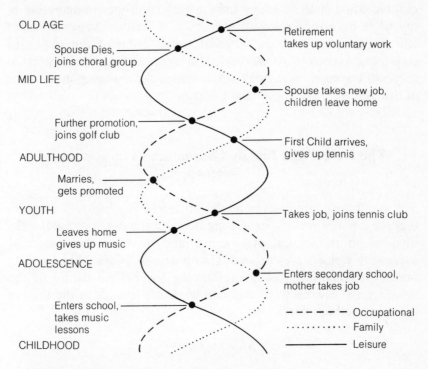

OLD AGE

Spouse Dies, ——————
joins choral group

————— Retirement
takes up voluntary work

MID LIFE

————— Spouse takes new job,
children leave home

Further promotion, ——————
joins golf club

————— First Child arrives,
gives up tennis

ADULTHOOD

Marries, ——————
gets promoted

YOUTH

————— Takes job, joins tennis club

Leaves home ——————
gives up music

ADOLESCENCE

————— Enters secondary school,
mother takes job

Enters school, ——————
takes music
lessons

– – – – – – Occupational
· · · · · · · · · · Family
————— Leisure

CHILDHOOD

Figure 8.2 Triple helix model: illustrative critical events
Source: Rapoport and Rapoport (1980)

confronts tasks that are new and specific to that phase, but simultaneously there is an interaction between past and present experience.

The whole life career is made up of work transitions. In addition, there is a helix for family and leisure. The three helical structures carry on through life, each with its own impetus and its own characteristics. Rapoport and Rapoport suggest that the three structures interact with each other in two distinct ways:

1 during steady states between transitions (the issue is balancing);
2 at transition points (the issue is the critical impact of events).

The triple-helix model of each life career must be constructed on the basis of that individual's experience. Adjustments for variables such as age of marriage, timing of childbearing and change of jobs must be made for each individual. Generally the helix looks like figure 8.2.

In a similar way to the sub-identity and network models, we may observe whether there is any unique pattern in the configuration of the triple helix for successful women. It is feasible that each strand will be given primacy at different times. Each of the suggested conceptualizations may be useful in representing the careers of successful women, as they all acknowledge the changing importance of different life arenas over the lifespan.

The Career and Family Commitments of Successful Women

The age-linked career stage model presented in chapter 5 suggests that the key features distinguishing between the developmental tasks involved in the typical male career and those in the careers of successful women are associated with family issues. This finding raises the importance of understanding the precise nature of the relationship between work and non-work life spheres in the lives of these female high flyers.

Marital status

Research data suggest that men benefit from the support provided by their wives. Cox and Cooper (1988) found in general that male chief executives felt that their careers and success would have been impossible without a supportive wife and stable home. Frieze et al. (1978) comment that men frequently benefit from their married status. It is suggested that 'the professional man's wife traditionally supports and aids him in his career in a way few men desire or are able to do for their wives.'

Providing emotional support may in fact act as source of strain for women, especially if they are pursuing a demanding career. Heckman et al. (1977) found that a source of stress for wives derived from the disproportionate amount of time that they devoted to supporting their husbands' needs rather than their own. Previous research has shown that the absence of family demands is beneficial for career success. Frieze et al. (1978) found that single professional women were more productive and successful than married women.

Marriage did not, however, appear to preclude success among the current sample. Indeed, 58 per cent of our sample of successful women were currently married, with only fourteen women divorced, seven of whom had remarried. The remaining twelve women were single, although five of these were cohabiting. These findings may be reconciled with earlier work by looking at the family as a social support system. With the exception of two, all the successful women described their partners as being very supportive of their careers. Like the male 'high flyers' interviewed by Cox and Cooper (1988), many believed that a supportive spouse provided the firm home base which was the secret of their success. As one said: 'Every woman needs the right husband, it's the secret of a successful career. I suppose my husband set me off in the first place because he said that he didn't want a coffee-drinking, bridge-playing wife, he wanted a wife who worked.'

Heckman et al. (1977) also found that when emotional support for the wife's career pursuits was evident, then the pressures of role conflict were attenuated.

Children

Fifty per cent of our group of successful women had children, and only five of these women had taken a career break, the average length of which was 9.4 years. This career break is somewhat longer than the national average which, is approximately five years (Equal Opportunities Commission, 1985). During this time the women were not idle. They engaged in voluntary work or they did freelance work from their homes. These women were among the older members of the sample, the mean age of the group being fifty-six years.

There is some evidence that the timing of family events appears to be changing among successful women. Nine women waited until their careers were well established before deciding to have children; the mean age of this group was thirty-five years. These women took minimum maternity leave. Ten of the women who did not have children were in the process of contemplating whether to have them; the mean age of this group was about thirty-three years. These women all felt that if they did have children they would continue to work and that they would employ a nanny. Several of them commented that they were intensely aware that if they did take a career break they would be stepping off the career track. For example:

> I haven't planned to have children so far and I haven't got long to make a decision. I've not had children so far because of my career but now I have seen my friends combining career and family, although with difficulty at times. If I decide that I want a family I will combine it with work because I could afford paid help.

As mentioned earlier, Rix and Stone (1984) feel that women are often justified in their fears that they will be at a competitive disadvantage if they step off the career track. The thirties appear to be the time when most successful young women are considering whether to have a family, and yet this is perceived as a critical make-or-break time in most careers. Adams (1984) has found that women who do become pregnant may be removed from the fast track, excluded from important meetings and reduced to a lesser role. Two of the successful women felt that they had been discriminated against when they became pregnant, as one of them explained:

As soon as I announced that I was pregnant my boss's attitude changed. He felt that women who worked were evil. He kept me locked in a corner for six months, which I found very frustrating because I wanted to carry on as normal. I took six months off because I was very ill, then on the day I was due to go back I was told that I had been made redundant. I knew that this wasn't fair but I didn't fight it because I didn't want to work for that person any more.

Gutek et al. (1981) suggested that women in managerial roles choose to avoid the conflict between family and career by remaining single. Successful women may marry, but many do choose to remain childless, as described by one of our respondents:

I decided that I didn't want children before I got married. I think I would have found it very difficult to do what I have done if I had children. My life wouldn't have been more complete with children because I would have abdicated the responsibility to a nanny.

These findings emphasize the importance of continuous employment for the achievement of career success. If women do expect to participate in both occupational and family roles, they can expect to encounter problems which relate to an implicit model of what a successful career looks like. Hirsh and Jackson (1990) have outlined a stereotyped pattern of managerial careers which incorporates continuous employment, working long hours, conforming to age-related concepts of careers, and being geographically mobile. This raises the question put forward by Gilbert (1984) once again: 'Can a concept of career that includes involvement in family and occupational roles realistically co-exist with social institutions that embody the values of a patriarchal society?'

The current conception of career makes the alliance between work and family lives somewhat uneasy. If successful women do have children, they almost certainly will not take a career break. Simply becoming pregnant may be enough to slow down career progress. These findings lend further support to the claims that it is time for organizations to rethink what constitutes a successful career. As Stone (1989) has pointed out, it is time to reassess the logic that equates long hours with superior performance and workaholism with commitment.

Processes linking work and family among successful women

As discussed earlier, Lambert (1990) has identified four main theories of work and family linkage: segmentation, compensation, spill-over and accommodation. In an investigation of these linkages, Evans and Bartolome (1984) conducted interviews with forty-four managers and their wives. They found that there was no single way of describing the relationship between family and work, and that attempts to resolve the spill-over–compensation debate were futile. Evans and Bartolome placed emphasis on the need to understand the social and psychological factors associated with the different relationships between family and work. They went on to suggest that there are two interacting factors which help to explain the occurrence of different work and family linkages. These two factors were:

1 *The emotional outcome of work.* Managers with positive feelings about work reported work and family to be conflicting or independent. In contrast, managers with negative feelings about work saw work as instrumental to family.
2 *Importance of work in the life of the individual.* Managers who found work very important experienced home–work conflict, or work spilled over into family life. In contrast, for those managers to whom work was not important, work was instrumental to family, or family was compensation for working life.

These findings provide strong support for the argument that the spill-over and compensatory hypothesis could be reconciled through Hall's (1976) concept of sub-identities. The compensatory hypothesis assumes that work is only one part of identity, not necessarily central; therefore work is unlikely to permeate other aspects of identity. As more of the individual's identity is invested in career through the process of career growth, then work may spill over into other less prominent sub-identities. Alternatively, the individual may accommodate the demands of his/her working life by limiting his/

her involvement in family life – that is, reducing the number of sub-identities.

Fifty per cent of the successful women in our sample claimed that work took priority in their lives. The centrality of work in their lives was also reflected in the definitions of career described earlier. A large proportion of the women felt that work was an integral part of their lives from which they derived their identity. A small proportion made the reservation that, although work had always taken priority in their lives, they were now beginning to regret it. They felt that they had missed their opportunity to have children or to enjoy their children while they were young. As one woman put it:

> Work has taken priority and that is part of my resentment. Although I am the one who takes too much on I think that the firm has allowed me to do it for too long. It was because of this that the decision not to have a family was made and I resent that.

The timing of the career sub-identity growth was discussed in relation to career centrality. Thirty-five per cent of the women were dedicated to a career from an early age. The development of career centrality was found to be delayed among other women until they rejected the role of housewife or were separated from a partner. The rejection of the traditional female role in favour of a career could represent the process of accommodation. It does seem, however, that a small proportion of successful women decide to compensate for failure in their personal lives by striving for success in their careers.

As the individual gains career competencies, Hall (1976) suggests that the career sub-identity will begin to expand. Bray et al. (1974) conducted a seven-year follow-up of MBA students who joined the American Telephone and Telegraph Company. They concluded that job success holds one to job-related themes, whereas lack of success permits or motivates one to turn to themes outside work. This is consistent with an argument put forward earlier, that success stimulates the growth of the career sub-identity. Bray et al. also comment that only career failures would be interested in devoting time and energy to family and leisure pursuits. This conclusion, however, ignores any choices that may be made on the basis of a value system.

Thirty per cent of our successful women said that they tried to achieve a balance, although they would put their family first in the event of a crisis. For example, one woman commented: 'Work comes first until it comes to a real conflict, then the balance tips – for instance, if my husband was ill. We each take events as they come and try to strike a sensible balance.'

Only 20 per cent of the successful women felt that their family took priority over their working lives. The results, therefore, provide only partial support for Marshall's (1984) contention that for women work does not take priority over all other life areas.

Role Conflict

O'Leary (1977), as we have seen, has identified three types of role conflict, of which two, inter-role conflict and role overload, are important for women's career development. Evidence of both types of conflict was found in the reports of the successful women.

Role overload

When asked whether there was any negative aspect to their work, 16.6 per cent of the women said that they did not have enough time to do everything, which they felt had negative repercussions for their family life. These reports were confirmed when the women were asked whether they felt they had enough time for their personal lives. Twenty-one per cent said that they did not feel that they had enough. They also felt that the spare time they did have was not used productively because they were exhausted after work. As one successful woman relates, 'I don't have enough time for my private life. I think that there must be a better way to organize life, because I'm always exhausted. This is a function of the company needing more staff.'

These women are clearly suffering the effects of role overload, or what Piotrkowski (1979) has termed 'energy deficit', whereby the individual does not have the psychological or physical energy to engage in family life. Similarly, Beutel (1986) found 'time-based conflict' to be the prevalent form of conflict in a sample of 113 married couples with children.

Inter-role conflict

Forty-two per cent of the women said that they did not have any family commitments which might influence their career plans. Of the remaining women, seventeen said that their family life had influenced their career plans. Eleven women believed that their progress had been slowed, or that their mobility had been reduced. One explained:

> My career plans have been influenced by having a family in terms of where I'm prepared to work – that is, a maximum of twenty minutes' drive from home so that I can see the children morning and evening on most days of the week.

Twenty-three per cent of the women claimed that their husbands' careers had taken priority, and that they had been forced to change locations to be with their husbands. This result may be a reflection of Atkinson et al.'s (1987) finding that over 80 per cent of male professionals and managers with working wives see their careers as taking precedence, compared to only 15 per cent of female professionals and managers.

A small proportion of the women said that they had restructured their working lives to accommodate their family. Ten per cent of the women had become self-employed to gain greater flexibility and control over their working lives. It is possible that self-employment represents a means for couples to achieve what Hall and Hall (1980) have described as a 'protean relationship', which is defined as a relationship in which the couple invent their own flexible way of managing their lives together, rather than simply responding to societal norms about how they should live. A protean career stresses autonomy and self-fulfilment. The individual should take charge of his/her own career and redirect it as required, rather than depending on organizational timetables. As described in the discussion of work history, most of the successful women in our sample were pro-active concerning the direction of their careers.

Several of the women described what Piotrkowski (1979) has labelled 'positive carry over' from family to work and vice versa. These women felt that career and family could be mutually enhancing. Being satisfied with their work, they were emotionally and interpersonally available to their families. The women felt that, having satisfied their need to achieve at work they were better humoured at home, which they felt was beneficial to their families and to themselves. This was illustrated by one woman:

> It is very hard to combine family and a career, but personally I would have found it much harder not having both. I find it mind-blowing

being at home because I find it difficult to identify anything that I can achieve at home. I need to strive for and work towards something.

As mentioned before, the women also found that the support of their families provided a secure base which was vital to their career success. For example:

Family and career can be combined providing you try to involve your family in your work. I know that my daughter has been very strongly influenced by my career in her own aspirations. They can be mutually enriching. I feel that you need a stable background to pursue a career.

In contrast, Evans and Bartolome (1980) found that 50 per cent of the male managers in their study described the effects of work on family as negative spill-over – that is, negative feelings such as worries, tensions and concerns generated at work spilled over into their home life. These authors suggest that individuals must learn to manage this negative emotional spill-over to achieve a healthy home life. The absence of evidence indicating negative emotional spill-over from work to family among the successful women might suggest that these women have developed effective ways of integrating their home and family lives.

Coping with role conflict

As described earlier in this chapter, Epstein (1970) and Hall (1972) have developed comprehensive lists of the coping mechanisms which people might employ to deal with role conflict. It is possible to examine the ways in which successful women distinguish between work and non-work time in terms of these coping mechanisms. Fifty-two per cent of the sample claimed that they did attempt to draw a distinction between their home and work time. Several of the women employed what Epstein has labelled 'compartmentalization'. These women felt that they could switch off from work, if they planned carefully and did not work at weekends. By timing their work, these women managed to avoid the intrusion of their work into their homes. They did comment that this was not possible all the time and that they occasionally needed to work at weekends to meet deadlines. Other women said that they preferred to work late at the office rather than taking work home. These women separated their home and working lives by physically distancing them, as described in this case:

On the whole I do make a distinction. I work very late at the office so
that I don't have to take work home, so I try to distinguish home and
work, but it gets very difficult. I try to keep weekends clear but I will
take work home if it's pressing.

Some women became more selective in their choice of friends,
mostly preferring not to socialize with work associates outside the
work environment. Epstein described this strategy as the 'elimination of social relations'. Thirty-five per cent of our sample of
successful women claimed that they did not have a strategy for
making a distinction between their work and non-work lives. The
majority of these women claimed to enjoy working and so working at
home was not arduous. This disinclination to separate their home
and work lives could be another symptom of the centrality of career
in the lives of these women. As one said:

I don't make a distinction between work and non-work time. Maybe I
should, but I don't want to. If you said what is an ideal evening out, it
would be talking shop. I suppose it is a luxury that I enjoy what I'm
doing so much that I want to do it in my social life.

What is concerning is that Gray (1982) found that the strategies
displayed by many of the successful women, such as keeping roles
totally separate, eliminating entire roles and the absence of a conscious strategy for dealing with role conflict, were all negatively
associated with satisfaction. Further research would be required
to establish whether the successful women who employ the above
strategies are satisfied.

Division of labour

Only 12 per cent of our successful women reported that their
partners helped in the running of the household. This finding is
consistent with earlier research which has shown that there is little
evidence of fifty–fifty accommodation. Wives, whether they work or
not, still perform the overwhelming majority of domestic tasks (Bird,
1979; Hall and Hall, 1980; Cunningham, 1981; Hochschild, 1989).

Although successful women took the responsibility for the domestic chore, 71 per cent did employ home help. As we have seen,
Longstreth et al. (1986) reported that the majority of self-employed
women hired a nanny, although only 8 per cent had cleaners. In
contrast, a much larger proportion of the successful women (56 per
cent) employed a cleaner.

It would seem that, in general, successful women do attempt to change the demands of their housewife role. Hall (1972) describes this as 'structural role redefinition', which is the coping mechanism most positively associated with career satisfaction. Some of the women have eliminated the maternal role and have placed priority on their working role. This coping strategy is said to be less effective than structural role redefinition, but more effective than reactive role behaviour, whereby one attempts to meat the demands of all roles. It is not clear from our data how many successful women adopted this maladaptive coping strategy, but they would seem to be in the minority.

Modelling the Careers of Successful Women

It was suggested earlier that women's careers may be represented as a triple helix composed of three strands: career, family and leisure (Rapoport and Rapoport, 1980). We may conceptualize Hall's (1976) model of sub-identities as a cross-section through the triple helix. Although there is not a direct correspondence in the diagrammatical representation, the thickness of the strands in the helix may be related to the size of the sub-identity. For example, as more of the total identity is invested in the career role, the thicker the career strand will become. It has been mentioned throughout the discussion that successful women have high career centrality. The timing of the growth of the career sub-identity varies among the women, but the majority have resolved the conflict and crystallized their career aspirations by their mid-twenties (the stage of entering the adult world). The points of cross-over in the helix equate to the overlap between the sub-identities. These points of cross-over correspond closely to the periods of transition in the lives of the successful women.

The data derived from the current study provide information on only the career and family strands in the helical structure. These data appear to confirm Rapoport and Rapoport's description of the interaction between the two strands. The successful women ex-perienced periods of stability during which they maintained a satis-factory balance between their work and family lives. These periods of stability are followed by periods of questioning and change. During these periods the women have a heightened awareness of the reciprocal impact of career and family upon each other. These periods of transition represent the main points of departure from the careers of men as described by Levinson et al. (1978).

A weaving metaphor

Hall (1984) has suggested a metaphor which incorporates the elements of both the triple helix and the sub-identity models. Hall depicts life as a process of weaving a complex fabric out of many threads. The threads may not be all the same length, ply, colour, texture or fibre. Some threads may be tightly woven, others loosely woven. The process of weaving involves a series of warp threads which are usually stationary. Weaving over and under the warp are

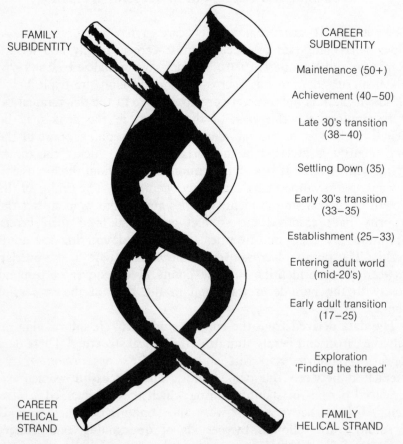

FAMILY
SUBIDENTITY

CAREER
SUBIDENTITY

Maintenance (50+)

Achievement (40–50)

Late 30's transition
(38–40)

Settling Down (35)

Early 30's transition
(33–35)

Establishment (25–33)

Entering adult world
(mid-20's)

Early adult transition
(17–25)

Exploration
'Finding the thread'

CAREER
HELICAL
STRAND

FAMILY
HELICAL STRAND

Figure 8.3   A double helix model illustrating the lifespan development of successful women

the woof and weft threads. Work may be the warp or the weft. The warp provides the structure around which other threads are woven. The finished fabric may highlight mainly warp, weft or both. The pattern may change as one moves through life and career stages. Hall proposes three stages in the weaving process:

1 finding the threads;
2 learning to weave;
3 managing the threads as a creative act.

The strands in the helix may be thought of as the threads in the fabric, while the sub-identity will represent the thickness of the thread. In the early adult transition, the women are in the process of finding the threads. This period might be extended in the case of some women who experience a period of identity diffusion and role conflict. The resolution of role priorities in the mid-twenties results in the growth of the career sub-identity.

From the age of twenty-five onwards, the career thread represents the warp in the lives of most of the successful women, which provides the structure around which the other threads are woven. The warp becomes a more prominent feature in the fabric throughout the lives of successful women as repeated career successes result in expansion of the career sub-identity.

The integration of the double-helix model with our findings concerning the age-linked structure of successful women's careers enables us to depict schematically the amount of the total identity invested in each life role over time, and the extent of the interaction between these roles over the lifespan. This schematic representation of the careers of successful women is shown in figure 8.3.

9
A Portrait of the Successful Woman

Introduction

In this final chapter we will summarize and bring together all the information gathered during this study, with the aim of presenting a picture of the successful woman. We will do this under the same broad headings as we have used throughout – namely, childhood, education, personality and motivation, work history, power and politics, and family relationships.

In doing this we have a dual purpose. First, to enhance women's understanding of their own careers and how they interrelate with other aspects of life, in the hope that this understanding will lead to the development of better coping strategies. Second, and just as important, we hope to provide men with a greater understanding of their female colleagues. If we are to progress towards a true and full equality in the workplace, both men and women must have clear concepts concerning the issues involved.

Childhood

Siblings

There is a predominance of first-born or only children among successful women. First-born children do not initially share their parents with siblings and, therefore, receive more attention, which should provide a secure environment in which to foster independent exploration. First-born children are often pushed harder to achieve, and they are also given responsibility for younger siblings at an early age. This pressure may force first-born children to test their ability while still quite young, thus gaining mastery experience and feelings of competence and self-confidence.

Later-born successful women tend to have older brothers with whom they have competed. Girls with older brothers are often more ambitious and aggressive than girls with sisters. Many will imitate and identify with an older brother, who is perceived as stronger, more competent and in control of important goals. As a result, these women may acquire what are traditionally thought of as masculine traits, such as an achievement orientation. It seems, therefore, that the sex of the older sibling may be an important variable in mediating the effects of birth order on achievement striving in women.

Parent–child relationship

A third of the women in the current study experienced a stable and trouble-free relationship with their parents. Their parents were supportive of their achievements, encouraging autonomy of decision-making. This represents the classic pattern of parent–child relations which is said to promote achievement striving and independence (Stein and Bailey, 1973). A larger proportion of the women, however, reported a problematic parent–child relationship. Several women felt that there had been a lack of bonding in their relationship with their mothers.

The various patterns of parent–child relations observed among the successful women all served to facilitate the development of a separate sense of identity, or a 'positional' identity, which is based on the individual's abilities and attributes. It has been argued that a positional identity is likely to engender a high need for achievement. Early experiences of coping independently with the environment generated a strong sense of competence and self-confidence in the women. An additional factor was the absence of excessive mother love; this is considered to aid the development of a tolerance to frustration in problem-solving and may well be crucial in dealing with stress in later life.

Kets de Vries (1980) has suggested that the lack of cohesive parental images, such as those experienced by several of the successful women, can lead to identity diffusion, followed by a desire to control an environment which in childhood has proved to be unpredictable. The need to have control over a tangible entity, and the rejection of authority figures, may be the motivation behind those who become entrepreneurs or strive to reach the top of organizations.

The majority of successful women identified one parent as being the more influential. Many successful women identified strongly with their fathers. They engaged in activities with their fathers which are normally reserved for sons. These activities are believed to create less constrained sex-role beliefs. A smaller number of women felt that their mother had been most influential in their development. Their mothers were described as strong characters with driving energy, who provided powerful feminine role models which may have helped the women to value positively and appreciate their own feminine traits. Maintaining femininity while operating in a predominantly male world may allow the women to form androgynous sex-role beliefs.

A large proportion of women described their parents as being ambitious for them to succeed, without pushing them in a prescribed direction. Democratic parenting styles are thought to lead to a 'constructed' career identify – that is, the consideration of a number of occupational alternatives, followed by a commitment to one partiuclar career choice.

Childhood events

Several women fought to overcome perceived character weaknesses during childhood. This early experience of acknowledging personal weakness and learning how to cope with it may have set a pattern of self-development throughout life. Many women also reported a family ethos of equity and a pattern of non-sexist socialization during childhood.

Social economic status and maternal employment

The majority of successful women have middle-class origins, which lends support to the contention that higher social economic status is related to stronger career orientation and innovation. A relatively large number of their mothers worked outside the home, when compared with the number of working women in their generation. This may have presented a less stereotyped view of sex roles, encouraging a career orientation. Maternal employment was not found to be predictive of plans to combine roles of career woman and mother.

Education

The majority of successful women attended grammar schools. It is not clear if this is a reflection of high ability or of their social class. Younger women were more likely to have a comprehensive education, which perhaps is likely to be the pattern in the future. Most of the women attended single-sex schools.

The successful women as a group achieved a high level of education. Fifty per cent had degrees, compared with only 6 per cent of women in general. The majority had specialized in traditionally female educational domains, which may indicate that they anticipated the subsequent sex segregation of the labour market. Only 50 per cent, however, chose their education with a career in mind. They tended to have occupational rather than organizational qualifications. This is well suited to the current economic climate, when continuous careers within the same organization cannot be guaranteed.

Personality and Motivation

Locus of control

Successful women have an internal work locus of control. Examination of the dimensional structure of this work locus of control showed them to the 'true internals'. They have a significantly stronger belief in their own ability to control the direction of their careers than a group of moderately successful women or secretaries. Scores on the scale of powerful others and chance did not differentiate the successful and moderately successful women. It is probable that 'internality' is a key factor in determining the extent of career success achieved. The majority of the women felt that luck was important in their careers, but they attributed their success to hard work, tenacity and a willingness to take advantage of the opportunities which luck presented.

Origins of locus of control

Not only warm and supportive parenting styles engender internal locus of control. In the case of many successful women, it seems that parental coolness may provide a push from the nest, leading to the exploration of cause-and-effect relations and the development of a sense of self as a causative agent. It is speculated that successful women have a low need for security, which enables them to explore the environment in the absence of a warm and supportive parent–child relationship.

Need for achievement

It is not clear whether need for achievement is a vital characteristic for obtaining outstanding career success, as the measure employed (Smith, 1973) did not distinguish between a group of highly successful and moderately successful women. This finding may be due to the lack of discriminatory power of the scale. Alternatively, the concept of need for achievement may not be as satisfactory in predicting women's career success as it has proved to be in predicting the career success of men. Successful and moderately successful women were, however, shown to have significantly higher need for achievement than a group of secretaries. On the basis of this finding, it was inferred that women in *careers* may have higher need for achievement than women in *jobs*.

The origins of need for achievement

As discussed in relation to childhood, a consistent theme seems to be emerging in the research on both male and female high flyers. All develop an early sense of independence and self-sufficiency. This separation of self from the parents facilitates the development of a positional identity, which in turn is thought to engender a need for achievement.

Self-efficacy

Management was considered to be a common factor among the wide-ranging jobs of the women in the study. Management has traditionally been stereotyped as a male domain; therefore, it was speculated that women who enter this domain would need high self-efficacy beliefs. No significant differences were observed between the successful women, moderately successful women and a group of management science students in overall managerial self-efficacy. All these individuals are committed to a career which involves a management function. Bandura (1977) claims that choice of behaviour is influenced by self-efficacy. Therefore we may infer that if individuals choose to pursue management they have relatively high managerial self-efficacy.

Successful women have high managerial self-efficacy relative to junior sales managers. This would seem to suggest that experience of success in management acts to raise self-efficacy beliefs. When asked how they had achieved their success, the successful women felt that tenacity and perseverence had been major factors. High self-efficacy may have enhanced this tenacity.

Origins of SE beliefs

Information derived from performance accomplishments may have been obtained during childhood. A family ethos of equity, described by several of the successful women, encouraged the women to believe that they could do what they wanted to do regardless of their gender. Non-sexist socialization practices would allow experimentation with a diverse set of roles, rather than forcing the women into prescribed nurturing roles. Successful performance in non-traditional roles would enhance self-efficacy beliefs in relation to these roles. Early challenges in their careers enabled the successful women to test their abilities. Successful performance provides a strong source of efficacy information.

The successful women make little mention of role models in their early lives or later in their careers. This would suggest that vicarious experience is not an important source of efficacy information for successful women. The women did, however, mention that their mentors had strengthened their self-confidence. Therefore verbal persuasion may be an important source of efficacy information for women.

Expectancy theory

The inclusion of the personality components locus of control, need for achievement and self-efficacy enhances the validity of 'expectancy theory' in predicting the behaviour of successful career women. High self-efficacy beliefs will enhance expectancy of success in managerial roles. A strong internal locus of control will act to increase the expectancy that rewards are contingent upon behaviour, rather than upon external factors such as luck or fate.

The expectancy of success resulting from performance is necessary, but not sufficient, to instigate action; the individual must also value the outcomes. If valence is determined by one's most salient needs, then individuals with a high need for achievement will place value upon successful performance. Need for achievement will be moderated by self-efficacy beliefs. Individuals with high need for achievement are motivated to increase the probability of success while minimizing the likelihood of failure. High self-efficacy beliefs will raise the individual's perception of the probability of success.

Creative style

Kirton (1976) has suggested that innovators are people who are willing to challenge existing systems and to cross boundaries. The women in the current study may be said to have crossed a significant boundary to occupy senior positions in commerce, industry and public life, which have traditionally been the preserve of men. The successful women were found to have a more innovative creative style than any group of male high flyers studied to date. This indicates an ability to think beyond existing paradigms, which may have enabled the successful women to question the traditional role of women in society. This argument is supported by examination of the adaptor–innovator scale sub-scores, which revealed that the successful women were less concerned with conforming to the rules than male high flyers. It is possible that this is because women must defy current conventions and transgress traditional sex roles if they are to be successful in a male-dominated environment.

Work History

Early careers

The position of the successful women in terms of Marcia's (1966) concept of 'identity status' was gauged by the degree of parental involvement in careers, and the extent of conscious career decision-making. A very small number of the women said that their parents had been involved in their choice of career. Parental attempts to prescribe occupational direction were often rejected and, therefore, did not result in 'foreclosed identity' – that is, commitment to occupational goals which are not personally selected. These women often drifted between jobs in their early careers, suggesting a period of 'identity diffusion'.

Women whose parents were ambivalent or permissive towards their career decision-making were less likely to make a conscious decision to have a career. Ambivalent parenting styles appear to generate role conflict, causing an extended period of exploration. Women experiencing such styles were often prompted to make late career decisions upon the realization that they did not want to be housewives, or following separation from a partner.

The majority of the successful women reported that their parents had no involvement in their choice of career, which allowed the consideration of a number of occupational alternatives. Waterman (1982) suggests that democratic parenting styles lead to 'achieved identity'. A conscious decision was facilitated by parents who were ambitious but not prescriptive. An early career decision was engendered by ambitious parents who are supportive and encouraging in relation to occupational pursuits.

As a group, the majority of successful women do make a conscious decision to have a career which is not parentally prescribed, from which we may infer that they have an achieved identity status. One third of the successful women made a late career commitment preceding a period in which they had no coherent career direction. This would seem to indicate that, for a large proportion of women, forging a vocational identity is a complex process involving role conflicts which may lead to an extended period of identity diffusion. Women who followed this pattern were classified as 'late starters' although some of the professionals experienced an extended exploratory phase.

Women who took early career decisions were more likely to enter their chosen occupation on the bottom rung. These women tended to be goal directed and had a planned route to achieve their goal. Women who made an early commitment to work were classified as 'go-getters' or 'entrepreneurs'.

The majority of successful women had not planned their careers in a structured or detailed form. Many regretted their poor career management, which they believed had lead to missed opportunities. Women who had no coherent direction in their early careers were less likely to engage in planning.

Development of career concepts

Several of the women experienced changes in their career concepts throughout their careers. Women who had no coherent direction in their early careers were said to have 'transitory' career concepts. These women developed a 'spiral' career concept, if and when they separated from a partner. The separation lead to a raised awareness of their own needs, and a redefinition of self in terms of their own abilites and attributes. This development of a positional identity may lead to the convergence of 'connected' and 'separate' selves. The spiral concept maintains the flexibility of the transitory concept, but integrates other aspects of the self into the career concept.

Some of the women who began their careers with a 'linear' concept, shifted to a spiral concept when confronted with role conflict generated by the need to balance work and family life. The career concepts of these women became more differentiated. A small number of the women who had a 'steady-state' career concept early in their working lives, investing their energy in their families, were prompted to develop a linear career concept following a divorce. This created the need for financial independence, which they achieved by striving for linear promotion.

The majority of our sample felt that career was an integral part of their identity. This is characteristic of a spiral career concept. It also supports the suggestion that in later stages of their careers successful women have developed a positional identity – that is, that they define themselves in terms of their career achievements.

Evidence of linear career concepts was found in the reports of several women. They perceived career to be a planned route from A to B, with each step becoming more challenging. These women incorporate both promotion and self-development into their linear career concept.

Aspects of a successful career

A large number of successful women experienced an early challenge in their careers. These women coped successfully with this challenge. The acquisition of evidence of their competence, through performance accomplishment and experience of psychological success, should raise self-efficacy beliefs and hence the setting of more challenging goals in the future. Therefore it seems true to say that, in the case of career women, success generates success. The successful women experienced a wide range of functions either in the same large organization, in different organizations or in an incubator organization. A more common path among professionals was to follow a career track within the same organization. It is possible that professional firms place greater emphasis on other aspects, such as loyalty and professional expertise, than on breadth of experience.

The most common prompt for movement between jobs was a blocked career path. Women made 'out-spiralling' moves to achieve promotion. This cannot be taken as evidence for the existence of the 'glass ceiling', as it is a strategy adopted by both men and women to achieve promotion.

Mentoring

None of the successful women had been involved in formal mentoring schemes, although most of them identified an individual who had been influential in their careers. The women mentioned both career and psychosocial benefits of having a mentor. The mentors had acted to raise confidence and belief in abilities, which suggests that the women have a need for psychological affirmation. Mentors also gave practical help, providing opportunities to demonstrate ability. The mentors did not act as role models.

Motivation

The motivations of successful women were found to be very similar to those of male high flyers (Cox and Cooper, 1988). Successful women were primarily motivated by the intrinsic desire to excel in their work. The demand for challenging and interesting work is stronger than the desire for promotion *per se*. They have a tendency to prefer challenging tasks, which could be interpreted as high mastery motivation. It has also been argued that successful women have high aspirations and career centrality, all of which indicate a high need for achievement. One third of the women claimed to be externally driven by the need to see the concrete results of their efforts and to obtain recognition from others for their successes. The need for concrete feedback is a characteristic which has often been associated with a high need for achievement (McClelland et al., 1953).

The theme of self-development was mentioned by a quarter of the successful women. By comparison, this was not a predominant theme among male high flyers (Cox and Cooper, 1988). The desire for self-development may be an artefact of high ego ideals, which means that the women are constantly striving to achieve high standards which are self-imposed. High ego ideals were evident in childhood reports of attempts to overcome personal weaknesses. The gap between ego and ego ideals provides a constant source of motivation activation.

Career orientation

The majority of successful women displayed a 'getting high' orientation. These women sought challenge and excitement from their work. Although Derr (1986) suggests that the getting high orientation is usually compatible with the spiral career concept, the current study showed that many women with a linear career concept also exhibited this orientation. In striving to achieve long-term goals, 'linears' seek constant challenge. This resembles Driver's (1988) description of 'active technical linears' who strive for the top and at the same time seek challenge achievement and recognition for their expertise.

Career stages

The careers of the successful women were classified into five basic patterns which represent the order in which tasks associated with career development emerged. These patterns were labelled: late starters, professionals, go-getters, entrepreneurs and unconventional. The issues observed in each of the five career patterns were integrated with issues concerning the combination of career and family roles, to create a model of career development for successful women.

An age-linked career-stage structure emerged from the work histories of the successful women. This career-stage model has strong similarities to the model of male careers proposed Levinson et al. (1978). It is suggested that continuous employment and correct timing of organization careers are perceived to be pivotal values which are a prerequisite for success. Women experience periods of stability and transition. The periods of transition represent the main points of departure from the male career model.

Power and Politics

Successful women of the 1990s do distinguish between formal and informal systems of influence. Almost the entire sample claimed to be aware of political processes operating in the workplace. Promotion was believed to involve both competence and selling oneself to those with the power to promote. A large proportion of the successful women had played team games, which are said to facilitate understanding of interpersonal relations.

The successful women were classified as 'wise politicians'. They were sensitive to the organizational systems of influence, but they avoided becoming entrenched in political games, which were frequently described in negative terms. It is difficult to ascertain the true extent to which successful women are willing to employ political strategies to further their own ends, owing to the negative connotations associated with politics and the desire, on the part of the respondent, to give socially acceptable responses.

Political styles

The successful women were classified as either 'team coaches' or 'visionaries'. Both operate on a system of personal or unshared meaning. This was also reflected in the adaptor–innovator scores, indicating low regard for rule conformity. These women seem to be able to think beyond existing paradigms. This may give them the ability to challenge the normative nature of power, and to think beyond the constraints allocated to women in society and organizational settings.

Family Relationships

Current family situation

Marriage does not appear to preclude success among women, since 58 per cent of the women in the study were married. Family seems to act as a social support system. Except in two cases, all the partners of successful women were described as supportive of their career pursuits. They all believed that a supportive partner was a secure base upon which they had built their careers.

Half of the women had children. Only the older women in the sample had taken career breaks. A common pattern was to wait until their career was well established, then have children in their early thirties. These women took minimum maternity leave, because a career break was perceived as stepping off the fast track. This emphasized the perceived importance of continuous employment among those who have achieved career success. This finding raises the issue of whether family and occupational roles can realistically co-exist within institutions which continue to embody traditional male values.

Processes linking career and family

Work takes a central role in the lives of successful women. The subordination of a family role in favour of a career suggests a process of accommodation. Very few women said that family took priority over their careers, which contradicts Marshall's (1984) contention that for women work does not take priority over all other life areas. In the case of most successful women, work clearly does take priority. A small number of women compensated for a failure in their personal lives by striving for success in their careers.

Role conflict

The majority of the successful women did not report role conflict between work and family. On the other hand, role overload did have an impact on home life. One fifth of the women found that they suffered what Piotrkowski (1979) has termed 'energy deficit' – that is, the successful women work so hard on their careers that they do not have the psychological or physical energy left to invest in their personal lives. Several women described positive carry-over from work to family, and vice versa. Family and work were perceived to be mutually enhancing. A small number of the women felt that their family lives and a negative impact upon their careers because of reduced mobility or following their husbands' careers.

Coping

Half of the successful women actively attempted to manage the conflict between the work and family roles. Several women practised compartmentalization as a means of separating work and home lives. This was achieved by careful planning or by physically distancing work from home (i.e. working late in the office to avoid taking work home). One third of the women had no conscious strategy for distinguishing between work and home time. This has been described as a dysfunctional approach to coping with role conflict (Hall, 1972). The successful women, however, enjoyed their work and the spill-over of work into their personal lives was not perceived to be a hardship. The disinclination to separate work and personal lives provides further evidence of career centrality.

Division of labour

In general the partners of successful women do not help with household chores or childcare. Although the successful women take the major responsibility for domestic chores, the majority do employ home help. In changing the demands of their family role, the women engage in 'structural role redefinition', which Hall (1972) suggests is the coping mechanism most positively associated with career satisfaction.

Exploiting Opportunities for Women in the 1990s

We suggested in chapter 1 that the prospects for women in the 1990s were favourable. A predicted growth in the traditionally female-dominated service sector, an increase in the numbers of high-level jobs, and a decline in the numbers of young people entering the labour force led the authors to suggest that the under-utilization of women would be economic suicide (see also Hansard Society Report, 1990). The so called 'demographic time bomb' was presented as a potential opportunity for women to strive for the top. It was suggested that organizations would have to begin to sell themselves to women and, as the Hansard Society Report suggests, employers would have to recognize that the best man for the job in the 1990s might be a woman.

These optimistic predictions have yet to be realized. The concern among employers about the demographic time bomb faded considerably during 1991. This is a reflection of the fact that, owing to economic recession, the bomb has yet to explode. The workforce in employment in the UK was 26,394,000 in March 1991. This represented a fall of 253,000 in the first quarter of that year. Unemployment in the UK rose by 67,000 between June and July 1991, to 2,368,100. This was the sixteenth consecutive month in which unemployment had risen, following the continuous fall in the forty-four months to March 1990. In September 1991 the level was 761,500 higher than March 1990 when the current upward trend began. Long-term unemployment among eighteen–twenty-four-year-olds is now 32 per cent higher than it was the previous year. The growth in the service sector peaked early in 1990, since which time it has seen a slight decline (*Employment Gazette*, September 1991).

Despite the recession and increased unemployment, Davidson (1990) reports that the female workforce has continued to grow. She suggests that this demonstrates that women are no longer 'political ping-pong balls' to be bounced in and out of the workforce with shifts in economic supply and demand. In addition, the opening of the free European market will pressurize British employers to comply with the European Community directives on equal opportunities. These factors lead Davidson to the optimistic conclusion that the advancement made for women over the next decade will not regress when the demographic tide turns against them in the 2000s.

A more pessimistic outlook might consider that any changes brought about by the skill shortage are likely to remain superficial and are unlikely to survive a reversal of economic need. Unless there is a qualitative change in organizational culture, personnel policies and practices, then it is doubtful whether women will continue to build on the opportunities created by the predicted demographic time bomb.

So far the experience of work has not allowed women to progress on their own terms. Women are still expected to conform to a 'male model' of a successful career. The model of successful women's lifespan development showed that the majority of successful women displayed high career centrality. These women worked continuously and full time, fitting their domestic responsibilities around their work or choosing to remain childless. Continuous, full-time employment is still perceived to be a 'pivotal' value which is a prerequisite for career success. The current research, therefore, confirms the observation made by Hirsh and Jackson (1990) that successful women are 'most realistically seen as a self-selected population of highly career oriented survivors.'

A qualitative change in the nature of 'successful career'

If we are to achieve 'genuine equality of opportunity in all aspects of life' then change is required in the prevailing stereotype of a successful career. As Hirsh and Jackson suggest, careers should be accommodated around the reality of women's lives, allowing them to make a meaningful investment in both occupational and family roles. It is necessary for equal opportunities policies, personnel and training practices to reflect the fact that many women's career patterns are still different from those of most men. Some examples of good practice are listed below:

1 Redesigning jobs to make part-time work and job-sharing realistic options, with benefits and promotion opportunities.
2 Flexible career-break schemes, retainers, and re-entry schemes.

3 Returner programmes, resolving practical issues and training managers to raise their awareness of family issues.
4 Family support and enhanced maternity and paternity leave.
5 Changing assumptions about the need for continuous employment and geographic mobility.
6 Encouraging late starters and changing attitudes about age-linked structures for promotion.
7 Improved childcare facilities.

The current statistics show that Britain still has a long way to go towards achieving these objectives. At present, the UK has the worst childcare and parental provision in Europe. Only 1.3 per cent of under-fives have a nursery place. Less than 1 in 5000 women can use nurseries provided by employers, and only 1 in 20,000 gets a childcare allowance from her employer. Fewer than 1 in 50 organizations have job-sharing schemes, home working or school-term deals. Only 25 per cent are offering some optional part-time working and flexitime, and only 18 per cent are allowing job sharing. Davidson questions how rapidly this is likely to change, given the results of a recent survey conducted by the Institute of Manpower Studies (Hirsh and Jackson, 1990), which showed that only 4 per cent of companies intended to reform their policies within the next two years.

Postscript – Successful Women's Advice to Other Women

We thought it would be interesting to ask our group of high achievers what advice they would give to other women who aspired to be successful. Most of the women pointed to the need to be single minded. They advised women to make their choices, to know what they wanted and what their priorities were. Having reached such a decision, they encouraged women to 'go for it' and to aim high. As one women put it:

Life's about choices and if you take a choice about having a serious career, then you've got to be honest with yourself and say you can't have everything and do it well. Those who think that they can are fooling themselves and they are going to come to grief. If you look at how men get on, it's because they're focused on their career and their wives assist them in getting on. Women have got to be as serious as that and if we're not going to take ourselves seriously then we are not going to succeed. Women have too many self-doubts. Once you make a choice, stick with it. I'm a strong believer that the stayers win. The race is for stayers and it's all about delivering excellence. Mediocrity does not count.

Many of our successful women mentioned the importance of persistence and stressed the need to 'keep battling' to achieve their objectives. They felt that success required making an extra effort and that the process of achieving success would be harder for a woman. Having made the point that success is harder for a woman to achieve, they also stressed that women should not allow their femininity to become an issue. Women were discouraged from having a 'chip on their shoulder'. Rather, it was advised that women should be aware that it would be hard, but that they should look for ways to overcome the obstacles in their path. As one woman suggested: 'You have to recognize that it will be harder for a woman than a fella. It's no good fighting against that – it's a fact of life. You need to look for ways of getting around it.'

In addition, a number of our successful women emphasized the need to let those in power know their ambitions, rather than waiting to be noticed. Aspiring women were discouraged from undervaluing themselves and as a result underselling themselves. As one women said:

> Don't underestimate yourself. Women have a dreadful tendency to underestimate how good they are. Women are often better, but they don't sing about it. I think that women feel that if they are really good then it will get noticed, but that really is no use. Blow your own trumpet! I've had to learn that the hard way.

Others advised that women should try to think about their image and to appear 'professional'. Several women stressed the importance of honesty and integrity, and still others felt that it was important to avoid copying men. They considered that women should attempt to be themselves rather than adapting to the male model. This was explained by one senior woman executive as follows:

> You have got to decide what you want. Women often expect other people to be psychic, but you have to tell people what you want. What we've got wrong is that many women have cloned to join, but I would say above all don't clone because you don't bring your own skills to the table, you bring a copy of other people's.

In summary, our successful group felt that women needed to be single minded, striving to meet their ambitions, persistent, professional, honest and, above all, to be themselves. In this process, they acknowledge that there are many 'ghosts' to overcome, within themselves, within others and within society. They also have a sense of optimism and hope that the ghosts inherent in all of us – as described by Henrik Ibsen in his play *Ghosts* – would welcome the light, and not be terrified by it:

But I'm coming to believe that all of us are ghosts. . . . It's not just what we inherit from our mothers and fathers. It's also the shadows of dead ideas and opinions and convictions. They're no longer alive, but they grip us all the same, and hold on to us against our will. All I have to do is open a newspaper to see ghosts hovering between the lines. They are haunting the whole country, those stubborn phantoms – so many of them, so thick, they're like an impenetrable dark mist. And here we are, all of us, so abjectly terrified by the light.

References

Acker, J. (1987) Women and work in the social sciences. In A. H. Stromberg and S. Harkess (eds), *Women Working: theories and facts in perspective*, Palo Alto, Calif.: Mayfield Publishing Co.

Adams, J. M. (1984) When working women become pregnant. *New England Business*, February, 18–21.

Alban Metcalfe, B. (1987) Male and female managers: An analysis of biographical and self-concept data. *Work and Stress*, 1, 207–19.

Allan, P. (1981) Managers at work: A large scale study of the managerial job in the New York City Government. *Academy of Management Journal*, 24, 613–19.

Almquist, E. M. (1974) Sex stereotypes in occupational choice: The case for college women. *Journal of Vocational Behaviour*, 5, 13–21.

Almquist, E. M. (1977) Women in the labour force. *Signs: A Journal of Women in Culture and Society*, 2, 843–55.

Almquist, E. M. and Angrist, S. S. (1971) 'Career salience and atypicality of occupational choice among college women'. *Journal of Marriage and the Family*, 32, 242–9.

Alston, A. (1987) *Equal Opportunities: a careers guide*, Harmondsworth, Middx: Penguin.

Andrisani, P. and Nestel, G. (1976) Internal–external control as contributor and outcome of work experience. *Journal of Applied Psychology*, 62, 156–65.

Archer, S. L. (1985) Career and/or family: The identity process for adolescent girls. *Youth and Society*, 16, 289–314.

Arnold, V. and Davidson, M. J. (1990) Adopt a mentor – The way ahead for women managers?. *Women in Management Review and Abstracts*, 5 (1), 10–18.

Arroba, T. and James, K. (1987) Are politics palatable to women managers? How can women make wise moves at work?. *Women in Management Review*, 10 (3), 123–30.

Ashburner, L. (1989) Men managers and women workers: women

employees as an under used resource. Paper to the Third Annual Conference of the British Academy of Management.

Association of University Teachers (1990). Cited in the report of the Hansard Society Commision on Women at the Top, January 1990.

Astin, H. S. (1968) 'The career development of girls during high school years'. *Journal of Counseling Psychology*, 15, 536–40.

Astin, H. S. (1984) The meaning of work in women's lives: A sociopsychological model of career choice and work behaviour. *Counseling Psychologist*, 12, 117–26.

Astin, H. S. and Myint, T. (1971) Career development of young women during the post high school years. *Journal of Counseling Psychology Monograph*, 18, 369–93.

Atkinson, J. W. (1958) *Motives in Fantasy, Action and Society*, Princeton, NJ: Van Nostrand.

Atkinson, J. W. (1964) *An Introduction to Motivation*, Princeton, NJ: Van Nostrand.

Atkinson, J. W. (1978) The mainsprings of achievement-oriented activity. In J. Atkinson and J. Raynor (eds), *Personality, Motivation and Achievement*, New York: Halsted.

Atkinson, J. W. and Feather, N. T. (1966) *Theory of Achievement Motivation*, New York: Wiley.

Atkinson, J. W. and Raynor, J. (1978) *Personality, Motivation and Achievement*, New York: Halsted.

Atkinson, J. et al. (1987) Relocating managers and professional staff. *IMS Report*, 139, University of Sussex: Institute of Manpower Studies.

Auster, C. J. and Auster, D. (1981) 'Factors influencing women's choice of non-traditional careers: The role of the family, peers and counsellors'. *Vocational Guidance Quarterly*, 29, 253–63.

Bakan, D. (1966) *The Duality of Human Existence*, Boston: Beacon Press.

Banducci, R. (1967) 'The effect of mother's employment on the achievement aspirations and expectations of the child'. *Personnel and Guidance Journal*, 46, 263–7.

Bandura, A. (1977) *Social Learning Theory*, Englewood Cliffs, NJ: Prentice Hall.

Bandura, A. (1982) Self efficacy mechanism in human agency. *American Psychologist*, 37 (2), 122–47.

Bandura, A. (1986) *Social Foundations of Thought and Action: a social cognitive theory*, Englewood Cliffs, NJ: Prentice Hall.

Bandura, A. and Cervone, D. (1986) Differential engagement of self-reactive influences in cognitive motivation. *Organisational Behaviour and Human Decision Processes*, 38, 92–113.

Bandura, A. and Wood, R. E. (1989) 'Effects of perceived controllability and performance standards on self-regulation of complex decision making'. *Journal of Consulting and Clinical Psychology*, 56, 805–14.

Bandura, A., Reese, L. and Adams, N. E. (1982) Microanalysis of action and fear arousal as a function of differential levels of perceived self efficacy. *Journal of Personality and Social Psychology*, 55, 805–14.

Barclay, L. (1982) Social learning theory: A framework for discrimination research. *Academy of Management Review*, 7, 587–94.

Bardwick, J. M. (1971) *The Psychology of Women: a study of biosocial conflict*, New York: Harper and Row.

Bardwick, J. M. (1979) *In Transition*, London: Holt Rinehart and Winston.

Barling, J. and Beattie, R. (1983) Self efficacy beliefs and sales performance. *Journal of Organisational Behaviour Management*, 5, 41–51.

Barnier, L. A. (1982) A study of the mentoring relationship: An analysis of its relation to career and adult development in higher education and business. *Dissertation Abstracts International*, 42(7-A), 3012–13.

Barron, K. D. and Norris, G. M. (1976) Sexual divisions and the dual labour market. In D. Barker and S. Allen *Dependence and Exploitation in Work and Marriage*, London: Longman.

Bartolome, F. (1972) Executives as human beings. *Harvard Business Review*, 50, 60–69.

Baumrind, D. (1971) Current patterns of parental authority. *Developmental Psychology Monograph*, 4(1, pt 2).

Bellaby, P. (1977) *The Sociology of Comprehensive Schooling*, London: Methuen.

Berk, R. A. and Berk, S. F. (1979) *Labour and Leisure at Home: content and organization of the household day*, Beverly Hills, Calif.: Sage Publications.

Bernard, J. (1971) *Women and the Public Interest: an essay on policy and protest*, Chicago: Aldine.

Bernard, J. (1978) Models for the relationship between the world of women and the world of men. In L. Kriesberg (ed.) *Research on Social Movements, Conflicts and Change*, Greenwich: JAI.

Bernard, J. (1981) *The Female World*, New York: Free Press.

Betz, N. E. and Hackett, G. (1986) Applications for self efficacy theory to understand career choice behaviour. *Journal of Social and Clinical Psychology*, 4, 279–89.

Beutel, N. J. (1986) 'Conflict between work–family and student–family roles: Some sources and consequences'. Working paper, Division of Research, W. Paul Stillman School of Business, Seton Hall University.

Bevan, S., Buchan, J. and Hayday, S. (1990) Women in hospital pharmacy. *IMS Report*, 182, University of Sussex: Institute of Manpower Studies.

Bird, C. (1979) *The Two Paycheck Marriage: how women at work are changing life in America*, New York: Pocket Books.

Bishop, R. C. and Bresser, K. (1986) Cited in R. A. Noe (1988) Women in mentoring: A review and research agenda. *Academy of Management Review*, 3 (1), 65–78.

Blaska, B. (1978) College women's career and marriage aspirations: A review of the literature. *Journal of College Student Personnel*, 19, 302–6.

Block, J. H. (1977) Another look at sex differences in the socialization behaviours of mothers and fathers. In *Psychology of Women: future directions of research*, New York: Psychological Dimensions.

Blum, L. and Smith, V. (1988) Women's mobility in the corporation: A critique of the politics of optimism. *Journal of Women in Culture and Society*, 13 (31), 528–45.

Boardman, S. K., Hartington, C. C. and Horowitz, S. V. (1987) Successful women: A psychological investigation of family class and educational origins. In B. A. Gutek and L. Larwood (eds) *Women's Career Development*, Beverly Hills, Calif.: Sage Publications.

Boecker, W., Blair, R., Francis Van Loo, M. and Roberts, K. (1985) 'Are the expectations of women being met?' *Californian Management Review*, 27 (3), 148–60.

Bray, D. W., Campbell, R. J. and Grant, D. L. (1974) *Formative Years in Business: a long term AT and T study of managerial lives*, New York: John Wiley.

Brief, A. P. and Oliver, R. L. (1976) Male–female differences in work attitudes among retail sales staff. *Journal of Applied Psychology*, 5, 266–88.

Brooks, L. (1984) *Counseling Special Groups: women and ethnic minorities*. In D. Brown and L. Brooks and associates (eds) *Career Choice and Development*, San Francisco: Jossey Bass.

Broverman, I. K., Broverman, D. M., Clarkson, F. E., Rosenkrantz, P. and Vogel, S. R. (1970) Sex role stereotypes and clinical judgement of mental health. *Journal of Consulting Psychology*, 34, 595–611.

Brockhaus, R. H. (1980) Psychological and environmental factors which distinguish the successful from the unsuccessful entrepreneurs. *Proceedings of the 40th Meeting of the Academy of Management*, 369–72.

Brown, R. (1982) Work histories, career strategies and class structure. In A. Giddens and G. Mackensie (eds) *Social Class and the Division of Labour*, Cambridge: Cambridge University Press.

Buchanan, D. and Boddy, D. (1983) *Organisations in the Computer Age: Technological imperatives and strategic choice*, Aldershot: Gower.

Burke, R. J. (1984) Mentors in organisations. *Group & Organisation Studies*, 9, 353–72.

Burlin, F. (1976) 'The relationship of parental education and maternal work and occupational aspiration in adolescent females'. *Journal of Vocational Behaviour*, 9, 99–106.

Campbell, D. (1971) The clash between beautiful women and science. In A. Theodore (ed.) *The Professional Woman*, London: Century.

Carter, S. and Cannon, T. (1988) *Women in Business*, Unviersity of Stirling: Scottish Enterprise Foundation.

Cartwright, L. F. (1972) 'Conscious factors entering the career decision of women who study medicine'. *Journal of Social Issues*, 28, 201–15.

Cervone, D. (1989) Effects of envisioning future activities on self efficacy judgements and motivation: an availability heuristic interpretation. *Cognitive Therapy and Research*, 13, 247–61.

Chodorow, N. (1978) *The Reproduction of Mothering*, Berkeley: University of California Press.

Chusmir, L. H. (1985) Motivation to manage: is gender a factor?. *Psychology of Women Quarterly*, 9, 153–9.

Clement, S. (1987) The self-efficacy expectations and occupational preferences of females and males. *Journal of Occupational Psychology*, 60, 257–65.

Clutterbuck, D. and Devine, M. (1987) Having a mentor: a help or a hindrance? In D. Clutterbuck and M. Devine (eds) *Business-women: Present and Future*, Basingstoke: Macmillan.

Collard, E. D. (1964) Achievement motive in the four-year-old child and its relationship to achievement expectancies of the mother. Unpublished doctoral dissertation, University of Michigan.

Collins, J. L. (1982) Self efficacy and ability in achievement behaviour. Paper presented at the annual meeting of the American Educational Research Association.

Colwill, N. (1984) Lucky Lucy and Able Adam: to what do you attribute your success?. *Business Horizons*.

Constable, J. and McCormick, R. (1987) *The Making of British Managers*, London: BIM/CBI.

Cooper C. L. and Hingley, P. (1983) *The Change Makers*, London: Harper & Row.

Coser, R. (1982) Where have all the women gone? Like the sediment of a good wine they have sunk to the bottom. In C. F. Epstein and R. Coser (eds) *Access to Power*, London: Allen & Unwin.

Coser, R. and Rokoff, G. (1971) Women in the occupational world: social disruption and conflict. In Kahn, Hut, Daniels and Colvard (eds) *Women and Work Problems and Perspectives*, Oxford: Oxford University Press.

Cox, C. and Cooper, C. L. (1988) *High Flyers*, Oxford: Basil Blackwell.

Cox, C. and Jennings, R. (1990) The foundations of success: the development, work experience and characteristics of British entrepreneurs and intrapreneurs. Paper presented at ENDEC International Entrepreneurship Conference, Singapore.

Crandall, V. C. (1969) Sex differences in expectancy of intellectual and academic reinforcement. In C. P. Smith (ed.) *Achievement-related Motives in Children*, New York: Russel Sage.

Crandall, V. C. (1973) Differences in parental antecedents of internal–external control in children and young adulthood. Paper presented at the American Psychological Association Convention, Montreal.

Crandall, V. J. and Rabson, A. (1960) Children's repetition choices in an intellectual achievement situation following success and failure. *Journal of Genetic Psychology*, 97, 161–8.

Crompton, R. and Sanderson, K. (1986) Credentials and careers: some implications of the increase in professional qualifications amongst women. *Sociology*, 20 (1) 25–42.

Crosby, F. J. (1982) *Relative Deprivation and Working Women*, New York: Oxford University Press.

Crowley et al. (1973) 'Seven deadly truths about women'. *Psychology Today*, March, 94–6.

Cunningham, I. (1981) Management development and women. *Management Education and Development*, 12 (1), 5–14.

Davidson, M. J. (1990) Exploiting the opportunities of the 1990s for women in the work place. Paper presented at Achieving Success as a Women Manager Conference.

Davidson, M. J. and Cooper, C. L. (1983) *Stress and the Woman Manager*, London: Martin Robertson.

Davidson, M. J. and Cooper, C. L. (1987) Female managers in Britain – a comparative perspective. *Human Resource Management*, summer, 26, 217–42.

Davies, J. (1985) Why are women not where the power is? An examination of the maintenance of power elites. *Management Education and Development*, 16 (3), 278–88.

Davis, W. L. and Phares, E. J. (1967) Internal–external control as a determinant of information seeking in a social influence situation. *Journal of Personality*, 35, 547–61.

Davis, W. L. and Phares E. J. (1969) 'Parental antecedent of internal–external control of reinforcement'. *Psychological Reports*, 24, 427–36.

Department of Employment (1989) *New Earnings Survey 1988*, London: HMSO.

Derr, C. B. (1986) *Managing the New Careerist*, San Francisco: Jossey Bass.

Devereaux, E. C. et al. (1969) Child rearing in England and the United States: a cross sectional comparison. *Journal of Marriage and Family*, 257–70.

Dex, S. (1984) *Women's Occupational Mobility: a lifetime perspective*, London: Macmillan.

Dickson, D. (1974) *Alternative Technology and the Politics of Technological Change*, London: Fontana.

Driver, M. J. (1979) Career concepts and career management in organisations. In C. L. Cooper (ed.) *Behavioural Problems in Organisations*, Englewood Cliffs, NJ: Prentice Hall.

Driver, M. J. (1988) Careers: a review of personal and organisational research. In C. L. Cooper and I. T. Robertson (eds) *International Review of Industrial and Organisational Psychology*, New York: John Wiley & Sons.

Driver, M. J. and Mock, T. (1975) Information processing, decision style theory and accounting information systems. *Accounting Review*, 50, 490–508.

Drucker, P. F. (1969) 'Management's new role'. *Harvard Business Review*, 47, 49–54.

Elias, P. and Main, D. (1982) *Women's Working Lives*, University of Warwick: Institute for Employment Research.

Epstein, C. F. (1970) Encountering the male establishment: sex-status limits on women's careers in the professions. *American Journal of Sociology*, 75, 965–82.

Epstein, C. F. (1981) *Women in Law*, New York: Basic Books.

Equal Opportunities Commission (1984) Nouth Annual Report, London: HMSO.

Erikson, E. H. (1968) *Identity: youth and crisis*, London: Faber & Faber.

Evans, P. and Bartolome, F. (1984) *Must Success Cost So Much?*, London: Grand McIntyre.

Eysenck, H. J. and Cookson, D. (1970) 'Personality in primary children: 111 – Family background'. *British Journal of Educational Psychology*, 40, 117–31.

Farmer, H. S. (1985) Model of career and achievement motivation for women and men. *Journal of Counseling Psychology*, 32 (3), 363–90.

Festinger, L. (1957) *A Theory of Cognitive Dissonance*, Evanston, Ill.: Row Peterson.

Fitzgerald, L. F. and Betz, N. E. (1983) *Issues in the vocational psychology of women*. In W. B. Walsh and O. H. Osipow (eds) *Handbook of Vocational Psychology*, 1, ch. 3.

Fitzgerald, L. F. and O'Crites, J. O. (1980) Towards a career psychology of women: What do we know? What do we need to know? *Journal of Counseling Psychology*, 27 (1), 44–62.

Forrest, L. and Mikolaitis, N. (1986) The relational component of identity: an expansion of career development theory. *The Career Development Quarterly*, 35 (2), 76–88.

Foster, J. (1988) 'Balancing work and the family: Divided loyalties or constructive partnership?' *Personnel Management*, 38–41.

Fraker, S. (1984) Why top jobs elude female executives. *Best of Business*, 6 (2), 44–50.

Frieze, I. H., Fisher, J. R., Hanusa, B. H., McHugh, M. C. and Valle, V. A. (1978) Attributions of the causes of success and failure as external barriers to achievement. In J. L. Sherman and F. L. Denmark (eds) *The Psychology of Women: future directions in research*, New York: Psychological Dimensions.

Fuchs, V. R. (1988) *Women's Quest for Economic Equality*, Cambridge, Mass.: Harvard University Press.

Garland, H. and Price, K. H. (1977) 'Attitudes towards women in management and causal attributions for their success and failure in a managerial position'. *Journal of Applied Psychology*, 62 (2), 29–33.

George P. and Kumnerow, J. (1981) 'Mentoring for career women'. *Training*, 18 (2), 44–9.

Gilbert, L. A. (1984) Comments on the meaning of work in women's lives. *Counseling Psychologist*, 12, 129–30.

Gilligan, C. (1979) Woman's place in a man's life cycle. *Harvard Educational Review*, 49, 431–46.

Gilligan, C. (1982) *In a Different Voice*, Cambridge, Mass.: Harvard University Press.

Ginzberg, E., Ginsberg, S. W., Atelrad, S. and Herma, J. L. (1951) *Occupational Choice: an approach to a general theory*, New York: Columbia University Press.

Goertzel, M. G., Goertzel, M. V. and Goertzel, T. (1978) *300 Eminent Personalities*, San Francisco: Jossey Bass.

Goffee, R. and Scase, R. (1985) *Women in Charge: the experience of female entrepreneurs*, London: George Allen & Unwin.

Goodale, J. G. and Hall, D. T. (1976) 'Inheriting a career: The influence of sex, values and parents'. *Journal of Vocational Behaviour*, 8, 19–30.

Goode, W. J. (1960) A theory of role strain. *American Sociological Review*, 25, 483–96.

Gottfredson, L. (1981) Circumscription and compromise: a developmental theory of occupational aspirations. *Journal of Counseling Psychology*, 28, 545–79.

Gray, J. D. (1980) Role conflicts and coping strategies in married professional women. *Dissertation Abstract*, 40, 3781–A.

Gray, J. D. (1980) The married professional woman: an examination of her role conflicts and coping strategies. *Psychology of Women Quarterly*, 7, 235–43.

Griffin, J. H. (1962) *Black Like Me*, London: Collins.

Grotevant, H. D. and Thorbecke, W. L. (1982) Sex differences in styles of occupational identity formation in late adolescence. *Developmental Psychology*, 18, 396–405.

Gutek, B. A., Nakamura, C. Y., and Nieva, V. F. (1981) The interdependence of work and family roles. *Journal of Occupational Behaviour*, 1, 1–16.

Gutek, B. A., Larwood, L. and Stromberg, A. (1986) Women at work. In C. L. Cooper and I. T. Robertson (eds) *International Review of Industrial and Organisational Psychology*, New York: John Wiley.

Gutek, B. A. and Larwood, L. (1987) *Women's Career Development*, Beverly Hills, Calif.: Sage Publications.

Haas, L. (1978) Benefits and problems of egalitarian marriage: a study of role sharing couples. ERIC Microfiche ED 165052.

Hackett, G. and Betz, N. E. (1981) A self efficacy approach to the career development of women. *Journal of Vocational Behaviour*, 18, 326–39.

Hakim, C. (1981) Job segregation: trends in the 1970s. *Employment Gazette*.

Hall, D. T. (1972) A model of coping with role conflicts: the role behaviour of college educated women. *Administrative Science Quarterly*, 17, 471–86.

Hall, D. T. (1976) *Careers in Organizations*, Santa Monica, Calif.: Goodyear.

Hall, D. T. and Hall, F. S. (1980) Stress and the dual career couple. In C. L. Cooper and R. Payne (eds) *Current Concerns in Occupational Stress*, New York: John Wiley.

Hall, F. S. (1984) Loose threads and life fabrics: an extended metaphor about personal, professional and organisational lives. In M. D. Lee and R. N. Kanungo (eds) *Management of Work and Personal Life*, New York: Praeger.

Halsey, A. H. (1977) 'Towards meritocracy? The case of Britain'. In J. Karabel and A. H. Halsey (eds), *Power and Ideology in Education*, New York: Oxford University Press.

Handy, C. (1976) *Understanding Organisations*, Harmondsworth, Middx: Penguin.

Handy, C. (1984) *The Future of Work*, Oxford: Blackwell.

Handy, C. (1987) The making of managers: a report on management education, training and development in the United States, West Germany, France, Japan and the UK. London: National Economic Development Council.

Hansard Society (1990) *Women at the Top*, London: A. L. Publishing Services.

Harlan, A. and Weiss, C. (1980) *Moving Up: Women in managerial careers: Third progress report*, Wellesley, Mass.: Wellesley Centre for Research on Women.

Hawley, P. (1971) What women think men think: does it affect their career choice?. *Journal of Counseling Psychology*, 18, 193–9.

Hayes, J. (1984) The politically competent manager. *Journal of General Management*, 10 (1), 24–33.

Haywood, H. C. (1968) Motivational orientation of overachieving and underachieving elementary school children. *American Journal of Mental Deficiency*, 72, 662–7.

Heckman, N. A., Bryson, R. and Bryson, J. B. (1977) 'Problems of professional couples: A content analysis'. *Journal of Marriage and the Family*, 39 (2), 323–30.

Heinstein, M. (1965) Child-rearing in California. Bureau of Maternal and Child Health, State of California, Dept of Public Health.

Helmreich, R. L., Spence, J. T., Beane, W. E., Lucker, G. W. and Matthews, R. A. (1980) 'Making it in academic psychology: Demographic and personality correlates of attainment'. *Journal of Personality and Social Psychology*, 39, 896–908.

Hennig, M. and Hackman, B. (1964) Men and women at Harvard Business School. Unpublished MBA research paper.

Hennig M. and Jardim, A. (1978) *The Managerial Woman*, London: Marion Boyars.

Herriot, P. and Winter, B. (1988) Aptitide, self-efficacy and situation as predictors of success in basic training of army recruits. British Psychological Society Annual Conference: Occupational Psychology Division, Manchester.

Herzberg, F., Mausner, B. and Snyderman, D. B. (1959) *The Motivation to Work*, New York: John Wiley.

Hirsh, W. and Jackson, C. (1990) Women into management: issues influencing the entry of women into managerial jobs. *IMS Report*, 158, University of Sussex: Institute of Manpower Studies.

Hisrich, R. D. and Brush, C. (1987) 'Women enrepreneurs: A longitudinal study'. In *Frontiers of Entrepreneurship Research*, Proceedings of the 7th Annual Babson College Entrepreneurship Research Conference Nc Churchill.

Hochschild, A. (1989) *The Second Shift*, New York: Viking.

Hoffman, L. W. (1972) Early childhood experiences and women's achievement motives. *Journal of Social Issues*, 28 (2), 129–55.

Hoffman, L. (1980) 'The effects of maternal employment on academic attitudes and performance of school-aged children'. *School Psychological Review*, 9, 310–35.

Holland, J. L. (1985) *Making Vocational Choices: a theory of vocational personalities and work environments* (2nd edn), Englewood Cliffs, NJ: Prentice Hall.

Holland, P. H. (1982) Creative thinking: an asset or liability in employment?. MEd dissertation, University of Manchester.

Horner, M. S. W. (1972) Toward an understanding of achievement related conflicts in women. *Journal of Social Issues*, 28 (2), 157–75.

Hunt, A. (1968) A Survey of Women's Employment, London: HMSO.

Hunt, J. (1979) *Managing People at Work*, Maideuhead, Berks.: McgGraw Hill.

Huston, A. C. (1983) Sextyping. In M. E. Hetherington (ed.) *Socialization, Personality and Social Development, Vol. IV of Handbook of Child Development*, New York: John Wiley.

Hutt, R. (1985) Chief officer profiles: regional and district nursing officer. *IMS Report*, 111, University of Sussex: Institute of Manpower Studies.

Ilgen, D. R. and Youltz, M. A. (1986) Factors affecting the evaluation and development of minorities in organisations. In K. M. Rowlnd and G. R. Ferris (eds) *Research in Personnel and Human Resource Management*, 4, Greenwich, Conn.: JAI Press.

Institute for Employment Research (1988) *Review of the Economy and Employment, Occupational Update 1988*, University of Warwick.

James, W. (1890) *Principles of Psychology*, New York: Holt.

Johnson, C. L. and Johnson, F. A. (1977) Attitudes towards parenting in dual career families. *American Journal of Psychiatry*, 134, 291–333.

Jones, S. (1987) 'Organisational politics...only the darker side?' *Management, Education and Development*, 18 (2), 116–28.

Kahn, S. E. (1984) Astin's model of career development: the working lives of women and men. *Counseling Psychologist*, 12, 145–6.

Kagan, J. and Moss, H. A. (1962) *Birth to Maturity*, New York: John Wiley.

Kakabadse, A. K. (1986) *The Politics of Management*, London: Gower.

Kakabadse, A. K. and Margerison, C. J. (1985) The management development needs of chief executives. In V. Hammond (ed.) *Current Research in Management*, London: Frances Pinter.

Kanter, R. M. (1977) *Men and Women of the Corporation*, New York: Basic Books.

Katkovsky, W., Crandall, V. C., and Good, S. (1967) Parental antecedents of children's beliefs in internal–external control of reinforcement in intellectual achievement situations. *Child Development*, 28, 765–76.

Kets de Vries, M. F. R. (1980) Stress and the entrepreneurs. In C. L. Cooper and R. Payne (eds) *Current Concerns in Occupational Stress*, New York: John Wiley.

Kirton, M. J. (1976) Adaptors and innovators: a description and a measure. *Journal of Applied Psychology*, 61 (5), 622–9.

Kirton, M. J. (1984) Adaptors and innovators: why new initiatives get blocked. *Long Range Planning*, 17, 137–43.

Kirton, M. J. (1987) *KAI Manual* (2nd edn), Hatfield: Occupational Research Centre.

Klauss, R. (1981) Formalised mentor relationships for management and development programs in federal government. *Public Administration Review*, July–August, 489–96.

Kohut, H. (1971) *The Analysis of Self*, New York: International University Press.

Kram, K. E. (1983) Phases of the mentoring relationship. *Academy of Management Journal*, 26, 608–25.

Kram, K. E. (1985) *Mentoring at Work: developmental relationships in organizational life*, Glenview, Ill.: Scott, Foresman.

Kram, K. E. and Isabella, L. A. (1985) Mentoring alternatives: the role of peer relationships in career development. *Academy of Management Journal*, 28, 110–32.

Kroeker, T. (1963) Coping and defensive function of the ego. In R. W. White *A Study of Lives*, New York: Atherton.

Lambert, S. J. (1990) Processes linking work and family: a critical review and research agenda. *Human Relations*, 43, 239–57.

Langer, E. J. (1979) The illusion of incompetence. In L. C. Perlmuter and

R. A. Monty (eds) *Choice and Perceived Control*, Hillsdale, NJ: Lawrence Erlbaum.

Larwood, L. and Blackmore, J. (1978) Sex discrimination in manager selection: testing predictions of the vertical dyad linkage model. *Sex Roles*, 4, 359–67.

Larwood, L. and Gattiker U. E. (1986) 'A comparison of the career paths used by successful women and men'. In B. A. Gutek and L. Larwood (eds), *Women's Career Development*, Newbury Park: Sage Publications.

Larwood, L. and Gutek, B. A. (1987) Working towards a theory of women's career development. In B. A. Gutek and L. Larwood, *Women's Career Development'*, Beverly Hills, Calif.: Sage Publications.

Lawler, E. E. (1973) *Motivation in Work Organizations*, Belmont, Calif.: Brooks/Cole.

Laws, J. L. (1979) *The Second X: sex role and social role*, New York: Elsevier.

Lee, C. (1982) Self efficacy as a predictor of performance in competitive gymnastics. *Journal of Sport Psychology*, 4, 405–9.

Lee, C. (1984) Accuracy of efficacy and outcome expectations in predicting performance in a simulated assertiveness task. *Cognitive Therapy & Research*, 8, 37–48.

Lefcourt, H. M. (1982) *Locus of Control* (2nd edn), Hillsdale, NJ: Lawrence Erlbaum.

Lenney, E. (1977) Women's self confidence in achievement settings. *Psychological Bulletin*, 84, 1–13.

Levenson, H. (1973) Perceived parental antecedent of internality, powerful others and chance locus of control orientations. *Developmental Psychology*, 9, 268–74.

Lever, J. (1978) Sex differences in the complexity of children's play and games. *American Sociological Review*, 43, 471–83.

Levinson, D. J., Darrow, C. N., Klein, E. B., Levinson, M. H. and McKee, B. (1978) *Seasons of a Man's Life*, New York: Alfred Knopf.

Levinson, R. A. (1982) Teenage women and contraceptive behaviour: focus on self efficacy in sexual and contraceptive situation. *Dissertation Abstracts International*, 42, 4769.

Lewin, K. (1951) *Field Theory in Social Science*, New York: Harper & Row.

Locke, E. A., Frederick, E., Lee, C. and Bobko, P. (1984) Effect of self efficacy, goals and task strategies on task performance. *Journal of Applied Psychology*, 69, 241–51.

Long, P. (1984) *The Personnel Professionals – a comparative study of male and female careers*, London: IPM.

Longstreth, M., Stafford, K., and Mauldin, T. (1986) Self-employed women and their families: time use and socioeconomic characteristics. *Journal of Small Business Management*.

Lukes, P. (1980) *Power: a radical view*, London: Macmillan.

Lynn, D. B. (1969) *Parental Identification and Sex Role*, Berkeley: McCutchan.

McCall, M. W. and Lombardo, M. M. (1983) Off the track: why and how successful executives get derailed. *Technical Report*, 21, Greensboro: Centre for Creative Leadership.

McCarthy, R. (1988) The relationship of cognitive style with coping as a member of a minority group at work. PhD thesis, Hatfield Polytechnic.

McCarthy, P. (1986) Effects of feedback on the self confidence of men and women. *Academy of Management Journal*, 29, 840–47.

McClelland, D. C. (1951) *Personality*, New York: William Sloane.

McClelland, D. C. (1955) *Measuring Motivation in Fantasy*. In D. C. McClelland (ed.), *Studies in Motivation*, New York: Appleton.

McClelland, D. C. (1961) *The Achieving Society*, New York: Van Nostrand.

McClelland, D. C. (1975) *Power the Inner Experience*, New York: Irvington Publishers.

McClelland, D. C. and Burnham, D. (1976) Power is the greatest motivator. *Harvard Business Review*, 54 (2), 100–10.

McClelland, D. C., Atkinson, J. W., Clark, R. A. and Lowell, E. L. (1953) *The Achievement Motive*, New York: Irvington Publishers.

McClelland, D. C. and Winter, D. G. (1969) *Motivating Economic Achievement*, New York: Free Press.

MacDonald, A. P. (1971) Internal–external locus of control: parental antecedents. *Journal of Consulting and Clinical Psychology*, 37 (1), 141–7.

Maehr, M. L. (1974) Culture and achievement motivation. *American Psychologist*, December, 887–96.

Mahoney, T. A., Jerdee, T. H. and Carroll, S. J. (1964) The job(s) of management. *Industrial Relations*, 4, 97–110.

Makin, P. (1987) Career commitment, personality and career development in organisations. PhD thesis, University of Bradford.

Marcuse, H. (1968) *One-dimensional Man*, London: Routledge.

Marcia, J. E. (1966) Development and validation of ego identity status. *Journal of Personality*, 3 (5), 551–8.

Marcia, J. E. (1980) Identity in adolescence. In J. Adelson (ed.) *Handbook of Adolescent Psychology*, 55, 19–30.

Margerison, C. J. (1980) How chief executives succeed. *Journal of European Industrial Training*, Vol. 3.

Marshall, J. (1984) *Women Managers: travellers in a Male World*, New York: John Wiley.

Maslow, A. H. (1954) *Motivation and Personality*, New York: Harper & Row.

Merton, R. K. (1957) *Social Theory and Social Structure*, New York: Free Press of Glencoe.

Metcalf, H. (1988) Employers' response to the decline in school leavers in the 1990s. *IME Report*, 152, University of Sussex: Institute of Manpower Studies.

Metcalf, H. and Leighton, P. (1989) The under utilisation of women in the labour market. *IMS Report*, 172, University of Sussex: Institute of Manpower Studies.

Mihal, W. L., Sorce, P. A. and Comte, T. E. (1984) A process model of individual career decision making. *Academy of Management Review*, 9 (1), 95–103.

Minzberg, H. (1973) *The Nature of Managerial Work*, New York: Harper & Row.

Missirian, A. K. (1982) *The Corporate Connection: why women need mentors to reach the top*, Englewood Cliffs, NJ: Prentice Hall.

Mitchell, J. (1971) *Women's Estate*, Harmondsworth: Penguin.

Moe, K. O. and Zeiss, A. M. (1982) Measuring self efficacy expectations for social skills: a methodological enquiry. *Cognitive Therapy and Research*, 6, 191–205.

Monk, D. (1973) *Joint industry committee for national readership surveys: social grading on the national readership survey*, JICNARS.

Morrison, A. and McIntyre, D. (1978) *Schools and socialisation*, London: John Wiley.

Moss, P. (1988) Childcare and equality of opportunity. Consolidated Report to the European Commission.

Mumford, A., Robinson, G. and Stradling, D. (1987) *Developing Directors: the learning process*, Sheffield: Manpower Services Commission.

Murray, H. A. (1938) *Exploration in Personality*, New York: Oxford University Press.

Mussen, P. H., Conger, J. J. and Kagan, J. (1979) *Child Development and Personality*, New York: Harper Row.

Neave, G. (1975) *How They Fared*, London: Routledge & Kegan Paul.

Neubauer, W. and Werner, L. (1979) Studies on the dimensionality of causal attribution amongst high school students. *Psychologie in Erziehung und Unterricht*, 26 (4), 199–206.

Nicholson, N. and West, M. (1988) *Managerial Jobs Change: men and women in transition*, Cambridge: Cambridge University Press.

Nightingale, K. (1985) Job satisfaction, locus of control and management turnover in a large wholesale organisation. MSc dissertation, UMIST.

Novarra, V. (1980) *Women's Work, Men's Work*, London: Marion Boyars.

Nye, F. (1974) Sociocultural factors. In L. Hoffman and F. Nye (eds) *Working Mothers*, San Francisco: Jossey Bass.

O'Leary, V. E. (1977) *Towards Understanding Women*, Monterey: Calif.: Brooks/Cole.

Osipow, S. H. (1975) *Emerging Women: career analysis and outlook*, Columbus, Ohio: Charles E. Merril Publishing.

Osipow, S. H. (1983) *Theories of Career Development* (3rd edn), Englewood Cliffs, NJ: Prentice Hall.

Parker, S. (1972) *The Future of Work and Leisure*, London: Paladin.

Parsons, T. (1965) Family structure and the socialisation of the child. In T. Parsons and R. F. Bales (eds) *Family Socialization and Interaction Process*, Glencoe, Ill.: Free Press.

Perun, P. J. and Beilby, D. D. V. (1981) Towards a model of female occupational behaviour: a human development approach, *Psychology of Women Quarterly*, 6, 234–52.

Piotrkowski, C. (1979) *Work and the Family System*, New York: Free Press.

Povall, M. (1983) *Managing or Removing the Career Break*, Sheffield: Manpower Services Commission Report.

Porter, L. W. and Lawler, E. E. (1968) *Managerial Attitudes and Performance*, Homewood, Ill, Irwin.

Procuik, T. J. and Breen L. J. (1975) Defensive externality and academic performance. *Journal of Personality and Social Psychology*, 31, 549–56.

Psanthas, G. (1968) Towards a model of female occupational behaviour: a human development approach. *Sociology and Social Research*, 52, 253–68.

Putnam, B. and Hansen, J. (1972) Relationship of self concept and feminine role concept to vocational maturity in young women. *Journal of Counseling Psychology*, 19, 436–40.

Putnam, B. and Heinen, J. S. (1985) Women in managment: The fallacy of the trait approach. In B. A. Stead (ed.) *Women in Management*, Englewood Cliffs, NJ: Prentice Hall.

Rajan, A. and Bevan, S. (1990) Socio-economic trends to 1995. *IMS Report*, 189, University of Sussex: Institute of Manpower Studies.

Rajan, A. and Pearson, R. (1986) *UK Occupation and Employment Trends to 1990*, London: Butterworth.

Rapoport, R. and Rapoport, R. N. (1980) Balancing work, family and leisure: a triple helix model. In C. B. Derr (ed.) *Work Family and the Career*, New York: Praeger.

Raynor, J. (1978) Motivation and career striving. In J. Atkinson and J. Raynor (eds) *Personality, Motivation and Achievement*, New York: Halsted.

Reed, S. E. and Fanslow, A. M. (1984) Household task performance in families of entrepreneurial women. *Journal of Vocational Home Economics Education*, winter, 80–92.

Regional Rewards Survey (1985) *Executive Performance and Rewards*, London: Regional Rewards Surveys.

Reif, W. E., Newstrom, J. W. and Monczka, R. M. (1975) Exploding some myths about women managers. *California Management Review*, 17 (4).

Rendel, M. (1980) How many women academics 1912–1970. In R. Dean (ed.) *Schooling for Women's Work*, London: Routledge & Kegan Paul.

Richardson, M. S. (1974) Vocational maturity in counseling girls and women. In D. E. Super, *Measuring Vocational Maturity for Counseling and Evaluation*, Washington DC: National Vocational Guidance Association.

Richardson, M. S. (1979) Toward an expanded view of careers. *The Counseling Psychologist*, 8 (1), 34–5.

Riley, S. and Wrench, D. (1985) Mentoring among women lawyers. *Journal of Applied Social Psychology*, 15, 374–86.

Rix, S. E. and Stone, A. J. (1984) Work. In S. M. Pritchard, *The Women's Annual (No. 4)*, Boston: G.K. Hall.

Robertson, J. (1985) *Future Work*, Aldershot: Gower/Temple Smith.

Roe, A. (1956) *The Psychology of Occupations*, New York: John Wiley.

Rodgers, C. R. (1959) Towards a theory of creativity. In H. H. Anderson (ed.) *Creativity and Its Cultivation*, New York: Harper & Row.

Rokeach, M. (1966) *Open and Closed Minds*, New York: Basic Books.

Rollnick, S. and Heather, N. (1982) The application of Bandura's self efficacy theory to abstinence-oriented alcoholism treatment. *Addictive Behaviours*, 7 (3), 243–50.

Roos, P. and Reskin, B. (1987) Institutional factors contributing to sex segregation in the work place. In B. Reskin (ed.) *Sex Segregation in the Workplace: trends, explanations, remedies*, Washington, DC: National Academic Press.

Rotter, J. B. (1966) Generalised expectancies for internal versus external control of reinforcement. *Psychological Monographs: General and Applied*, 80 (609).

Russo, N. F. and O'Connel, A. N. (1980) Models from our past: Psychology's foremothers. *Psychology of Women Quarterly*, 5, 11–53.

Rutter, M., Maughan, B., Mortimore, P., Ouston, J. and Smith, A. (1979) *Fifteen Thousand Hours: secondary schools and their effects on children*, London: Open Books; Cambridge, Mass.: Harvard University Press.

Ryecroft, T. (1989) *Survey of women managers – Interim report*, London: British Institute of Management.

Sadri, G. (1988) The construction and validation of a scale to measure managerial self-efficacy. PhD thesis, UMIST.

Scase, R. and Goffee, R. (1989) *Reluctant Managers: their work and lifestyles*, London: Unwin Hyman.

Schein, E. H. (1978) *Career Dynamics: matching individual and organisational needs*, Reading, Mass.: Addison Wesley.

Schein, E. H. (1979) *Organizational socialization and the profession of management*. In D. A. Kolb, I. M. Rubin and J. M. McIntyre (eds) *Organisational Psychology*, Englewood Cliffs, NJ: Prentice Hall.

Schein, E. H. (1982) Individuals and career. *Technical Report*, 19, Office of Naval Research.

Schein, V. E. (1973) Think manager: think male. *Atlantic Economic Review*, March–April, 95–100.

Schein, V. E. (1977) Individual power and political behaviour in organisations. *Academy of Management Review*, 2, 64–72.

Schumpeter, J. A. (1934) *The Theory of Economic Development*, Cambridge,

Mass.: Harvard University Press.

Seeman, M. (1967) On the personal consequences of alienation in work. *Sociological Review*, 32 (2), 783–91.

Seiber, S. D. (1974) Towards a theory of role accumulation. *American Sociological Review*, 39, 567–78.

Shapero, A. (1975) The displaced, uncomfortable entrepreneurs. *Psychology Today*, November, 83–8.

Smith, E. L. and Grenier, M. (1982) Sources of organisational power for overcoming structural obstacles. *Sex Roles*, 8, 733–46.

Smith, J. M. (1973) A quick measure of achievement motivation. *British Journal of Clinical Psychology*, 12, 137–43.

Snyder, M. (1973) On the influence of individuals on situations. In N. Cantor and J. F. Kilstrom (eds) *Personality, Cognitive and Social Interaction*, Hillsdale, NJ: Lawrence Erlbaum.

Sobol, M. (1963) Commitment to work. In F. Nye and L. Hoffman (eds) *The Employed Mother in America*, Chicago: Rand McNally.

Social Trends (1989), London: HMSO.

Social Trends (1990), London: HMSO.

Social Trends (1991), London: HMSO.

Sonnenfelt, J. and Kotter, J. P. (1982) The maturation of career theory. *Human Relations*, 35, 19–46.

Spector, P. E. (1988) Development of the work locus of control scale. *Journal of Occupational Psychology*, 61, 335–40.

Spence, J. and Helmreich, R. (1978) *Masculinity and femininity: their psychological dimensions, correlates and antecedents*, Austin, Texas: University of Texas Press.

Stahl, M. J. (1983) Achievement, power and managerial motivation: selecting managerial talent with the job choice exercise. *Personnel Psychology*, 36, 775–89.

Staines, G., Travis, C. and Jayarante, T. E. (1974) The queen bee syndrome. *Psychology Today*, January, 55–60.

Standley, K. and Soule, B. (1974) Women in male dominated professions: contrasts in their personal and vocational histories. *Journal of Vocational Behaviour*, 4, 245–58.

Stein, A. H. (1973) The effects of maternal employment and educational attainment on the sex typed attributes of college females. *Social Behaviour and Personality*, 1, 111–14.

Stein, A. H. and Bailey, M. M. (1973) The socialisation of achievement orientation in females. *Psychological Bulletin*, 80, 345–66.

Stewart, L. P. and Gudykunst, W. B. (1982) Differential factors influencing the hierarchical level and number of promotions of males and females within an organisation. *Academy of Management Journal*, 25, 586–97.

Stone, N. (1989) Mother's work. *Harvard Business Reveiw*, September–October, 50–6.

Super, D. E. (1957) *The Psychology of Careers*, New York: Harper & Row.

Super, D. E. (1980) A life span, life space approach to career development. *Journal of Vocational Behaviour*, 16, 282–98.

Super, D. E. (1984) Career and life development. In D. Brown, L. Brooks and Associates (eds) *Career Choice and Development*, London and San Francisco: Jossey Bass.

Sussman, J. A. (1979) *Korn/Ferry International Executive Profile: a survey of corporate leaders*, New York: Korn Ferry International.

Tangri, S. S. (1972) Determinants of occupational role innovation among college women. *Journal of Social Issues*, 38, 177–99.

Taylor, K. M. and Betz, N. E. (1983) Applications of self-efficacy theory to the understanding and treatment of career indecision. *Journal of Vocational Behaviour*, 22, 63–81.

Terborg, J. (1977) Women in management: a research review. *Journal of Applied Psychology*, 62, 647–64.

Tinsley, D. and Faunce, P. (1980) Enabling, facilitating and precipitation factors associated with women's career orientation. *Journal of Vocational Behaviour*, 17, 183–94.

Tinsley, H. E. A. and Heesacker, M. (1984) Vocational behaviour and career development, (1983): a review. *Journal of Vocational Behaviour*, 25, 139–90.

Tyler, L. (1967) The encounter with poverty – Its effect on vocational psychology. *Rehabilitation Psychology Bulletin*, 11, 61–70.

Valdez, R. and Gutek, B. A. (1987) Family roles: a help or a hindrance to working women? In B. A. Gutek and L. Larwood (eds) *Women's Career Development*, Newbury Park, Calif.: Sage.

Valliant, G. E. (1977) *Adaptation to Life*, Boston: Little, Brown.

Veroff, J., Wilcox, S. and Atkinson, J. W. (1953) The achievement motive in high school and college age women. *Journal of Abnormal and Social Psychology*, 48, 108–19.

Vetter, L. (1973) Career counseling for women. *Counseling Psychologist*, 4, 54–66.

Vondracek, F. W., Lerner, R. M. and Schulenberg, J. E. (1986) *A Life Span Development Approach*, Hillsdale, NJ: Lawrence Erlbaum.

Vroom, V. H. (1964) *Work and Motivation*, New York: John Wiley.

Waddel, F. T. (1983) Factors affecting choice, satisfaction and success in the female self employed. *Journal of Vocational Behaviour*, 23, 294–304.

Walsh, W. B. and Osipow, O. H. (1983) *Handbook of Vocational Psychology*, vol. 1, Hillsdale, NJ: Lawrence Erlbaum.

Warihay, P. D. (1980) The climb to the top: is the network the route for women? *Personnel Administrator*, 25 (4), 55–60.

Warr, P. and Parry, G. (1982) Paid employment and women's psychological wellbeing. *Psychological Bulletin*, 91, 498–516.

Waterman, A. S. (1982) Identity development from adolescence to adulthood: an extension of theory and a review of research.

Developmental Psychology, 18 (3), 341–58.

Watkins, J. M. and Watkins, D. S. (1983) The female entrepreneur: Her background and determinants of business choice – some British data. In J. A. Hornaday et al., *Frontiers of Entrepreneurial Research*, Wellesley, Mass.: Babson College.

West, J. (1982) *Women, Work and the Labour Market*, London: Routledge & Kegan Paul.

Weston, L. C. and Stein, S. L. (1977) The relationship of the identity achievement of college women and campus participation. *Journal of College Student Personnel*, 18 (1), 21–4.

Wheeler, K. G. (1983) Comparison of self efficacy and expectation models of occupational preferences for college males and females. *Journal of Occupational Psychology*, 56 (1), 73–8.

White, J. (1982) *Rejection*, Reading, Mass.: Addison Wesley.

White, B. L. (1989) A study of the characteristics of female managers and female entrepreneurs. Unpublished MSc dissertation, UMIST.

White, R. W. (1960) Competence and the psychosexual stages of development. In M. Jones (ed.) *Nebraska Symposium on Motivation*, Lincoln, Nebr.: University of Nebraska Press.

Williams, S. and Watson, N. (1985) Perceived danger and perceived self-efficacy as cognitive determinants of acrophobic behaviour. *Behaviour Therapy*, 16, 136–46.

Wolfson, K. P. (1976) Career development patterns of college women. *Journal of Counseling Psychology*, 23 (2), 119–25.

Women in Enterprise Directory (1989).

Woodlands Group (1980) Management development roles: Coach, sponsor and mentor. *Personnel Journal*, 59, 918–21.

Wortley, D. B. and Amatea, E. S. (1982) Mapping adult life changes: a conceptual framework for organising adult development theory. *Personnel and Guidance Journal*, April, 476–82.

Wright, J. (1978) Are working women really more satisfied? *Journal of Marriage and the Family*, 40, 301–13.

Zytowski, D. G. (1969) Toward a theory of career development of women. *Personnel and Guidance Journal*, 47, 660–4.

Index